FAMILIAR GARDEN BIRDS OF AMERICA

FAMILIAR
GARDEN BIRDS

OF AMERICA

By HENRY H. COLLINS, JR.
and Ned R. Boyajian

Illustrated by John C. Yrizarry
and Nina Williams

Harper & Row, Publishers, New York

LIBRARY OF CONGRESS CATALOG CARD NUMBER: 65-21006

Contents

Publisher's Note

Bird watchers are legion on this continent which houses some 680 individual species. In the century and one-half since the writings and paintings of Alexander Wilson and John James Audubon the American naturalist has been favored with a regular stream of precise descriptions of our rich avian population.

In conceiving the idea behind this book Henry Hill Collins, Jr., was aware that for many of us the large, scholarly tomes on bird behavior simply cover too many unfamiliar species and reveal more esoteric information than we want. The author reasoned that a selective list of perhaps 100 species, the most familiar birds from all parts of this vast land, could be assembled. The opinions of field and laboratory ornithologists, feeding station operators, directors of bird sanctuaries, and bird clubs across the United States were sampled. After some hot discussion a list of America's familiar birds was drawn up. Further refinement resulted from the author's concentration on the birds that are common to American gardens or their winter equivalent in the North, the bird feeder.

The book that follows offers complete life histories for more than 70 major species, including briefer notes on a number of related species. It serves to provide the significant details on breeding, migration, range, voice, food, habitat, while contrasting trends in distribution and bird populations. The reader learns the essential factor behind the behavior of a particular species: the reason individual birds breed, nest, mate, eat, or sing as they do. And the book calls into question certain widely-held notions about the biology of birds. Even the common belief that the mockingbird imitates the songs of other birds is persuasively challenged.

Henry Hill Collins, Jr., died before this book was completed. Author of *Complete Field Guide to American Wildlife,* among other books, he always addressed himself to the questions homeowners and other amateurs, young and old, ask about the wildlife around them. Ned R. Boyajian, who contributed a number of the species accounts and completed notes on nests and eggs, is president of New York's famed Linnaean Society. As a field ornithologist Mr. Boyajian has combined methods of the scientist with a feeling for the special habitats of birds that sheds light on native plants and the diversity of the American landscape.

John Cameron Yrizarry's color paintings provide a guide to identification and a rich gallery of bird art; the characteristic pose of each bird is rendered faithfully in its natural setting. Mr. Yrizarry also assisted Nina Williams in putting the finishing touches on her delicate pen and ink drawings.

Footnoting has been eliminated. Reference to sources and notes on the literature are included in the bibliography assembled by Mr. Boyajian.

FAMILIAR GARDEN BIRDS OF AMERICA

PIGEONS, DOVES / *Columbidae*

MOURNING DOVE (*Zenaidura macroura*)

The mourning dove was described in 1731 by Mark Catesby, the first important writer on American birds, as "the Turtle of Carolina," meaning, of course, "the Turtle *Dove* of Carolina." In the past century it was widely known as the Carolina dove. It breeds throughout North America from southern Canada to Mexico and winters from south of the Great Lakes to Panama. Since 1920 it has become much more common in the northern part of its range. Mourning doves migrate, at least in the North, and the birds you see in winter may be birds from the North, not the same individuals you saw in summer.

This dove is a bird of lawns, shade trees, orchards, open woodlands, suburbs, roadsides, barnyards, farmlands, sand dunes, beaches, and open meadows. In the West it frequents plains and mountains, and breeds to an elevation of 8,000 ft. The species has benefited by the settlement of North America. Fields, woodlots, hedgerows, and farm ponds are more favorable to its increase than unbroken forest. So also are overgrazed pastures and abandoned farms.

On the ground the mourning dove walks rather than hops; it bobs its head as it walks. The gravel it picks up is used in its crop as an aid to

1

digestion. Like other doves and pigeons, but unlike most birds, it can drink without raising its head. It likes to bask in the sun on a sandy spot, with its breast flat on the ground and its head bent back over its shoulder. It sometimes tries to lure intruders from its nest by limping along the ground, pretending it has a broken wing.

Its flight is swift, 55 mph, and is usually direct, but may at times be erratic, particularly in the wind. The rather long pointed wings and tail distinguish it at a considerable distance. Normally the wings beat 147 times per minute, but occasionally on approaching a perch, the bird will glide in on set wings. Doves often fly in groups of three, which one expert believed represents a pair and one offspring. In arid regions the species makes daily flights to water in early morning and late afternoon. In doing so the doves follow narrow local flyways along which, in season, gunners find it profitable to hide. In the Old West thirsty travelers learned to follow these dove flights to water.

Because of its value as a game bird and its relative abundance, the mourning dove has been intensively studied.

In the North the average weight of an adult is 140 grams, in the South, 100. This follows Bergmann's rule that individuals of the same species tend to become larger in cooler climates.

Males outnumber females by 13 percent when immature, by 28 percent when adult.

In the southern United States, where its numbers are increased each fall by migrants from the North, this species is classified as a game bird. It is widely hunted and highly esteemed for food. Dove shooting is popular partly because of the bird's swift flight and partly for the wide variety of shots it offers the hunter. These include oblique shots, side shots, and shots at towering or descending birds.

Eugene Murphey, well-known poet and ornithologist of Georgia, has stated that at Augusta "great numbers are killed annually for sport —in years gone by I have known of 1,500 to 2,000 to be slaughtered in a single day." The total kill for the state of Georgia was nearly 2 million birds per year from 1949 to 1952. Such harvests impose a heavy strain on the bird population, and constant government vigilance is required to see that the dove's numbers are maintained.

Like other birds the mourning dove has its normal quota of parasites and diseases. The disease called trichomoniasis, caused by *Trichomonas gallinae,* made sufficiently heavy inroads on the doves in the southeast to cause a marked decline in the population in 1950.

The loving behavior of male and female supports the popular belief in their affectionate nature; they do bill and coo. In spring, one bird, presumably the male, occasionally engages in a "tower dance" apparently associated with courtship. In this performance a bird will fly up almost vertically 30 ft. or more above treetop level. It flutters at the top of its ascent, facing in various directions. After descending somewhat, it ascends again to flutter once more, facing this time in different directions.

Other authors have written of the male in courtship circling above his mate, with tail fanned, and on the ground with feathers spread, strutting and nodding his head before her.

Another courtship performance has been described as the "nest-calling attitude." Wallace Craig, who made a study of posturing and displays in pigeons, writes:

The male [sits] with his body tilted forward, tail pointing up at a high angle, the head so low that bill and crop may rest on the floor, or if the bird be in the nest, the head is down in the hollow. Both the voice and the attitude of the male serve to attract the female, for in all pigeons the nest-call is accompanied by a gentle flipping of the wings, ogling eyes, and a seductive turning of the head. In addition to these general columbine gestures, *Zenaidura* has a special bit of display of his own, for during the first note of the nest-call he spreads his tail just enough to show conspicuously the white marks on the outer feathers; soon as this first note is past, the tail closes and the white marks disappear, to flash out again only with the next repetition of the nest-call, before which there is always a considerable interval.

The mourning dove builds a frail platform nest of twigs, lined loosely —if at all—with smaller twigs, pine needles, or grasses. This is placed on a horizontal branch, low tree, or bush from 3 to 20 ft. above the ground (occasionally higher). Conifers are often preferred early in the season. The two white eggs are laid 36 hours apart and can be frequently seen through the twigs from below. The female may lay the first eggs before the nest is fully constructed. In open country she may lay her eggs on the ground, usually without constructing a nest. Some-times she places her platform on top of an old nest of another species such as a robin, grackle, blue jay, mockingbird, or even a black-crowned night heron. She raises two broods in the North, three or occasionally four in the South; and she usually builds a new nest for a second brood.

The female alone builds the actual nest, but unlike most other birds, the male is the only one of the pair that collects the twigs. He delivers them to the female at the nest and she works them into position. One male at Columbus, Ohio, was observed to make 82 trips in $3\frac{1}{2}$ hours. Nest building is an early morning occupation and stops by 10 or 11 o'clock.

Both sexes share in incubation and brooding. The male sits on the eggs during the day for about 8 hours, the female sits the remainder of the time. The mourning dove is a devoted parent and practically never deserts its nest. In an experiment, eggs in a number of nests were painted various colors in different combinations and designs. The par-ents continued to sit and the eggs hatched. Few birds are able to dis-tinguish between their own eggs and those of other species, or even other objects. If, in this experiment, marbles or moth balls had been substituted for the eggs, in all probability the doves would have attempted to brood them also. Unlike most land birds, the mourning dove broods its young almost constantly until they are fledged. Also unlike most land birds, the parents make no attempt to keep the nest clean. The species has a long breeding season which lasts in the warmer parts of the country from February or March into October. Occasionally the birds breed in loose colonies.

Young mourning doves are hatched blind, naked, and helpless. They are fed for several days largely on pigeon's milk, a secretion from the lining of the parent's crop, which is regurgitated into the mouths of the young. Both parents produce the secretion and both feed the young. In this process the young bird pokes its bill into one corner of the mouth of the parent. The parent closes its beak over that of the young one and makes a pumping motion with its head. Whereupon the muscles of its throat are seen to twitch and the pigeon's milk comes up for the young to swallow. The procedure may last from 15 to 60 seconds. The first nestling then withdraws its bill and the other nestling inserts its bill in the other corner of the parent's mouth. After this one has had its turn, the first one comes back for a second helping.

As the squabs develop, the parents also bring them seeds to eat and some insects and worms. Pigeon's milk gradually assumes less importance in their diet. By the time they are ready to leave the nest, 98 percent of their food may be seeds.

After the main breeding season, often by the end of July, mourning doves commence assembling for the night at common roosts, sometimes as many as 600 birds in one roost. At dawn they scatter widely to feed. Throughout their range in fall and winter these doves are found in various-sized flocks that are actually aggregations of mated pairs. Audubon Society Christmas census records show that the mourning dove is among the 25 most common species in winter in the United States. At the approach of the breeding season the winter flocks break up into their constituent pairs.

The usual call of this dove is a low, mournful *coo-ah, coo, coo, ooo,* or *ah-coo'-roo-ooo,* which can be heard 250 yds. away. Despite its mournful quality, it is actually a love song.

The bird also makes a *whee-whee-whee* sound as it springs into flight. This is usually attributed to the sound of its wings, but some authorities claim that the bird can also make this noise when it is perched.

The mourning dove feeds primarily on weed seeds, but it also takes grain, beechnuts, and small acorns. It is very fond of buckwheat. Researchers found in one stomach 6,400 seeds of foxtail grass (*Chaetocloa*), in another 7,500 seeds of yellow wood-sorrel (*Oxalis stricta*), and in a third 9,200 mixed weed seeds. In season, wheat seeds are much eaten and so is acorn. These are largely waste seeds which the bird gleans from the ground, although the dove does do some occasional damage to grain and peas in the South.

At feeders this species likes the seeds of hemp and millet. It is attracted by salt and, in the breeding season, lime that helps in the production of egg shells.

Description: Length, 12 in. Small head; bill, slender and swollen at the base; wings and tail, long and pointed; legs, short. Brown head; buffy gray body with a bluish cast on wings; black spot below ear. *Note*:

The rock dove is heavier and chunkier and has a fanshaped, not pointed, tail. The sparrow hawk has a heavier head and shoulders, and a squared tail; its wings in flight lack the sharp downstroke of the dove. The now-extinct passenger pigeon was larger and bluer, had longer wings and tail, and lacked the black spot below the ear.

Incubation, 14 to 15 days; young stay 13 to 15 days in nest.

Size of eggs, 1.1 x 0.9 in.; two broods per year in the North; three or occasionally four in the South.

SPOTTED DOVE (*Streptopelia chinensis*)

Of the very few species of birds domesticated by man, almost all have come from three groups: Anatidae (ducks and geese), Galliformes (chickens, turkeys, etc.), and Columbidae (pigeons and doves). Most of them have been with man so long that the circumstances and location of their domestication have long been forgotten.

In the case of ducks, chickens, and similar fowl, there seems no doubt that the reason for their domestication was for food, and their capture and retention was entirely premeditated. But man's association with various species of pigeons and doves might have begun quite differently. It seems unlikely that anyone would go out of his way to capture and maintain these relatively small, meatless birds as a food supply. It may be that the Columbids themselves began the feeding on the waste grain of stockyard and thrashing floor. Perhaps at first they were tolerated simply because they were harmless and constituted a handy, if unsubstantial, source of food. This is certainly true today. In every part of the world where there are permanent human settlements, one or more species of Columbids can be found in a domesticated or feral state, and though occasionally used for food they are far more likely to be considered as communal pets.

None of the native American Columbids has been domesticated, but three Old World species have been introduced and either by escape or deliberate release have become established in a feral state: the rock dove, or common pigeon, the ringed turtle dove, and the spotted dove.

The terms *pigeon* and *dove* are synonymous, and though the larger species are usually called "pigeons" and the smaller are called "doves," the two terms are used interchangeably.

The spotted dove is a medium-sized, brownish pigeon with a long, rounded, white-tipped tail. Adults have a conspicuous band of black-and-white spots across the nape of the neck which distinguishes them from all other species. Immature and adult birds in flight are best distinguished from the native mourning dove by the shape and pattern of the tail. The tail of the spotted dove is rounded, with very conspicuous white corners. The mourning dove's tail is sharply pointed, with white tipping confined to the sides at the widest part.

Another introduced species, the ringed turtle dove, is established in a few parks in Los Angeles. Though similar to the spotted dove in shape and tail pattern, it is easily identified by its very pale creamy-tan coloration and narrow black line across the nape of the neck.

The spotted dove is a native of southeastern Asia. It was introduced in the vicinity of Los Angeles at about the end of World War I and quickly became the most common species of pigeon in metropolitan Los Angeles. Today it is well established in Los Angeles and Orange counties and is found in lesser numbers south to Oceanside and east to Bakersfield and Santa Barbara. Much more recently it was introduced around Miami, where it occurs chiefly in the vicinity of Bayshore Park.

Pigeons drink by plunging the bill into water beyond the nostrils and inhaling in long draughts, a method unique among birds. Consequently a permanent source of standing water is absolutely essential for their existence, though this does not prevent some species from inhabiting the most arid regions. They need drink only once or twice a day and are strong, swift flyers, capable of traveling many miles to waterholes. Nevertheless, a water supply is the single most important factor governing the distribution of pigeons, and many species, including the spotted dove, are seldom found far from it.

The dove inhabits only moist areas that have a number of tall trees and an assured water supply close by. In California it has spread to some extent into streamside woodlands and irrigated agricultural areas, but for the most part it remains a bird of parks and residential districts.

To those who have studied the behavior of the Columbidae, the false reputation of this family for gentleness and innocence must be amusing.

During the mating season, males especially are among the most pugnacious and ill-tempered of birds, seldom behaving as symbols of
peaceful coexistence. They indulge in furious battles, buffeting each
other with powerful wings in a deadly earnestness seldom encountered
among other species of birds. In the wild, these battles usually end with
the loser escaping unharmed, but in captivity it is not unusual for a
bird to be killed or seriously injured in the encounters.

The spotted dove is no exception to the behavior. During the breeding season, which begins as early as February and lasts throughout the
spring, the males are constantly involved in battles with their rivals.
Their spectacular courtship performance hardly jibes with the gentle
billing and cooing ascribed to doves, but rather it resembles the wild
and exuberant performances of hawks. From the top of a high conspicuous perch the male will suddenly whirr straight up 100 ft. or
more and then, with wings held stiffly motionless, plummet almost per-
pendicularly downward in an accelerating spiral.

The call of the spotted dove is similar to that of the mourning dove,
but harsher, more vigorous, and with a burry quality: *wook-ko-whoooo*,
the first and last notes accented, the final *whooo* drawn out and falling
slightly in pitch. It may be heard any time of day throughout the year,
but more frequently during the breeding season and more often in
early morning and late evening.

The nest is a shallow platform of sticks across a sturdy horizontal
fork. It is usually in a deciduous tree, though conifers are used also
and occasionally a nest is found balanced on the broad frond of a palm.
The eggs are white, two to a cluch, and hatch in about 15 days. Both
parents participate in nest building, incubation, and care of the young.

For the first several days after they hatch, young pigeons are fed
entirely by regurgitation. Thrusting their heads down the adult's
gullet until they seem about to be swallowed, the fledglings feed on a
thick, syrupy fluid sloughed off from the swollen lining of the crop and
forced up by the parent bird. As they grow older, they obtain partially
digested food from the parent's crop, but receive no raw food until
they leave the nest and are on their own.

The spotted dove forages on the ground, feeding on weed and grass
seed and occasionally waste grain. As far as is known, it takes no animal

food of any kind, nor does it seem particularly fond of fruit. It has
inhabited our agricultural areas only a relatively short time and so far
has not been known to attack cultivated crops. Spotted doves are highly
sedentary, seldom wandering far from their own neighborhood, and
though occasionally a large number can be found together in some
place with an especially abundant food supply, they do not normally
travel in flocks.

Spotted doves are quick to visit a feeding station if one happens to
be within their regular foraging territory, but they seldom congregate
in numbers and apparently are not attracted from any great distance.
Usually it is only the same local few individuals that return constantly.
They feed mostly on cracked corn, hemp, millet, and other small seeds.

Description: Length, 13 in. Adults distinguished from all other species
by broad band of black and white spots on nape of the neck. The immature distinguished from mourning dove by shape of tail, from turtle
dove by much darker coloration and from white-winged dove by slim-
mer build and uniformly dark wings.

Incubation, 12 to 15 days; young stay 14 to 15 days in nest.

Size of eggs, 1.05 x 0.85 in.; two to three broods per year.

COMMON GROUND DOVE (*Columbigallina passerina*)

The ground dove is a bird of wayside and dooryard throughout
much of the deep South. It is characteristic of the country road, the
packed earth about the sharecropper's cabin, and the farm and plantation barnyard. It is a tame, confiding species.

This tiny dove is only about the size of a large sparrow. It has soft,
gray-brown plumage, a black-tipped tail, and a big flash of chestnut in
its wings. It is found along the coastal plain from South Carolina to
Texas, west to southern California, south to the Florida Keys, and
throughout northern Central America. Other subspecies range from
Venezuela and Colombia to Brazil and Ecuador. It is also widely distributed and well known in Bermuda and the West Indies.

In Georgia and South Carolina the ground dove is common on the coastal plain, south of the "fall line," but is rare or absent north of this line. This is the boundary, marked by the first waterfalls on rivers flowing into the Atlantic, that separates the tidewater from the piedmont. In some parts of its range, without known cause, the dove has disappeared or become scarce in areas where it was once abundant.

Although in much of its range this sedentary species is a permanent resident, it exhibits some seasonal movement. In South Carolina it is less common in winter than in summer, some individuals apparently moving south. Many birds from the West shift southward and eastward to winter along the Gulf coast, which is the reason the species is locally common as a resident in Louisiana in winter, but rare in summer.

The habitat of this terrestrial dove includes horse corrals, gardens, pea patches, sandy fields (cultivated and abandoned), cotton fields, overgrazed grasslands, bare stony stretches, open pine woods, forest edges, hammocks, lake shores, beaches, quiet village streets, and the outskirts of towns. In Georgia it appears in thinly timbered woodlands with thick low undergrowth. In Louisiana it often inhabits old cane-fields. In the Southwest it frequents ranches, mesquite flats, willows along irrigation ditches, and river bottom woodlands. It is seldom found far from water.

The ground dove cuts a rather comical figure walking rapidly on short legs. With head nodding and tail held high, it has a bantamlike appearance. On the woods road it manages to stay just ahead of us. If we approach too closely, it flies farther on, alights, and keeps on going down the path, perhaps flitting its wings as it runs, always just out of reach.

When this dove rises from the ground, its short, rounded wings make a whirring sound. Its flight is usually short, low, and direct. Although it feeds on the ground (sometimes in the barnyard with the chickens), it often perches on a branch, fence, rooftree, or telegraph wire, where the male coos from the elevated location.

In Florida a favorite roosting place of this dove is among thickly leaved orange trees where, as Frank M. Chapman writes, "frequently when the bird is hidden in their depths one may hear its mellow, crooning *coos* uttered so softly that they float on the air as though born of the wind." The principal enemies of the species are common ground predators such as opossum, skunk, fox, and feral cat.

The courtship of this species reminds us of the domestic pigeon. The male, with puffed feathers and trembling wings, struts before the female, bows his head, and coos. He may take short flights in pursuit of the female as she keeps flitting ahead of them. Often two or three males will chase one female.

Certain authorities say that a pair mates only on a low perch, not on the ground. W. Leon Dawson, author of *Birds of California,* writes that the birds mate during their daily visits to a water source, at which time the male, with quivering wings, utters a special *kool, kooul* note. When mated, the two birds often sit side by side on a branch in an attitude of apparent affection. Some pairs, perhaps most, remain together for life.

The nest is usually placed within 6 ft. of the ground, although sites as high as 12, 20, and even 25 ft. have been reported. Many nests are on the ground itself, usually in fields or weed patches. In such cases a few grasses or weed stalks serve to line the slight depression.

However, if the nest is aboveground, it is usually placed in a vine or bush, on a stump, fence post, or horizontal branch of a low tree. The frail structure consists of a loose foundation of twigs or pine needles, lined with rootlets and grasses. Eggs often project above the low rim. In addition to constructing a nest of its own, this species frequently uses or builds onto an old nest of another species, such as the mourning dove. Favorite nesting sites in the sea islands of Georgia are wax myrtle bushes, and mesquite thickets in the Southwest.

Two unglossed white eggs make up the clutch. Both parents incubate. The ground dove is a close sitter and does not easily flush from its nest. If an intruder nears the homesite when the male is brooding, he ruffles up, raises his wings over his back, and emits a rough, angry nasal note.

If actually disturbed at the nest, the incubating parent tumbles onto the earth, feigns lameness, and drags itself along the ground with drooping wings. When these actions have succeeded in luring the intruder far enough away, the bird takes wing and disappears. The eggs hatch about two weeks after they are laid. The parents brood the young until they are able to fly, which is long enough for them to dirty the nest and area around it to a shocking degree.

The ground dove has the longest breeding season of any of our birds. In New Mexico it nests from May to October. Egg dates in Florida range from February 27 to October 22. In Georgia, January to October is the nesting period. A parent brooding a healthy squab was once found four days before Christmas in a nest in Imperial County, California; and a January 22 breeding date has also been reported from southern California. This species uses the same nest for the second, third, and sometimes fourth brood in the same season.

The voice of the male is a mournful *cooo-oo, cooo-oo, cooo-oo* note that sounds at a distance like *cooo* with a rising inflection. Ralph Hoffman, well-known writer about birds, describes it as a series of single *coo*'s repeated 7 to 20 times without interruption, followed by a pause, and then another series of *coo*'s, each one sounding like *coo-ook* run together. The notes are low but penetrating.

This species lives largely on weed seeds, waste grain, wild berries, and some insects. On occasion it comes to feeders. Like all members of its family and unlike most other birds, this dove drinks without raising its head.

Favorite feeder foods include grain and wild bird seed.

Description: Length, 7 in. Wings rounded; tail short and slightly rounded; smoky pink forehead, cheeks, and underparts; bluish gray crown and nape; gray-brown upperparts; scaly throat and breast; chestnut wing lining; tail with black band at end; red bill; orange eye; pink feet. Female browner above, grayer below. Females and young generally paler, less spotted. In contrast to the long-tailed Inca dove, which is scaled all over, the ground dove is scaled only on head, neck, and breast.

Incubation, 12 to 14 days; young stay 14 to 16 days in nest.

Size of eggs, 0.86 x 0.64 in.; two to four broods per year.

INCA DOVE (*Scardafella inca*)

The Inca dove is smaller and more slender than the mourning dove, of which it looks like a miniature edition. It has a small head and a long, white-edged tail. The sexes are similar in plumage. It is a permanent resident in the Lower Sonoran and Tropical life-zones. Its original home was semiarid plains. Now it is also common about ranches, town, and cities. It ranges from Texas, southern New Mexico, southern Arizona, and Lower California south along the lowlands on both coasts to northwestern Costa Rica and Nicaragua.

The spread of civilization has opened up much favorable terrain for this species. From its original south Texas home (San Antonio south) it has spread north and east as far as Kerrville, Austin, and Columbus. In Arizona it is found north to Wickenburg and is common in Yuma, Phoenix, Tucson, and the Gila Valley. In New Mexico it occurs north to Silver City.

The Inca dove forages, seldom far from water, on open ground or areas of scattered trees with little understory. It likes parks, lawns, gardens, corrals, zoo enclosures, and chicken yards. In these latter it often seems almost as domesticated as the hens themselves. In walking on its short legs, the bird's breast and tail almost touch the ground. Its favorite breeding territory includes urban parkland and stream valleys, and the neighborhoods of villages and houses.

The habits of the Inca dove in New Mexico, Texas, and Sonora, Mexico, were intensively studied from 1956 to 1958 by Richard F. Johnston. Much of the following description of its behavior is taken from his researches.

In foraging, the Inca dove whisks its bill back and forth through dry soil to bring to light any hidden seeds. A tiny puff of dust rises into the air with each swipe of the bill. After three or four swipes the bird eats any seeds thus brought to light. But if the soil is moist, the dove directly picks up any seeds that lie exposed.

Each pair of Inca doves in the breeding season establishes its own territory, which the male defends from intrusion by other Inca doves. Such an area varies in size from 30 x 50 yards to 70 x 100 yards. Territories may be strung out along a river valley or they may be scattered about the countryside in conformity with the suitability of the terrain. The two requirements for a territory are a clear area on which to forage and trees in which to hide, court, nest, and roost.

The male begins to defend his territory two to three weeks after the start of courtship and one to three weeks before the first egg is laid. Three types of vocalizations are used to help maintain a pair on a territory. The first is the courtship call, *cut-cut-ca-doah,* directed toward the female. The second is the *coo-coo* song with which the male first tries to repel an intruder.

Failure of the intruder to withdraw is followed by the resident male uttering his aggressive *cut-cut-cut, ca-dóah* call, which he may repeat continuously when highly excited, accompanying it by incompletely raising and fanning his tail. If this fails to dislodge the intruder, the home male then chases the other, usually at an angle and with the far wing raised. If the intruder still does not leave, the occupant will attack him with bill and wings, and the birds will come to blows, jumping up and down a foot in the air as they fight.

A male "drives" his mate when an intruding male is nearby. This means that the mated male attempts to occupy the spot where the female is; she moves off to another spot; he proceeds to occupy this spot, and she moves on again. This may happen from 3 to 12 times before the male stops driving her. Driving apparently has the immediate objective of removing a female from the attentions of a rival male.

The Inca dove is a social bird. Rarely does an individual do anything alone. In the nonbreeding season the birds flock and (unlike during the breeding season) are singularly lacking in aggressiveness. In areas where much food is available, 100 or more doves may be found together. Such a flock is usually composed of several subflocks of from 10 to 40 birds each. But in regions where there are no great concentrations of food, the doves may assemble in flocks of only a dozen individuals.

The daily routine of flock members is quite ritualized. They start foraging from 8:30 to 9:30 A.M., leaving the roost earlier on clear, warm days and later on cool, cloudy ones. After an hour of feeding they sun for an hour. Then there will be more foraging, following by more sunning and loafing. When sunning, a group of birds will perch side by side in strong sunlight, partially roll over facing the sun, and slightly raise the half-fanned upper wing. This stance lasts from 10 seconds to 2 minutes, whereupon the birds sit upright again and preen. Alternate sunning and preening may occur two, three, or four times in short order. The birds normally go to roost about half an hour before sunset. Evergreens, both conifers and broadleaved, are preferred roosting places. A number of doves usually spend the night close together; at times, some perch on the backs of others.

Within a flock there is no peck order and no leader. The doves do not maintain individual distance. On the contrary they frequently touch each other when roosting, sunning, or resting. The principal mechanism for holding a group together seems to be intermittent *coo coo* calling. Every 10 to 30 minutes perhaps four birds from a group of a dozen will give this call. A human imitation, if uttered immediately after the birds have called, will fail to elicit a response. If uttered 10 minutes after the last round of calling, it may bring forth an answer; if given 20 minutes afterwards, it will almost certainly arouse a reply. The assumption is that this calling keeps each member of a group in touch with the whereabouts of others.

The flight of the Inca dove, for any distance, is strong and rapid, with red-brown conspicuous in the wing. But short flights of a few feet are jerky; the tail opens and shuts and swings up and down, and the wingbeat is irregular. The wings in flight make a flat, buzzing sound that can be heard 30 yards away. This may serve as a form of species advertisement. About 1 second after alighting, the Inca dove suddenly pumps its tail up and down 2 or 3 in. When perched and at rest, the head is sunk on the breast and the tail is drooped. Females under stress raise their tails about 1½ in.

Courtship in its early stages consists of cooing, head bobbing, and mutual preening. In New Mexico pair formation starts in late January, in Sonora somewhat later and nearer the beginning of the rainy season. Head bobbing involves much raising and lowering of the head while keeping the bill horizontal. At first a male bobs at any dove, male or female. Within a few days the females start bobbing back; but a male does not answer the bob of another male. These doves apparently identify each other as to sex largely by behavior. After bobbing, the male preens the head and neck feathers of the female, following which the female preens the male. Such public caressing has won this species the reputation of being very affectionate.

Mounting is another part of the courtship performance. In this a male perches on the back of a female and may, or may not, attempt to mate. But if the female is not ready, she goes on foraging and ignores him. The act of mounting also helps a male determine which individuals are females. If a male mounts another male, the latter throws him off, whereas a female tolerates a male on her back even when not ready for mating.

In a winter flock, courtship activities start among the older birds. As pairs are formed, they split off from the flock and commence to establish nesting territories. Later the birds of the year start pairing. Thus at any one time in early spring it is possible to find in a suitable area, such as a college campus, some birds still in a winter flock, others beginning to court or recently paired, some already established as early territorial pairs, and still others with nests and eggs.

In March and April the vertical tail fanning display marks the height of courtship. In this a male assumes a horizontal position a foot or two in front of a female. Uttering a throaty *cut-cut-ca-dóah* he raises his tail to a vertical position and fans it out so as prominently to display the black-and-white markings on the outer tail feathers. After the display the female preens him. About a week after the start of display the pair commences to build. But mating begins before building and continues during construction and probably while the clutch is being laid. Full courtship behavior lessens as nesting proceeds, but head bobbing and mutual preening go on until the end of the breeding season.

The nest is built in a vine, tree, or bush, usually on a horizontal fork or broken limb from 5 to 10 (but up to 25) ft. above the ground. Often it is placed near human habitations, sometimes even in or on a man-made structure. Usually, however, a shade tree, or thorn, cactus, mesquite, or acacia is chosen. Favorite shade trees include elm, live oak, sycamore, umbrella tree, and cottonwood.

Both male and female help build the nest. The female carefully places each twig in position and shapes the interior of the nest with her body. The male, following a rigid behavior pattern, searches on the ground until he finds a suitable stick, then flies with it toward the female. Alighting nearby, he walks to the female, climbs on her back, and when he reaches her shoulders passes the twig to her. She accepts it and puts it in place.

Nest building is normally a morning activity and usually stops by 10 A.M. The male spends three times as long looking for materials as he does passing them to the female. In a period of intense activity a male once made 12 trips to the nest in 12 minutes. Building usually takes place on three successive days. Often nests are constructed, or partly constructed, and then abandoned. A pair may start one or even two nests before putting together the final one. When building, a pair becomes quite preoccupied, and the near presence of a human being does not disturb them.

The nest is a loose, shallow, cupshaped platform of twigs, grasses, rootlets, and plant fibers. It is usually unlined. In it the female deposits two white, unglossed eggs, which hatch in 14 days. Egg dates for Arizona range from February 28 to October 21, with the bulk between April 15 and May 25. Egg dates for Texas are from April 16 to August 10, with the bulk between April 19 and May 28.

The young are fed at first by regurgitation. Droppings are not removed from the nest. Instead they accumulate and serve as a binder to cement the twigs more firmly together. The second and subsequent broods continue to add this kind of cement to the nest, which thus often becomes strong enough to last through the winter and be used the following season. One nest under study was occupied for four successive years and sheltered 11 broods. Sometimes the birds use an abandoned nest of another species, such as mourning dove or mockingbird.

The female dove incubates from late afternoon through to the next morning; the male sits during the heat of the day. Inca doves are close sitters and do not flush until almost touched. After the eggs hatch, the parents brood the young for about a week; after another week the young leave the nest; and for still another week the parents continue to feed them. The old birds start renesting shortly thereafter, while the young assemble in juvenile flocks. In New Mexico the post-nuptial molt takes place in September and early October. In late October and November there is some recrudescence of sexual behavior, but no nesting.

The Inca dove produces four kinds of sounds: (1) the song, *coo-coo*; (2) the aggression call, *cut-cut-cut, ca-dóah*; (3) the courtship call, *cut-cut-ca-dóah*; and (4) the alarm note, *cut*. Simmons describes the song as a "monotonous, tiresome, extremely mournful, rather short two-syllabled, hard little *coo,* quite different from the soft, soothing manner of the western mourning dove."

The Inca dove feeds on weed seeds and waste grain.

Description: Length, 8 in. Tail: long, narrow, and double rounded (i.e., outside and middle feathers are shorter than those between); legs short. Adults: gray-brown above, grayish pink below, buff belly; much red-brown in wings; brown and black tail, two outer tail feathers largely white, next two with white tips; entire plumage scaled; black bill, pink legs and feet. Young: duller, mottled above with pale gray-buff. The ground dove also shows red-brown in its wing in flight, but its tail is dark and stubby.

Incubation, 14 days; young stay 14 days in nest.

Size of eggs, 0.88 x 0.66 in.; two to five broods per year.

HUMMINGBIRDS / *Trochilidae*

Anatomically, hummingbirds are among the most remarkable birds. They are the smallest and have the most rapid heartbeats and wingbeats. These wingbeats make a humming noise from which the birds get their name. The hummingbird's breastbone is deeply keeled to permit the attachment of exceedingly powerful flight muscles. Hummers have great mobility of flight; they can hover, fly forward, sidewise, or backward. This mobility is due in part to the extraordinary development of the muscles that control the upstroke of the wing. In most birds only the downstroke is powered, weak muscles sufficing to raise the wing; but in the hummingbird, both upstroke and downstroke are powered strokes; the elevator muscles controlling the upstroke are almost half as heavy as the depressor muscles that power the downstroke, instead of being only one-ninth as heavy, as in the robin. The iridescence of the plumage is due to the structure of the feather and the angle at which the light strikes it; it is not pigment in the feather itself.

We usually first see a hummingbird hovering before a flower, darting its bill and tongue into the center of it, and then moving on to another. Hummers are attracted by bright colors. Hence these birds are especially fond of red flowers. But in woodland shade or swamps, orange

19

often appears brighter than red. In the desert, where everything is brown, they go quickly to a green blossom. The birds thrust their bills far into the flower; thus, like bees, they aid in pollination. Sometimes a hummer's head will emerge from a bloom all gilded with yellow grains of pollen, "the amorous anther's golden grime" of the poet.

Hummingbirds have a long, extensible, and double-tubed tongue that captures insects by its stickiness and takes up nectar by capillary action. These birds have the highest relative food consumption of any in the world and daily can consume twice their own weight in syrup alone. So active is their metabolism by day that some have to "hibernate" by night, when they assume a temporarily torpid condition in which their body temperature falls almost to that of the surrounding air.

Males display before the females in elaborate courtship performances, but their interest in the females is restricted to courtship and mating. Once mating is over, the males are off to further adventures in polygamy. Nest building, incubation, and care of the young devolves on the female.

Hummingbirds are confined to the New World. They originated in Central and South America; northwest South America today has the largest number of the 319 species known to science. Only 17 species enter the United States. All are at least partially migratory.

Hummers are readily attracted to preferred food flowers. Plant a few in your garden and have the pleasure of hummingbird company all through the warmer months. Here are some of their favorites: azalea, basswood, scarlet runner bean, bearberry, bee balm, bellflower, wood betony, Virginia bluebell, highbush blueberry, lowbush blueberry, bottlebush, bouncing bet, dwarf buckeye, flame buckeye, butterflybush, canna, cardinal flower, catnip; century plant, columbine, coralbells, cornflower, cotoneaster, ref-flowering currant, daylily, eucalyptus, figwort, four-o'-clock, foxglove, fuchsia, gladiolus, scarlet hamelia, hibiscus, hollyhocks, honeysuckle, cape honeysuckle, red horse chestnut, iris, jasmine, jewelweed, lantana, larkspur, lilac, lily, loquat, manzanita, matrimonyvine, milkweed, mint, monkeyflower, morning glory, nasturtium, new jersey tea, paintedcup, siberian peashrub, pelargonium, pentstemon, petunia, cape plumbago, flower fence poinciana, royal poinciana, oriental poppy, prickly pear, flowering quince, ragged-robin, rattlesnakeroot, redhotpoker, scarlet sage, scabious, snapdragon, great solomonseal, sourwood, spiderflower, scarlet starglory, sweetwilliam, thistle, tigerlily, tree tobacco, trumpet creeper, waxmallow, weigelia.

RUBY-THROATED HUMMINGBIRD (*Archilochus colubris*)

The ruby-throated hummingbird breeds over a larger expanse of territory than any other hummingbird in North America. It is the only hummer in the East.

The male and female are both dark green above and white below. The male, however, is distinguished by its iridescent ruby throat which in various lights or at a distance may appear black. The male weighs $\frac{1}{8}$ oz., the female $\frac{1}{7}$ oz. In the fall before migration each adds in fat half again as much to its weight. Its heart beats 615 times per minute.

This species breeds throughout North America east of the Plains from Alberta to Nova Scotia. It winters in Mexico and Central America. One of the most impressive feats in the bird world is the semiannual migration of this mite across the Gulf of Mexico. Thousands must perish each year in such a perilous adventure, but tens of thousands survive, and the species maintains its numbers despite the toll levied by wind, fog, rain, and fatigue.

The ruby-throat under straightaway conditions flies at a speed of about 30 mph and beats its wings 75 times a second.

The distance from the tip of Yucatan to the coast of Louisiana is 575 miles. If a hummer encountered no adverse winds, 10 hours would be required for the flight. Ten hours is 600 minutes or 36,000 seconds. Multiply this by 75 wingbeats per second and those tiny wings must beat with hardly a stop some 2,700,000 times in order to carry the migrant to its shore. All this is done on less than $\frac{3}{40}$ oz. of fat as fuel. The bird weighs, on the average, $\frac{1}{5}$ oz. before leaving one shore and $\frac{1}{8}$ oz., barely the weight of a copper cent, when it arrives at the other.

In spring migration, after it reaches its landfall on the Gulf coast, it proceeds northwards as rapidly as its favorite flowers come into bloom. The sexes migrate separately, the males preceding the females by several days. In fall migration the adult males start south a month before the females and immature birds. Except when artificially fed, ruby-throats are usually seen singly or in pairs, but occasionally in migration a group of up to a dozen of one sex will be found swarming over a favorite food tree.

In the autumn migration at Point Pelee, Ontario, this hummingbird is one of the most fearless species to plunge out over the waters of Lake Erie. Flying swiftly down the peninsula to the sand spit at its end, the hummer speeds straight out, low over the waves, toward Pelee Island and the American shore some 30 miles away.

The habitat of the ruby-throated hummingbird is woods, clearings, and gardens. It nests in woods or orchards and does most of its feeding on flowers that grow in the open.

The flight of the species is straight, but the bird may suddenly turn sharply, veer, rise, or shoot downward. In migration it seldom flies more than 25 ft. above the ground or water. It attacks birds much larger than itself and drives them off. Kingbird, crow, hawk, and eagle all retreat before a hummingbird's onslaught. It also spends much time in aggressive behavior toward other members of its own species. Its disposition is irascible, pugnacious, and fearless.

The ruby-throat's enemies are few. No other bird can catch it. Spider webs, however, occasionally snare one; some have been caught on thistles; occasionally one is grabbed by a frog and unconfirmed reports have indicated that when flying over water, the birds may be jumped at and swallowed by fish. Weather may sometimes be a dangerous enemy. Late frosts that kill the flowers on which hummingbirds feed may cause many to starve.

When the male ruby-throat arrives at his breeding grounds, he selects an exposed perch and watches day after day for a female. When one arrives he tries to attract her interest with a pendulum-like courtship flight in which he describes a parabolic, tilted or U-shaped curve with a radius of 3 to 40 ft. With various pauses, this performance may last from 2 to 20 minutes.

Other forms of courtship flight have been noted: (1) a male facing north makes a sideways flight 25 ft. from east to west and back again, with stops every 3 ft. to hover and hum; (2) a male and female about

2 ft. apart fly up and down 10 ft. vertically for 2 or 3 minutes; he is at the top of this aerial arena while she is at the bottom, and vice versa; their paths cross as one ascends and the other descends. Nuptial flights may continue as much as a month, until mating has been thoroughly consummated. Despite the male's protracted courtship the female shows interest in him for only 3 or 4 days before egg laying. After mating, the male disappears and does not aid or trouble the female further until the next breeding season.

Like the nests of other hummingbirds, the ruby-throat's is the size of an eyecup and is unusually beautiful. The walls are bud scales covered with lichens and lined with plant down; the structure is held together by the silk of spiders and caterpillars. An inch in diameter and an inch deep, it is saddled with glue of the bird's own saliva on a small horizontal or downward sloping limb from 5 to 50 ft. up, often near or over the water. At a distance it looks like a knot or gall. The nest is built by the female alone. Old nests are often renewed and remodeled the next season.

The two tiny white eggs, the size of peas, are laid about 48 hours apart, sometimes before the nest is completed. The eggs are so small that it would take 5,000 to equal the volume of an ostrich egg. Young hummingbirds are hatched blind and naked. They are fed five times an hour by regurgitation.

The ruby-throat, either in aggression or in defense of his territory, gives voice to a variety of sharp, clear, high-pitched, testy notes, chips or squeaks, emphatic but not loud, in groups of one, two, or three, or in phrases, the last note usually accented. Sometimes these notes might be written as *zzzt-zzz* or as a rhythmic *z,z,z,z,z,z,zzt*. A. A. Saunders, the bird-song expert, writes them as *tsit tsit tsit* or *tsidit tsidit tsidit*. A single bird is usually silent.

Flower nectar and small insects are the chief natural foods of this hummer. In front of blooms the bird hovers on fast beating wings. As it thrusts its bill into the center of the flower, it sticks out its long tongue to gather in both insects and nectar. The bird also feeds on sap exuding from maple trees or from the bark of a tree punctured by a sapsucker. Sometimes hummingbirds go flycatching amid swarms of little insects dancing in the air.

The ruby-throated hummingbird will readily accept a man-made nectar of 1 part honey and 3 parts water offered in a tilted test tube or hummingbird feeder. Sugar may be substituted for honey, but it lacks the proteins and vitamins that the birds need. Individual feeders may be hung on your porch or placed about your garden, or they may be set in a revolving stand with one or more decks and a dozen or more tubes. A perching wire in front of the tubes will make it unnecessary for hummers to hover while feeding. Keep ants away from the vials, as they will tend to drive away the birds. A ruby-throat may consume two teaspoonfuls of honey a day. It can be trained to come for food and perch on one's finger.

Description: Length, 3½ in. Long and needle-like bill; black bill, legs, and feet; wings pointed and relatively long; feet, small and weak; plumage, iridescent. Adult male: forked tail; bronze-green upperparts, whitish underparts; ruby or coppery throat, appearing black in some light. Female and immature: tail rounded; white throat and tips of outer tail feathers. *Note*: Tail feathers lack rufous edges; flight relatively silent for a hummer.

Incubation, 11 to 14 days; young stay 14 to 31 days (average 20) in nest.

Size of eggs, 0.52 x 0.35 in.; two broods per year.

BLACK-CHINNED HUMMINGBIRD (*Archilochus alexandri*)

The black-chinned hummingbird is the western counterpart of the ruby-throated hummingbird. It breeds west of the Rockies in the juniper and yellow-pine zones from southwestern British Columbia and northwestern Montana to Lower California and Texas, where it ranges east to Dallas and San Antonio. It winters from southeastern California south into Mexico.

The species is sparingly distributed in summer over its northern breeding range, but is relatively common from southern Utah south, and is quite abundant in southern New Mexico, Arizona, and around San Diego. The northward migration coincides with the blooming of its favorite food plants; the females arrive at summer territories a day or two before the males. This hummer breeds from sea level and the

bottom of the Grand Canyon to an altitude of 8,500 ft., advancing up
the mountainsides with the season, as drought withers its favorite
feeding flowers at lower elevation. In New Mexico it is most commonly
found in summer from 5,000 to 7,000 ft.

The black-chinned is the least brightly colored of our hummingbirds.
The male has a white collar below a squarish black chin and a violet
gorget. Female black-chins, ruby-throats, and Costa's hummingbirds
are best identified by the males they accompany; they cannot readily
be distinguished in the field.

The favorite habitat of the black-chinned hummingbird in spring
and summer is the Transition life-zone, i.e., the zone of yellow pines;
but the bird also thrives in semiarid country, particularly in hillsides,
watercourses, and towns. It often inhabits gardens, canyons, canyon
mouths, dry washes, and dry foothills, cedar-oak, mesquite, and juniper
associations; and mountainsides. Preferred nesting sites are in willows,
sycamores, and cottonwoods that mark underground watercourses or
which flank running streams in semidesert country. In breeding season
both sexes stake out a territory. The female defends a territory around
the nest while the male maintains his own feeding territory. Birds in
the irregular valleys of the Southwest often raise a first brood and then
depart for cooler regions, leaving their adolescent progeny behind.

As with other hummingbirds, the black-chin has a straight, swift
flight and the ability to hover and fly backward. At rest, it perches on an
exposed twig. The bird has extraordinary control of its wingbeats.

One of the courtship flights of the black-chinned hummingbird resembles one of the ruby-throat. In a typical performance the female is
perched on a low twig. The male, from an elevation nearby of perhaps
15 ft., swoops down in front of her and up again 15 ft. in a U-shaped
curve, his wings making a whizzing noise, particularly at the bottom
of the curve. At the top of the U-flight, he claps his wings together,
making a distinctive sound, then swoops down again, whizzing past her
and up to the top of the U, where he claps his wings again, and so on.
One such performance consisted of five U-shaped swoops and ascents in
the space of 1½ minutes. Except for the whizzing of the wings, both
birds were silent. Other observers, however, have noted during this
performance "a long-drawn, pulsating, plaintive, liquid note, probably
the most pleasing utterance of any of our hummingbirds" (Woods).

There is considerable variation in this nuptial flight. Sometimes the male's arc will have a chord of only 3 ft.; sometimes he will indulge in a high, vertical dive with gorget puffed and tail feathers widely spread. In another type of courtship flight the male, in a shuttling movement accompanied by a heavy droning of wings, describes the pattern of a Figure 8 on its side.

The nest of this species, like that of other hummingbirds, is dainty and beautiful. It is composed of budscales, small leaves, plant down, and spider webs, and is fastened on a horizontal or downsloping branch, usually from 4 to 8 ft. above the ground but sometimes as high as 30 ft. The nest is often found near or over water. The color of its plant-down walls often makes it look like a small yellow sponge. The structure differs from that of the ruby-throated hummingbird by the customary absence of lichens on the outside, except around San Antonio.

The birds usually build in shrubs or trees, particularly willows and sycamores, that border watercourses in dry regions; but sometimes they choose trees in orchards or build on horizontal branches of oaks. Occasionally the birds select unusual man-made situations for their nests such as the loop of a rope hanging in a garage, a porch in use day and night, a steel rod in the roof of a blacksmith's shop, a piece of haywire in the wall of a barn, and an electric wire near a porch light.

The black-chin builds a nest that is more elastic than most birds' nests. In it the female lays two white eggs, the size of a pea. The semi-globular shape and the size of the nest resemble a hollow golf ball with the top third removed; the middle is wider than the rim. This is supposed to have the effect of keeping eggs and young from tumbling out in a high wind. The plant down from thistles, milkweed, willows, and young sycamore leaves, which makes up the nest, is soft and spongy. If you squeeze your fist over even an old nest, it will come back into shape when released. The rim of the nest is especially elastic. This gives the nest a rather unique feature of expansion; as the young grow larger, they push the rim outward to make more room.

The song of the male is a faint, pleasant, high-pitched warble that some authors compare to whistling through one's teeth. The pursuit notes are similar to the song, but are louder and more "chittery," like light, rapid lipsmacking.

Flower nectar and small insects are staple food of this hummingbird. Nectar is secured by hovering in front of a flower and probing the bloom with the bill. Insects are often captured on the wing in the manner of flycatchers or may be picked off vegetation while the bird is hovering. Black-chins delight in man-made feeders, where they relish honey-water or sugar-water. Favorite feeding plants of this species include Texas buckeye, century plant, pink cleome, honeysuckle, iron-wood, red larkspur, Texas mountain laurel, mescal, ocotillo, palo verde, purple pentstemon, Texas redbud, and tree tobacco.

Description: Length, 3¾ in. Plumage, iridescent; dark bronze-green upperparts; spot behind eye; white tufts on sides of rump; light grayish underparts. Male: chin black and squarish; gorget violet (sometimes hard to see); white collar; greenish sides. Female: tail rounded, two middle feathers longest; white tips of three outer tail feathers; brown flecks on throat. *Note*: Male ruby-throat has ruby throat and lighter underparts. Female Costa's has less green in outer tail feathers than in black-chin; female ruby-throat has two central tail feathers shorter than other tail feathers; but these three females cannot be accurately distinguished in field.

Incubation, 13 to 16 days; young stay 21 days in nest.

Size of eggs, 0.49 x 0.33 in.; two or three broods per year.

ANNA'S HUMMINGBIRD (*Calypte anna*)

Anna's hummingbird is unique in several respects. It is the largest California hummingbird. The male is our only hummer with a red crown and gorget, the female the only one with red on the throat. Its nuptial flight is the most elaborate, its nest is found in the most unusual situations, and it is the only species that starts breeding as early as December. It is named for a woman friend of the zoologist Lesson, who first described the species.

Anna's hummingbird is California's own, the only one that lives primarily in the Golden State. It is resident from northern California to northern Lower California, west of the Sierra Nevada. It is also found on Santa Cruz Island. In fall and winter some wander northward to Humboldt Bay, west to the Farallone and other Santa Barbara islands, and a few go east through southern Arizona to northern Sonora.

The preferred habitat of this hummer is the Upper Sonoran life-zone, the zone of junipers and chaparral. Here it is found in canyons and wooded bottomlands and on hillsides, particularly among live oaks. After breeding, some individuals move up the mountains to pine forests. It is also widely distributed in the most populous parts of California, especially in city parks and gardens. It frequents urban window boxes and will enter a room through an open window in search for flowers. Joseph Grinnell, the California bird authority, tells how the presence of hummers depends on favorite flowers:

Like all the hummingbirds this species follows the flowers, and its local presence or absence is governed by their abundance or scarcity. Thus, in August and September hundreds of Anna hummers are to be found over the stubble fields and sunflower patches attracted by the flowers of the "tar-weed." During the winter months they are found in profusion about the blossoming eucalyptus trees. In January and February when the weather is mild, they appear high on the mountain sides among the flowering manzanitas; and in March and April in the blossoming orange groves in the valley, and about the currant bushes on the hillsides.

The habits of this striking species are similar to those of other hummingbirds. It feeds on nectar that is secured by probing with a long bill deep into the corolla of trumpet-shaped flowers, while it hovers before them on rapidly beating wings and pumping tail. It flies backward as it disengages its bill from the bloom.

This hummer likes to perch on exposed limbs, where it moves its head from side to side, dashing out every so often to catch its protein requirements on the wing from the swarms of midges and other tiny insects that dance in the air. It also picks small insects off leaves or stalks, while hovering.

Females maintain a nesting territory, males a feeding territory. From one or more strategically located jutting bare twigs, a male will drive off any other hummingbird that dares trespass on this domain. In other situations the supposedly aggressive behavior of this species may not be so vicious as it seems. In the course of daily activity, Anna's hummingbird puts forth as much energy, scientists calculate, as would be the equivalent of that supplied by the nectar of 1,000 fuchsia blossoms.

Like most hummingbirds this one is not afraid of bees, but strongly dislikes ants. It will poke its way through a mass of bees to get at the nectar of a flower; but a few ants crawling around the lip of a feeder will keep it away.

Studies of Anna's hummingbird in flight have shown that its wings are in almost constant motion; only very occasionally does it permit itself a short glide. Sometimes its wings beat from almost vertically above its body to almost vertically below, i.e., through an arc of almost 180 degrees. At other times the wings seem to beat only below the midline of its body. Normal flight produces a low hum that grows louder and higher in proportion to the speed of flight. "In wet weather," Woods tells us, "one may often hear from a flying hummingbird a sort of clapping sound of short duration, as if it were striking its wings together to rid them of moisture."

On the subject of its courtship, Woods writes:

The bird mounts upward until almost lost to sight then shoots vertically downward at tremendous speed, finally altering his course to describe an arc of a vertical circle, which carries him as closely as possible past the object of his attention as she sits quietly in some bush or tree. At the lowest point of the circuit he gives utterance to a loud, explosive chirp, which so nearly resembles the "bark" of a California ground squirrel (*Citellus beecheyi*) that one who is familiar with that sound may easily be deceived. From this point he continues along the arc until he arrives at a point directly above his mate, where he hovers for a few seconds with body horizontal and bill directed downward, rendering his squeaky "song." Then, without change of attitude, he begins to rise rapidly and vertically, repeating the entire maneuver until he tires or the other bird departs, with himself in hot pursuit.

The Anna's nest resembles that of other species of hummingbirds, but is likely to be more varied in composition. Its walls are composed of plant down, moss, vegetable fibers, and delicate stems. The outside is covered with lichens or mosses; the inside is often lined with feathers or fur and the whole is held together with spider silk.

A favorite nesting locality is an oak grove in a narrow canyon, where the nest is often placed on a branch near or overhanging a watercourse.

Orange and lemon trees in orchards are also chosen. The bird frequently nests in most unusual places in downtown Los Angeles and other California cities, on ladder rungs, advertising signs, and the wires under the crossarms of electric light poles. The nest is placed from 2 to 30 ft. above the ground.

In the nest, usually before it is completed, the female deposits two tiny white eggs. She continues building while she incubates. An observer at one nest noted that for several days the female spent almost exactly 2 minutes on the eggs and then 2 minutes off gathering more nesting material. The structure did not reach its full height until incubation was half completed, and the mother was still adding lichens to the outside when the first egg hatched.

Donald R. Dickey, a well-known California ornithologist, describes the growth of the young in the nest:

Finally, on the fourteenth day of incubation—a long period for so small a bird—the young hatched into black, grubby caterpillars, with smoky fuzz in two lines down the back, and squat, yellowish mouths that gave no hint of the future awl-like bills. Now the mother's care was redoubled, and on the fifth day their eyes opened. Two days later respectable pin feathers transformed them from loathsome black worms into tiny porcupines.

Now we saw more and more often the gruesome-seeming spectacle of their feeding. The female's foraged burden of small insect life, culled from the flowers' corollas, and doubtless nectar-sweetened, is transferred to the young by regurgitation, and to avoid waste the mother's needle bill is driven to its hilt down the hungry youngster's throat. It suggests, as someone has said, a "major surgical operation," but the young so obviously enjoy and thrive upon it that we outsiders slowly lost our fear for them. At last the feathers broke their sheaths and the wee mites took on the semblance of real hummers.

Only the male Anna sings. The song, enthusiastically and persistently delivered at virtually all times of the year, is a squeaky thin warble that has been likened to the filing of a saw or the whetting of a scythe. When singing, the bird sticks its neck forward and keeps its bill closed. Another note, also heard from the female, includes a little *chip* as the bird moves from flower to flower. This may be uttered more rapidly as a territorial defense warning note, when the bird is perched on one of its lookouts. While chasing another bird, both male and female often give voice to a series of shrill chittering notes, *ztikl-ztikl-ztikl*.

Anna's hummingbird is a regular visitor at hummingbird feeding stations, where it takes its quota of honey-water or sugar-water.

During the day a bird may come to the feeder at half-hour intervals, but toward sunset and immediately after will feed much more frequently. Its food plants are many. W. Leon Dawson, author of *The Birds of California,* says: "A catalogue of Anna's favorite flowers would be nearly equivalent to a botany of southern California. But if one had to choose *the* favorite it would probably be *Ribes speciosum,* the handsome red flowering gooseberry, for it is upon the abundance of this flower that Anna relies for her early nesting." Other special favorites include century plant, eucalyptus, and tree tobacco.

Description: Length, 4 in. Bronze-green back; wings and tail largely black; grayish underparts. Male: rose red crown and gorget with purplish reflections (look black in poor light); underparts washed with green; gorget pointed; tail forked. Female: tail rounded, middle feathers longest, white tips of outer feathers; resembles female ruby-throat, but throat usually has some red or bronze like immature male ruby-throat, though this may be absent in some individuals. Upperparts are darker green and underparts grayer than other hummers.

Incubation, 14 to 19 days; young stay 21 days in nest.

Size of eggs, 0.52 x 0.34 in.; two broods per year.

RUFOUS HUMMINGBIRD (*Selasphorus rufus*)

In the spring this species migrates northward along the lowlands and foothills west of the Rockies, particularly along the Pacific slope, the males a week in advance of the females. The rufous is the most northerly ranging of our hummingbirds. It breeds in the Canadian and Transition life-zones from latitude 61 degrees in southeastern Alaska, east to Alberta and Montana, and south to northwestern California. It winters in western and central Mexico. In the fall, in addition to the mountain route, a number move south over the plains, east of the Rockies through Wyoming, Colorado, and the Texas Panhandle, appearing along the Gulf coast as far east as Florida.

Within its range, in season, the rufous hummingbird is found wherever its favorite food flowers are blooming in gardens, orange groves, chaparral, streamsides, alpine meadows and other open spaces in the wild. All hummingbirds seem to be drawn toward red flowers, but particularly the rufous.

The rufous hummingbird, next to Allen's (p. 34) is perhaps our most aggressive hummer. When several species are together, it tends to dominate the assemblage. It attacks other rufous hummingbirds, other species of hummingbirds, and other species of birds with fine impartiality.

G. D. Sprot, in an article in the *Condor,* thus describes its courting and mating:

In the displays I have witnessed, which have been many, a careful survey of the ground beneath the performer invariably revealed the female sitting motionless on some twig of the low-growing underbrush, and as the aerial acrobat reached the limit of his upward flight she was seen to turn her head slightly and glance admiringly aloft. The male ascended usually with his back towards his mate, then turning, faced her, and with gorget fully expanded descended swiftly until within an inch or two of her, when spreading both wings and tail he checked himself and soared aloft again to repeat the performance, or else settled on some near-by bush. As he so checked his flight the whining note was produced, undoubtedly by the rush of air through the outspread feathers.

On two occasions, in May, 1925, and May, 1926, I witnessed in connection with the above performance what I believe to be the actual mating of the birds. After one or two towering flights by the male, the female rose from her perch and the male immediately closed with her. Then over a distance of some ten or twelve feet, and horizontally, they swung together backwards and forwards through the air, just as one often sees insects so doing. The regular swinging hum of the wings is hard to describe but is just what one might expect. So fast is this swinging flight, and so close was I, not over four or five feet away in one instance, that I was totally unable to see the birds except as a blurred streak of color. As the flight ceased I saw them separate, and in one instance the female was seen to fall to the ground, but later to regain her perch, while the male continued his towering flights.

L. L. Haskins, who made extended observations of this bird in the Willamette Valley, Oregon, reports:

Besides the diving act it has another modified performance. In this act the male "teeters" in the air above the female who is hidden in the grass below. It is like the dive, but the arc is much shorter and flatter—a shallow curve of only 6 or 8 inches. The male in this stunt shoots forward with the tail spread and much elevated, followed by a quick backward dart, tail lowered, and twittering and buzzing to his utmost. This is repeated again and again.

The well-built nest of this species follows the general hummingbird pattern. The walls are of plant down strengthened with vegetable stalks and moss. The outside is covered with moss, bud scales, bark shreds, or lichens; the inside is lined with plant down; and the whole is held together with cobwebs.

The nest is firmly saddled on a branch, usually one that hangs down, from 2 to 20 ft. above the ground. Drooping conifer limbs such as lichen-covered dead spruce branches are common sites, but a variety of deciduous trees, bushes, and even ferns are also chosen. Vines over-hanging embankments are preferred locations. The bird may use the same site year after year. It will often attach a second nest to the branch on top of the nest of the year before, and sometimes a third nest above the two old nests. In some places, rufous hummingbirds tend to colo-nize, and several nests may be found very close together.

The female builds the nest, incubates the two tiny white eggs, and rears the young without help from the male. There are, however, occasional exceptions to this rule, general among hummingbirds.

The rufous hummingbird enjoys two principal kinds of food: nectar and insects. The nectar it obtains from flowers. It also enjoys hovering before holes made by sapsuckers in the bark of various trees and drink-ing the nectarlike sap as it exudes. It secures insects flycatcher-fashion by sallying forth from its perch to chase them in mid-air, by hovering to pick them off vegetation or by licking them up from the corollas of flowers along with the nectar.

Favorite food flowers of the rufous hummingbird include those of the century plant, cherry, red columbine, crimson-flowered currant, fireweed, gilia, wild gooseberry, hibiscus, honeysuckle, tigerlilies, lupines, madrona, nasturtium, ocotillo, paintbrush, scarlet pentstemon, redhotpoker, salmonberry, salvia, and thimbleberry.

Description: Length, $3\frac{1}{2}$ in. Feet, small, weak; tail at rest, pointed. Male: fiery iridescent scarlet throat, looks orange or green in some lights; white chest; red-brown upperparts; head with faint greenish tinge; pale rufous underparts. Female and immature: bronze-green upperparts; white underparts and feathers, thus similar to female ruby-throat, but with base of tail and rump rufous, and light rufous flanks and underparts. *Note*: In fall the female broadtailed hummingbird also has rufous on sides at base of tail, but not in center of rump; male Allen's has rufous rump and checks, but a green back; female rufous in field indistinguishable from female Allen's.

Incubation, 12 to 14 days; young stay 20 days in nest.

Size of eggs, 0.52 x 0.35 in.; two broods per year.

ALLEN'S HUMMINGBIRD (*Selasphorus sasin*)

Allen's hummingbird is closely related to the rufous hummingbird and resembles it except for a green back. Instead of ranging over the entire West, however, Allen's is restricted in the breeding season to a narrow strip along the Pacific coast from southern Oregon to Ventura County, California. It migrates through Arizona and Lower California to winter in northwestern Mexico. In the same manner as its rufous cousin, Allen's comes north in spring through the lowlands, but in summer ascends the mountains to return southward along the ridges. A subspecies, slightly larger than the mainland form, is resident on the Santa Barbara islands and does not migrate.

The preferred habitats of Allen's hummingbird are canyons, ravines, gardens, parks, and stands of eucalyptus trees in the Transition and Upper Sonoran life-zones. In suitable areas the birds may sometimes be seen in considerable numbers, 100 or more having been reported one February in a single eucalyptus grove near Salinas, California.

This species seems to be even more aggressive than the rufous, and when the two are together, Allen's is dominant and will drive the other off. It is also shyer and at the same time more active than the rufous. It often perches on an exposed dead twig from which it can survey its territory.

During courtship the male defends a breeding or, more properly, wooing and mating territory. Later he defends a feeding territory of his own. He has no part in building the nest, incubating the eggs, or raising the young.

In his courtship flight, the male Allen's mounts 75 ft. in the air and dives down precipitously just over the female, who is perched on a twig. He emits a low buzzing sound as he passes her and suddenly swoops up. He then rocks back and forth in a 25-ft. semicircular arc in front of his prospective mate, uttering the while a series of mouselike squeaks. At the top of each arc he spreads his tail, violently shakes his body, and swoops down again. After several such pendulum-like swings back and forth, the bird mounts again 75 ft. in the air and repeats the performance.

Different observers have noted variations in this courtship display. Sometimes the arc is reduced to the design of a shuttle only a foot or two wide, which the male traces in air in front of the female.

The nest is a well-built structure of moss and plant stems, lined with plant down, decorated on the outside with lichens and bound together with spider silk or fine shreds of eucalyptus bark. The female often continues to dress up the outside with lichens long after incubation has started.

The nest is usually saddled on a small limb of a sapling, away from the main stem; but sometimes large trees, bushes, blackberry tangles, or vines are chosen, particularly if they are along a stream. In San Luis Obispo County, willow stands are a favorite location. Nests have been found from 1 to 90 ft. above the ground, but most are placed at elevations under 12 ft. At times the bird selects as a nest site an odd man-made object such as a hanging pulley, an iron hook, or the loop of a rope. Like the rufous hummer, this species often nests in colonies, frequently in conifers. The female lays two tiny white eggs.

The buzz that the male Allen's hummingbird produces at the bottom of his high dive during courtship flight is presumably made by air rushing through his wings or tail feathers. The noise may last for as long as a second, unlike the short, sharp, metallic clink of Anna's hummingbird. The ornithologist Henry W. Henshaw, who first described this species, pointed out other buzzing sounds. There is, for example, the buzzing from its wings when the bird is fighting. This is louder and more rasping than the soft, low hum when the bird is merely feeding. All these mechanical buzzes or hums are distinct from the vocal mouselike squeaks that the male Allen's utters as he swings back and forth in his pendulum-like arc.

The diet of Allen's hummingbird—nectar and insects—is like that of other North American hummers. Its favorite food plants include ceanothus, century plant, columbine, madrona, mint, monkey flower, scarlet sage, and tree tobacco.

Description: Length, 3½ in. Plumage, iridescent; feet, small, weak. Male: bronze-green upperparts; rufous rump, tail, and flanks; red or orange-red throat; white breast and underparts. Female: indistinguishable in field from female rufous.

Incubation, 14 to 15 days; young stay 21 days in nest.

Size of eggs, 0.50 x 0.34 in.; two broods per year.

WOODPECKERS / *Picidae*

YELLOW-SHAFTED FLICKER (*Colaptes auratus*)

The flicker is conspicuous, noisy, and well known. In the days before ornithologists standardized bird names, it had many colorful local appellations. F. L. Burns, who wrote a monograph on the flicker in 1900, listed 125 different names. Some of the more striking were: clape, yarup, highhole, wake-up, yocker-bird, wilcrissen, harry wicket, yellow hammer, gaffer woodpecker, partridge woodpecker, and pigeon woodpecker.

The yellow-shafted flicker belongs to the woodpecker family. As with other woodpeckers, stiff feathers in its tail help it cling upright to a tree trunk. Unlike almost all other species the plumage of the young resembles that of the father, not of the mother. Thus a young female has a black mustache like the adult male; but she loses this in her first autumn molt.

The flicker has a powerful bill that can chisel wood from a tree in search of wood-boring insects or in building its nesting hole. Its skull is constructed so that the root of the long sticky tongue, good for catching ants, curls over the top of the skull, forward into a groove above its right nostril. When needed for ant catching, the tongue can be shot out 2 or 3 in. beyond the end of the beak.

This species breeds east of the Rockies from the limit of trees in Alaska and Canada, south to the Gulf. It is found throughout the year in most of its range, but leaves the northernmost parts in winter; some birds migrate as far south as southern Texas and southern California, east of the Sierras.

The flicker migrates in loose flocks, largely by night. Along barrier beaches and mountain ridges, however, and at bottleneck peninsulas on flyways, many are seen traveling by day. In winter, flickers in northern states are occasionally found in swamps and on southern slopes of hills with staghorn sumacs or dense groves of cedars; they are principally seen along the coast, where they feed upon bayberries and forage in poison ivy.

The red-shafted flicker (*Colaptes cafer*) is found from the eastern foothills of the Rockies, west to the Pacific, spreading eastward onto the plains. It has red wing shafts and tail feathers; the male has a red mustache. There is a considerable area where the ranges of two kinds of flickers overlap, and hybridization takes place.

Yellow-shafted and red-shafted flickers are closely related. The latest official check list of the American Ornithologists' Union designates them as separate species; but since they interbreed readily, some scientists feel they are only subspecies. The habits of the two are similar, and most of the observations in this sketch apply to the red-shafted as well as to the yellow-shafted.

Of all our woodpeckers, the flicker adapts itself to the most varied habitat. It breeds in woods, edges of woods, swamps, brushlands, and open country with scattered trees. It is a bird of lawn and garden as well as of remote clearing. It nests with equal facility in Central Park, New York City, and the wilderness of northern Canada.

Flickers, especially in spring, beat a loud tattoo with their bills on a dead branch or tree trunk, or even on a telephone pole or roof.

These woodpeckers rise and retire early. One observer found that they habitually went to roost a half-hour, sometimes an hour, before sunset. As a roost they use the nest cavity, a sheltered spot on a tree trunk, a hiding place against some building, or another protected nook. They will also roost in an artificial roosting box.

The flicker spends more time on the ground than any other woodpecker. It progresses awkwardly by hopping and running. It often runs a short distance and then stops, as does a robin. It has a passion for ants, and whenever it locates an anthill, tears it open and laps up the inhabitants. On long flights the flicker flies straight and strongly, with fairly rapid wingbeats and slight undulations. Its short flights, however, are undulating and consist of rapid wingbeats on the rise, slower beats on the dip, then a short glide. In flight the bird displays a big white rump and yellow underwings.

These conspicuous marks cause it to be one of the first birds that beginning bird watchers learn to identify in flight. When it lands, swooping up against the trunk of a tree or perching on a branch, the white rump suddenly disappears, covered over by other feathers and wings. Scientists regard this as a form of protective coloration. They hypothesize that an enemy in pursuit would follow the prominent white rump. When this suddenly vanishes, the baffled pursuer would lose sight of its intended victim.

One enemy of the flicker is the peregrine falcon, which from high on a cliff can spot a flicker flying across the valley. If the falcon can swoop successfully before the woodpecker reaches safety, a collection of brown, red, and yellow feathers will soon adorn his nest. Other hawks, notably sharp-shinned and Cooper's, also prey upon flickers. In the competition for nesting sites, the starling dominates this woodpecker.

The courting of the flicker is a noisy, amusing, and complicated performance. In spring two courting flickers on the ground hop about each other with their bills raised at an odd 30-degree angle. First one hops, then the other. One or both may go clockwise or counterclockwise; the two seem to be held together by an invisible string, and the playing goes on within a circumscribed area. After a time, one hops out through the charmed circle and the play is over.

In flicker courtship the female often takes the dominant role. A common pattern is for two females to go after one male. The females perform in front of the male and fight between themselves for his favor. A male, however, will fight off a rival male. The male spends much time looking for a nesting site, but the final selection is apparently made by the female. Females recognize a male by its black mustache; males recognize females by absence of the mustache.

The long, ringing *yuk, yuk, yuk* calls are often given as part of the courtship performance, but we sometimes hear them at other seasons, too. Typical sounds also include a loud *wake-up, wake-up*; an inquiring, slightly threatening cry that suggests the French word *bien*; and a wide variety of other notes.

The flicker usually nests from 2 to 90 ft. above the ground in a dead tree trunk or branch, in a cavity that the bird chisels out with its sharp bill. It has been known to nest in telephone poles, buildings, chimneys, haymows, hayricks, kingfishers' burrows, on the ground, and in a variety of other places.

The entrance hole is about 3 in. wide and leads several inches in and about a foot down to the nesting cavity, which is 7 to 8 in. in diameter. The nest itself is nothing but a thick layer of wood chips hacked from the inside of the cavity. On this the female lays six to eight eggs. A flicker's egg is "pure lustrous white, with a brilliant gloss; the shell is translucent and, when fresh, the yolk shows through it, suffusing the egg with a delicate pinkish glow, which is very beautiful" (Bent). The egg is normally laid between 5 and 6 o'clock in the morning. The male incubates by night; male and female take turns by day. The sitting partner is fed by the other. The flicker readily accepts an artificial nesting box. This should face south on a pole, and the bottom should be covered with a layer of wood chips.

Birds fall into two groups as far as egg laying is concerned. The female may be capable of laying a definite or an indefinite number of eggs. Pigeons, doves, herring gulls, and most shorebirds lay a definite number of eggs. If anything happens to an egg or to the clutch, the female does not lay more eggs that season. Other birds, such as the domestic hen, are indefinite or "indeterminate" layers. With the proper stimulus they will keep on laying a long time—the hen, in fact, all year under conditions of domesticity.

Young flickers spend a relatively long time in the nest. When first born, according to A. R. Sherman, who did a study of this species:

The pellucid color of the newly hatched flicker resembles that of freshly sunburned human skin, but so translucent is the nestling's skin that immediately after a feeding one can see the line of ants that stretches down the bird's throat and remains in view two or three minutes before passing onward. This may be witnessed for several days.

If you tap on a nesting tree, the young will make a hissing noise like a swarm of bees. As the nestlings develop, they use their claws to climb and hold to the inside walls of the nest cavity. The parents feed them by regurgitation, the adult poking its bill far down the throat of the young, or the young holding the parent's bill crosswise. Very young flickers have growths at the corners of the gape, which some students think help to channel the regurgitations down the nestling's throat to keep the food from spilling. One student believes the black crescent on the parent's breast serves as a target for the young to strike at in soliciting food. When this area is touched by the young, it seems to act as a stimulus for regurgitation.

The excreta of the young is discharged in a gelatinous bag called a fecal sac. For the first ten days these are eaten by the parents. Later the parents pick them up in the bill and drop them at a distance from the nest. After feeding the young, if the parent finds no fecal sac in the nest, it stimulates the nestling to discharge one by poking the stub of its tail with its bill.

Three-fifths of the flicker's food is of animal origin, two-fifths vegetable; three-fourths of the animal food is ants; 5,000 of these were once found in a single flicker's stomach. The flicker eats more ants than any other bird. The flicker's animal diet also embraces wood-boring beetles, wasps, grasshoppers, crickets, woodlice, and caterpillars. Occasionally it flies out to catch insects like a flycatcher. Its vegetable diet includes berries of goodwood, mountain ash, black gum, poison ivy, sumac, and Virginia creeper, as well as blueberries, blackberries, pokeberries, serviceberries, elderberries, barberries, mulberries, hackberries, wild grapes, wild cherries, and acorns.

Suet is a favorite food of the flicker at the feeder.

Description: Length, 13 in. Bill strong, pointed; stiff tail; feet with two toes forward and two pointing back. Brown plumage; white rump; yellow underwings; red crescent on nape; black crescent and spots on breast. Male and young have black mustache, lacking in adult female.

Incubation, 11 to 12 days; young stay 25 to 28 days in nest.

Size of eggs, 1.1 x 0.9 in.; one to two broods per year.

RED-BELLIED WOODPECKER (*Centurus carolinus*)

Many people believe the red-bellied woodpecker is as representative of the South as the mockingbird. Scientists have confirmed this conviction by designating the red-belly as one of the typical birds of the Carolinian life-zone, which covers most of the South.

The red-belly is resident of most of the United States, east of the plains. It ranges northward into Ontario, but is not found in the Northeast. It has no regular migration; but there is some fall wandering. There is also some southward shift in winter, and in the southern states at that season the bird becomes much more common.

With the climate warming of recent years, the species is gradually pushing its way northward. Bird watchers now see it regularly in areas north of its range of only 30 years ago.

Open woods, the edges of woods, orchards, swamps, woods along watercourses, farms and residential suburbs are habitats favored by the red-belly. So are roadside fence posts, yards, gardens, and shade trees. In Florida it also likes wet bottomlands, orange groves, and hummocks, as the clumps of hardwoods surrounded by grassy everglades are called.

In northern portions of its range this bird shows some preference for deciduous or mixed woodlands, but in the South it is commonly found amid the pines.

The red-bellied woodpecker, like other woodpeckers, is adapted to clinging to the trunk of a tree and chopping out holes in the wood with its strong, sharp beak. It chisels holes to secure insects and to excavate its nesting cavity. Its skull and the membrane around the brain are thickened to enable it to withstand the shock of its beak chopping on hard wood. When it locates an insect it shoots out its extensible, barbed, sticky tongue, impales the insect, and devours it.

The yoke-toed feet of this woodpecker, two toes forward and two toes back, and its stiff tail feathers enable it to cling to the vertical trunk of a tree, to hitch its way up, or to sideslip its way down. As do other woodpeckers, it has an undulating flight.

The red-belly is so vocal we usually have little difficulty in finding

it. Like the flicker it is often seen on the ground eating ants. Like some
other woodpeckers and jays, it has the habit of storing acorns, beechnuts, and other food in various crevices and hideaways for future use.

The nest of the red-belly is gourdshaped, 12 to 18 in. deep in a dead
tree or telegraph pole or in a partly decayed tree branch or stub. The
entrance hole is 1¾ to 2 in. in diameter. Both male and female work
on the excavation. The species is not averse to height, and nesting holes
130 ft. above the ground have been reported; but most are not above
50 ft.

The red-belly prefers to nest in soft-wooded deciduous trees such as
sycamores, basswoods, elms, maples, poplars, and willows rather than
in the harder-wooded oaks, ashes, and hickories. In the South the dead
stub of a cabbage palm is a favorite location. In southeastern Georgia
and in other areas it often nests in pines. In Texas the dead upper parts
of backyard hackberries are much used.

Seven to ten days are usually required for the excavation of a nesting
cavity, and this may be used more than one season. The depth of the
cavity seems to vary with the amount of light that can enter, darkness
apparently being preferred. In a protected position, such as the underside of a branch where less light can enter, the cavity is usually shal-
lower.

Like all woodpeckers, this species lays glossy white eggs. Four to six
is the usual number.

The red-belly will lay again if disaster overtakes the first set of eggs.
Such disasters, in former years, sometimes appeared in the form of
egg collectors. The nest of one red-belly was once robbed by collectors
until the female had laid four sets, or a total of 19 eggs. Male and female
both incubate the eggs and both feed and help care for the young.

C. J. Maynard, a New England ornithologist who wrote about birds
in Florida, has this to say of the red-belly in winter:

I found the red-bellied woodpeckers quite abundant in winter in the
piney woods which border the plantations on the Sea Islands off the Caro-
linas but as I proceeded south, their numbers increased and in Florida, they
fairly swarmed, actually occurring in flocks. They accompany the cockaded
woodpeckers in the piney woods and also associate with the yellow-bellies
in the swamps and hummocks; in fact, it is difficult to remain long in any

portion of Florida where there are trees, without hearing the discordant croak of these woodpeckers and I even found them on the Keys.

The most common sound made by this bird is often written *cha cha cha*. Another frequently heard sound is usually written *churr, churr, churr*. This note is similar to but harsher than the note of the red-headed, and it has more of a scolding quality. The red-belly is somewhat exceptional among woodpeckers in the variety of its notes.

RED-HEADED WOODPECKER

Like other woodpeckers, the red-belly, especially in spring, drums a tattoo on a dry, resonant branch. This serves both as a mating call and as a warning to other red-bellies to keep away. On a still day this drumming can be heard for half a mile.

The diet of the red-bellied woodpecker is about one-third animal in origin and two-thirds vegetable. Animal food consists primarily of ants, beetles, caterpillars, grasshoppers, and on occasion the larvae of a coddling moth. The vegetable food includes acorns, beechnuts, various berries and fruits, some seeds and occasionally corn. The red-belly also likes oranges, both on the ground and on the tree.

Favorite feeder foods are suet and meat scraps, but bread crumbs, nuts, and scratch are also taken.

Description: Length, 10 in. Skull, strong; bill, strong and pointed; tongue, extensible; tail, stiff; two toes pointing forward and two backward. Red nape; barred back and wings; white patches on rump and wing, conspicuous in flight; gray underparts; reddish wash on belly. Crown: red in male, gray in female; the young are duller and have the all-gray head.

Incubation, 14 days; young stay 14 to 15 days in nest.

Size of eggs, 1.0 x 0.8 in.; one brood per year in North and two to three in South.

HAIRY WOODPECKER (*Dendrocopos villosus*)

Except for size, the hairy and downy woodpeckers are nearly identical in appearance. The hairy averages half again as long as the downy. Its bill is also much larger and heavier than the downy's; it is twice as long as the distance from the base of the bill to the eye. The hairy weighs two to three times as much as the downy. These two woodpeckers are sympatric species; i.e., are closely related and occupy much the same range, but have slight but critical differences in habits, ecological requirements, etc., which prevent them from interbreeding and maintain their status as distinct species.

The range of the hairy woodpecker is the forested and orchard regions of North America, from Alaska south through the mountains of Central America to Panama. It occurs from sea level to timber line. It is largely a resident species and hardly has a true migration. However, there is some shift southward in winter, and in the mountains some vertical movement to lower levels. There is also considerable wandering in colder months. Hence, the individuals you see in winter may not be the same ones you see in the same locality in summer.

Isolated populations of hairy woodpeckers, especially those in the tropics, tend to look less like races of the species living adjacently. This is the classic way in which speciation occurs. It is theorized that if populations remain apart long enough that when reunited with other hairy woodpeckers, each behaves toward the other as a separate species.

The hairy woodpecker is not common. Except in the forests, mountains, or South, most people see five times as many downies in a given time as they do hairies. This is partly because downies are more common throughout the country as a whole and partly because they are much more common near the haunts of man.

The home range of the hairy is a relatively few acres. Over the country as a whole the bird is found in hardwoods as well as in conifers, and in bottomland as well as mountain forests. Random observations show that it inhabits roughbarked more than smoothbarked trees.

This woodpecker clings upright to a tree trunk, supported by its stiff tail and by feet that have two toes forward and two back. (Most birds have three toes forward and one back.) From time to time it drives its hard sharp beak into the trunk to chop out the hole it wants. Then it sticks out its long barbed tongue, impales the larva of a wood-boring beetle, draws back the tongue, and swallows the morsel. In order to withstand the force of the hard repeated shocks of the bill, the skull is unusually strong and the brain is enclosed in an unusually thick membrane.

Just how the woodpecker knows where and when to strike into the wood for a grub is not known. In summer when the beetle larvae are actively boring through the wood, the faint crunching noise they must make may well be audible to a sensitive woodpecker ear. But in winter when the larvae are dormant, how then? One theory is that the woodpecker's senses can detect the difference in sound between a tap on solid wood and a tap on hollow wood that contains a dormant larva.

Day after day much of the hairy's time is spent clinging to the bark, making short jumps up or around the trunk, ever ready to drive in its bill for food. Frequently it progresses up the trunk in spirals and continues out along a horizontal branch, often pausing while clinging beneath the branch to deliver blows from this inverted position.

When flying from tree to tree the hairy woodpecker has an undulating flight. The longer the flight, the greater the undulations. The bird beats its wings on the rise, then holds them beside its body for the downward glide. The beating wings make a distinct noise that sounds like *prut-prut-prut*. When the bird lights on a trunk, it clings vertically. When it perches on a horizontal branch, it perches crosswise.

In winter the hairy will sometimes—but less often than the downy— join mixed groups of nuthatches, chickadees, and other small birds. In the West its associates may also include Cassin's finches and juncos. At this season the hairy comes closer to the habitations of man, is more frequently seen in settled districts, and will visit the feeder. In Alaska, in winter it frequents trees in village streets.

The hairy is noisier, shyer, and more restless than the downy. However, you can sometimes attract one by knocking with a stick on a dead limb or tree trunk in imitation of its tattoo.

The female, it is thought, selects the nest site. Usually, but not always, it is a new one each season. Both birds help in the excavation. In a week they may dig out a cavity in a soft-wooded species such as poplar, but it may take them three weeks to do so in the hard wood of a sound maple. Telltale chips are sometimes seen on the ground at the foot of a nesting tree. The male has the somewhat unusual habit of digging out a shallow sleeping hole for himself in a tree nearby.

The nest tree may be either living or dead, and the hole (usually about $1\frac{7}{8}$ x $1\frac{1}{2}$ in.) may be from 5 to 60 ft. from the ground. The gourdshaped cavity is about a foot in depth. The bottom is covered with fresh chips of wood in which the eggs are partially buried. The eggs, normally four in number, are pure white. When freshly laid they are translucent enough for the yolk shining through to give them a beautiful orange-pink color.

Major Charles E. Bendire, the bird biographer of the 1890s, wrote:

The duties of incubation are divided between the sexes and last about two weeks. The young when first hatched are repulsive-looking creatures, blind and naked, with enormously large heads, and ugly protuberances at the base of the bill, resembling a reptile more than a bird. They are totally helpless for some days, and cannot stand; but they soon learn to climb. They are fed by the parents by regurgitation of their food, which is the usual way in which the young of most woodpeckers are fed when first hatched.

. . . The young remain in the nest about three weeks. When disturbed they utter a low, purring noise, which reminds me somewhat of that made by bees when swarming, and when a little older they utter a soft "puirr, puirr." Even after leaving the nest they are assiduously cared for by both parents for several weeks, until able to provide for themselves.

At first the parents enter the nesting cavity in order to feed the young. As the latter grow larger, however, they poke their heads out of the entrance hole to be fed. The partly grown young make considerable noise in the nest.

The hairy has a kingfisher-like rattle that resembles that of the downy, but is louder. To my ear its notes seem to be all on the same pitch, and it has been so described by such ornithologists as Ralph Hoffman and others. A. A. Saunders, the great bird song expert, however, says that the rattle, more slurring than a kingfisher's, rises a little at first and then drops considerably. The call note, a hard *peenk,* is similar to, but louder and harder than, the downy's.

The tattoo that the hairy beats on a resonant dead limb differs from that of the downy by being louder and shorter and by having a greater interval between beats. In the mating season the hairy utters a flicker-like *kuweek, kuweek, kuweek.*

About three-quarters of the hairy's diet is of animal origin, principally insects; about one-quarter is of vegetable origin, mostly fruits and seeds. The chief single item is the larvae of wood-boring beetles. Next in importance are ants and caterpillars. Such nuts as acorns, beechnuts, and hazelnuts are favorite foods in fall and winter. So are pinyons and pine seeds.

The favorite feeder food of this species is suet and meatbones.

Description: Length, 8 to 10½ in. Skull and bill, strong; length of bill, twice distance from base of bill to eye; tail, stiff; feet zygodactyl, two toes forward, two back. Black and white upperparts and wings; white underparts and three outer tail feathers. Males have red spot on back of head; young males have reddish crown.

Incubation, 15 days; young stay three to four weeks in nest.

Size of eggs, 0.9 x 0.7 in.; one brood per year.

DOWNY WOODPECKER (*Dendrocopos pubescens*)

Next to the chickadee at the winter feeding station the downy woodpecker is probably the favorite bird, with its trim lines, poised carriage. conservative colors, and businesslike actions. It is fascinating to watch the way it clings to the trunk of a tree; hitches its way up, down, or over; chops at the bark; or drums away on a resonant branch.

The range of this woodpecker includes the wooded parts of the continental United States and Canada except southern Texas and the extreme Southwest; it is absent or rare in the deserts and deep forest and is not common in the mountains. The downy and hairy woodpeckers are a similar and closely related species that occupies much the same range, but does not interbreed. As is usually the case with sympatric species, the range of the larger of the two extends somewhat farther north, especially in winter.

The downy is a resident species and has no regular migration. From the North and the mountains, however, there is some shift of population southward and downhill in the colder months; after the breeding season, some individuals wander. Therefore the birds you see in winter in any area may not necessarily be the same ones you see in summer.

The downy, a dooryard woodpecker, is much more sociable than the hairy. It is common near the haunts of man where it frequents shade trees, city parks, and orchards. It is found also in pine woods in Florida, in old river beds, and swamps in the Northwest, in willows and alders in Alaska, and in stream bottoms and small woodlots everywhere. The home range of an individual downy is not large. One study near Yonkers, New York, showed that in the breeding season about 4 acres was the average foraging area per pair.

This woodpecker is not usually a conspicuous bird. Normally we hear it before we see it. It spends its time climbing or spiraling up the trunks of trees or horizontally along their branches. After working its way up the trunk of one tree, it drops down to start over again at the base of another. The bird is supported when vertical by the stiff feathers in its tail and by feet that have two toes pointing forward and two backward, instead of the usual arrangement of three toes forward and one toe back.

As it climbs, it inspects the surface of the bark for insects and their eggs, and chops into the wood for larvae burrowing within. These it impales and extracts with a barbed, sticky tongue that it can shoot out a distance of 2 in. One bird once spent 13 minutes going up only 10 ft. of trunk. In that time it pecked the bark, virtually without stopping, at the rate of 100 strokes a minute, netting 52 grubs. In fall and winter the downy often works over weed stalks, corn stalks, and shrubbery.

"Industrious," "vivacious," and "confiding" are favorite adjectives for describing this species. It is also agile and versatile. It will cling to the underside of a pine cone or branch. It can snatch insects on the wing, and at a feeder will sometimes catch nut kernels that are tossed to it. If there is snow on the ground, it indulges in a snow bath.

The courtship of the downy has been variously described. William Brewster, the well-known ornithologist, observed this behavior one May near Concord, Massachusetts:

At 8 A.M. saw a pair of downy woodpeckers in young oaks behind Ball's Hill, behaving very strangely. They kept flying from tree to tree, flapping their wings slowly and feebly like butterflies, sometimes moving on a level plane, sometimes in long loops, occasionally sailing from tree to tree in a long *deep* loop. Their wings had a strange fin-like appearance due, probably, to the way they were held or flexed. They both uttered a low, harsh, chattering cry, almost incessantly. No doubt this was a love performance, but they were male and female and both "showed off" in the same way.

The downy woodpecker nests in a gourdshaped cavity from 8 to 12 in. deep in a dead tree, dead branch, or telegraph pole at a height of 5 to 30 ft. above the ground. Rarely is a living tree chosen. Occasionally the nest is placed up to 60 ft. above the ground. The female generally selects the site. The pair chisels out the cavity afresh each year through a symmetrically round entrance hole about 1¼ in. in diameter. The bottom of the cavity is lined with wood chips on which four to six white eggs are laid. The bird will also nest in a bark-covered man-made nesting box.

Both male and female incubate the eggs. The young are hatched blind, naked, and ugly. Whether in their earliest stages they are fed by regurgitation is unknown. But in four or five days they are taking whole insects. As the young grow older, they also grow noisier. At times they chipper in the nest like a hive of bees.

When young woodpeckers leave the nest they are capable of making a long flight and landing well up in another tree. In order to attain such proficiency on the wing, they remain in the nest longer than the young of ground-nesting birds such as sparrows. These latter may flutter about on the ground or low limbs for several days after leaving the nest before achieving their full powers of flight.

In winter, downies roam the woods in loose association with chickadees, titmice, nuthatches, creepers, kinglets, juncos, and others. A continual conversational chipping and calling seems to help keep the birds together as the flock moves slowly through the woods. At night the downy may roost in its nesting cavity, in a man-made nest box, or in a roosting cavity it has specially chiseled out in a protected spot.

A common sound made by the downy woodpecker is a distinctive rattle or whinny. It is somewhat like the hairy's rattle, but is not so loud and has a characteristic regular drop in pitch. The notes are separable and can be counted. They are not slurred as are those of the hairy. The bird's call note is a short, sharp *pink,* which has been likened to the sound of a marble quarrier's chisel. The note is often heard in flight.

In the spring the downy's mating call is a steady tattoo, drummed with its bill on a resonant dead limb. (The similar tattoo of the hairy is louder and has pauses.) Both sexes do this drumming, although it is thought that the males do it more. The same drumming serves to establish property rights over a foraging or nesting area. The drumming constitutes an audible "no trespassing" sign for other downies.

The food of the downy is about three-quarters animal in origin, largely insects, and about one-quarter vegetable. The principal insects are beetles, wood-boring ants, and caterpillars; but it also takes larvae of coddling moths and wood-boring beetles (though fewer than does the hairy) and eggs of tent caterpillars. The vegetable part of its diet includes sap, seeds, berries, fruit, and a cambium layer of bark.

The favorite feeder food of the downy is suet. It may be hung in mid-air as a ball or placed in a container on the side of a tree.

Description: Length, 5½ to 7¼ in. Strong, pointed bill, and as long as distance from base of bill to eye; tail, stiff; feet, two toes pointing forward and two back. Black and white plumage; white back; three outer tail feathers have black bars; male has red patch on back of head; young male has red crown.

Incubation, 12 days; young stay two weeks in nest.

Size of eggs, 0.7 x 0.6 in.; one to two broods per year.

CROWS, JAYS, MAGPIES / *Corvidae*

GRAY JAY (*Perisoreus canadensis*)

The gray jay, known also as Canada or Oregon jay, is a resident species of boreal forests. It occurs from northern New England, northern New York (mountains) and northern Minnesota to Newfoundland, British Columbia and the Yukon, and also in the mountain forests of the West. It does not migrate, though from the northern parts of its range a few may shift southward in autumn and in severe winters. Within most of this range the birds are found throughout the year, usually in pairs or in small groups of three to ten.

The gray jay is our only jay that is primarily gray in color. It looks like an overgrown chickadee. In very cold weather it appears bigger because it keeps warm by fluffing out its feathers.

The Indians called the gray jay "wiss-ka-chon," which the white man corrupted to "Whiskey John" and then "Whiskey Jack." "Moose bird," "camp robber," "meat bird," "grease bird," and "Hudson Bay bird" are other names by which it is known.

The species is inquisitive, tame, and bold. It follows the trail of the trapper, frequents the camps of logger, miner, sportsman, and tourist. It comes to the sound of an ax and, unlike most birds, is also attracted by the noise of a gun. It eats from the camper's table and steals from his tent.

Its "thieving" habits are often annoying. It takes bait from a trap line and sometimes eats a trapped dead animal. But the "moose bird" is a dependable companion of man in the wilderness. Its cries break the silence of the forest.

The flight of a "Whiskey Jack" is deliberate, quiet, light, and rather slow. On broad wings the bird seems to float in the air. It seldom flaps, except when making one of its rare long flights.

A common sight is to see one glide gracefully from the top of one tree to a lower branch of another nearby. It usually coasts to a perch at the end of each glide. Then it hops up the tree, often in a spiral around the trunk, as does Steller's jay (p. 58). On the ground it hops rather than walks.

Little is known of its courtship. It nests, with snow still on the ground, from late February to April, sometimes with the temperature at 32 degrees below zero. When breeding, the birds are shy and secretive. They forsake the haunts of man for sites deep in the wilderness. A favorite spot is in a thick clump of conifers, often near a sphagnum bog. But where the forest is open, the bird will build in an isolated tree. If there are no evergreens, it may use a willow.

The nest is bulky and high-walled. It is carefully and warmly constructed of twigs, grasses, and bark strips. Inside it is lined with mosses, lichens, and plant down, and with feathers often from several different kinds of birds. Cocoons and spider webs hold the structure together. It is placed from 4 to 10 (or occasionally 30) ft. up in a crotch or on a horizontal branch of a tree, generally near the trunk. The three or four eggs have a grayish or greenish ground color and are evenly or irregularly spotted with olive-buff. Only the female sits; but both parents feed the young.

This jay is less noisy than either the blue jay (p. 55) or Steller's jay (p. 58). One of its notes resembles somewhat the cry of the blue jay. Another suggests the cry of the red-shouldered hawk (but less so than does the similar note of the blue jay). Brewster recognized a succession of eight or ten short, rather mellow whistles, all in the same key; also a loud *cla, cla, cla, cla, cla, cla cla,* not unlike the cry of the sparrow hawk; and a scolding note like that of a Baltimore oriole. Seton heard a *chuck, chuck* note, like that of a robin. Bent credits this jay with being something of a mimic. DeMille says that as one comes gliding to a perch near its mate, there is a series of rapid, grating cries, changing abruptly to a soft, high-pitched purring.

In spring some of these jays have a low, pleasant song somewhat like the catbird's. This may be delivered from a treetop or from a well-concealed branch. It is a *sotto voce* song, and many who think they know the jay well have never heard it.

The gray jay will eat anything from soap to plug tobacco. In spring, summer, and fall it prefers insects, especially grasshoppers, wasps, bees, beetles, and caterpillars, but also takes buds, seeds, fruits, berries, or scattered grain.

From camp grounds or feeders gray jays often take more than they eat. One of their favorite feeder foods is baked beans.

Description: Length, 12 in. Stout, pointed bill; rounded wings and tail; white forehead, throat, and collar; black cap on back of head; rest of plumage gray, darker above. Young: dark slate, head blackish. *Note*: Northern shrike has longer hooked beak and black wings and tail.

Incubation, 17 days; young stay 15 days in nest.

Size of eggs, 1.1 x 0.8 in.; one brood per year.

BLUE JAY (*Cyanocitta cristata*)

The blue jay is our only bright blue and white bird with a crest. The combination of its spirited, aggressive ways and loud, varied calls gives the species a highly distinctive character.

East of the Rockies, this is one of the first brilliantly colored birds the beginning bird watcher learns. It is an easy bird to recognize because there is no similar species and it is found throughout the year over most of its range.

Originally the blue jay was a bird of the forest and the forest edge.

Today it also frequents lawn and garden, ranch, suburb, and city park. Although it is found all year over most of its range, the same individuals may not be present both winter and summer. There is a general southward shift of the population in autumn; and the migration of hundreds or thousands of blue jays frequently attracts general attention.

Many people object to the jay's bad manners. It frequents feeders and, when feeding, drives most other birds away.

The jay is an alert, wary bird. Whenever you hear its loud *cla cla cla cla,* you may be sure something is afoot, a cat on the prowl, a hawk, an owl, or a human nearby. Other birds recognize these notes also, so that in effect the jay, without any intent on its part, acts as a kind of sentinel.

The blue jay's flight is usually straight and level, recognizable at a considerable distance. The bird flies with outspread "fingered" flight feathers. Except in migration it seldom travels in a group across an open space. First one goes, then another after a short time, and then another, as if each one were waiting to see if anything happened to those ahead of it. Sometimes something does, if a peregrine falcon is at hand. These duck hawks are fond of swooping down on birds flying across a valley, and blue jay's feathers are not infrequently found in a peregrine eyrie.

Blue jays and some other species have the peculiar habit of "anting." A bird will pick up ants, one at a time, from an anthill, and insert them in its body and wing feathers and in the feathers at the base of its tail. The reason for this has not been satisfactorily explained, but it is speculated that the ant's juices may tend to keep parasites off the jay's body.

In Dallas, Texas, F. W. Miller raised a fledgling in his home. The bird developed the fascinating habit of seizing a burning cigarette in its bill and "anting," or in this case, dressing the under surface of its wing feathers with the burning end. This lasted 10 or 12 seconds each time until all the burning end of the cigarette had been worn off.

The courtship of the jay is not conspicuous, nor easily identified. Bent, early one morning in late April, saw eight jays chasing each other around in the top of a tree, bobbing up and down, making a musical note. One, perhaps a female, finally flew off with the others in pursuit. Bent thought this performance might have been a form of courtship.

At nesting time the jay changes character. The vociferous, boasting bird of winter now is silent. It goes about its business quietly, and slinks to and from its nest on furtive wing. It is partial to conifers for a nesting site, but does nest in other situations. Sometimes it builds in vines about porches and chimneys and in other locations near the haunts of man.

Lawrence Kilham describes a mating he witnessed in Bethesda, Maryland:

A pair of jays appeared in the yard on March 18, 1953, and on March 31 began nest-building in a clump of honeysuckle hanging 12 feet up in a pine tree. At 7:30 A.M. on April 9 both jays were 15 feet up in a hickory, about 25 feet from the nest tree. The female sat on a limb while the male hopped from one limb to another, keeping within a foot of her, with his feathers ruffled up and making *quick, quick* notes. She perched stiffly upright. After a few moments the jays stood facing each other on the same limb with bills open and touching briefly. Then the male mounted and (after) several seconds flew away. The female, however, remained on the same limb, fluttering her wings. That evening one jay was observed to feed the other, a performance witnessed on subsequent days but not prior to mating. (Mutual feeding among adults is an act often associated with courtship and mating.)

A blue jay's nest is a coarse, carelessly built, cupshaped structure with a ragged brim, usually placed in a crotch of a. limb 10 to 20 ft. above the ground. It is woven together of twigs and rootlets, and often contains such ingredients as paper, rags, or string. The inside is lined with strips of bark, grass, leaves, and feathers. The four or five eggs have an olive or buff background and are marked with dark dots and blotches. The young are hatched naked, as is the case with most other land birds.

This species has many calls and cries. One of the most common is a *jay, jay*. Another sounds somewhat like the call of a red-shouldered hawk. The jay also has a pleasant whistled *tea-cup, tea-cup* note, a *tull-ull* note, and a "creaking wheelbarrow" call note in which the bird twice raises and twice lowers its head. It also utters a *kuk, kuk, kuk* sound, a pebbly growl, and a series of bell-like notes.

The blue jay has a seldom-heard song, usually uttered when the bird is well hidden. It is a subdued mixture of sweet low notes and whistles remotely suggesting a robin, mockingbird, or goldfinch. But for a hundred persons who recognize its calls, hardly one has heard this song.

Like most jays, this one eats almost anything edible. Department of Agriculture biologists have found that about 25 percent of its food is animal and 75 percent vegetable in origin. The animal food consists largely of insects, occasionally including termites. Sometimes a jay will eat a small fish, salamander, tree frog, or mouse. Very rarely will it take a bird. Its former reputation as a robber of birds' eggs and nests seems to have been exaggerated. It loves to eat acorns and also hides and stores them.

In their autumn migration, blue jays often congregate in considerable numbers at special funneling areas such as Point Pelee, Ontario, and Cape May, New Jersey. Other birds do, too, because these peninsulas point south and project out into the water; but the blue jays and other larger birds such as flickers and hawks are particularly conspicuous. Hundreds of jays gather in the woods about the point of land as they wait for favorable winds before launching themselves aloft to cross the water to the South.

Jays also assemble at Inwood Park, New York, and at Hawk Mountain Sanctuary in Pennsylvania.

Description: Length, 12 in. Crested; tail, long and wedgeshaped. Violet-blue above; azure on wings and tail; white on face, throat, wing bars, and outer tail tips; black hood line; pale below and under tail.

Incubation, 17 days; young stay 17 to 21 days in nest.

Eggs size, 1.1 x 0.9 in.; one brood per year.

STELLER'S JAY (*Cyanocitta stelleri*)

Steller's jay—our only jay that is black and blue in color—has the curious habit of hopping up the branches of a tree in spirals around the trunk.

Called also crested jay, this bird, which comes readily to feeders, is named for George Wilhelm Steller, a naturalist on the Russian expedition that discovered Alaska. On July 20, 1741, while on Kayak Island,

Steller saw this bird, which he had never seen before. His discovery constituted the first bird record for Alaska, perhaps the first for the Pacific coast of North America.

Steller's jay has a prominent crest, which the bird can raise or lower at will. Its foreparts are black. Its lower back, wings, and tail are dark blue and conspicuous in flight. Adults look much alike, but the female is a little smaller and has less distinct barring on the secondaries and tail feathers. Immatures tend to resemble the female, but often have some brown on the back. Some subspecies have a white eyebrow and bluish white streaks in the crest.

This jay is a bird of the pine forests of the West. Its original habitat was mountainsides, canyons, and forest edges, where it is still found. It has adapted well to civilization, however, and is also found about ranches, clearings, orchards, cabins, camps, picnic grounds, city parks, and suburban yards. It breeds in the mountains up to 11,000 ft., and in late summer may wander higher. But it does not go above the timber line and in summer is seldom seen below the lower limit of the pines. Because it is a bird of the pines, it occurs at higher elevations in the South than in the North, where these forests are found at lower altitudes.

When approached too closely, this jay utters a derisive shriek and takes off in strong and direct flight. Its wing beats, except when it is alarmed, are slower and deeper than the blue jay's. On the ground it hops or takes long bounds, but does not walk. It has a habit of flicking its wings and tail. It likes to mob owls and frequently quarrels with Cassin's kingbird, the western wood pewee, and various woodpeckers. When bird watchers make whistling or squeaking noises to attract birds, this is one of the first species that comes to investigate.

Steller's jay, as do other jays, sometimes picks up ants in its bill and rubs them along the feathers of its wing or tail.

The species does not seem to have elaborate courtship rites. As the breeding season approaches, the birds become secretive and retire to secluded sites to nest.

It builds a large, bulky bowlshaped nest of sticks, mud, and grass, often with some light-colored material near the base. It is lined with rootlets, pine needles, or grasses. The entrance is on one side. The nest is frequently built on a platform of old leaves in the crotch of a tree usually from 8 to 25 ft. high, but sometimes as low as 2 ft. or as high as 100. Occasionally the nest is placed in a troughlike hole in the trunk.

The birds prefer conifers early in the season. Later, when the leaves are out, they will nest in deciduous trees. Sometimes they build in man-made structures, such as inside the Sierra summit snowsheds of trans-continental railroads.

The three to five eggs are pale greenish blue, spotted or dotted rather evenly with brown, purple, or olive. Incubation takes 16 days. Both male and female sit on the eggs. The young stay in the nest about 16 days after they are hatched. One brood a year is the rule.

Steller's jay is a noisy bird and acts rather like a sentinel. Its usual cry is a low-pitched, raucous *shaak, shaak, shaak* that serves to warn the wildlife of approaching danger. It also has a variety of other notes. One resembles the scream of the red-tailed hawk. Dawson describes another as a mellow *klook, klook, klook.* Dickey writes of "wheezy magpie-like notes, such as *ca-phee, ca-phee, pheeze-ca.*"

Studies by Department of Agriculture biologists show that about a quarter of the jay's food is of animal origin and about three-quarters vegetable. The animal food is largely insects, notably wasps, wild bees, and (in the breeding season) some eggs and young birds.

About 40 percent of the jay's yearly diet is acorns, a figure that rises in January to 99 percent. The bird carries off and stores acorns in localities that are often uphill from the tree from which they came. Many of these acorns are not found again by the jay, and in time they germinate and grow into oaks. This (and similar activity by squirrels) may be an important way of propagating oaks that spread up the mountain.

The bird also likes other nuts, pine seeds, and berries. Of the vege-table food about one-fifth is fruit, and sometimes these jays become a pest to the orchardist. They are well known habitués of picnic areas and feed on scraps left by camper and tourist.

The species is resident within its range, but engages in considerable local movement, seasonably, depending presumably on the food sup-ply. Except when paired off and breeding, it is usually found in family parties or small groups. In autumn it descends to lower altitudes and in winter is commonly seen in the valleys and about human habitations. Its diet then is omnivorous. It often drives other birds away from feeders, until it has finished eating. It particularly relishes crackers, bread, and meat.

Description: Length, 12 in. Stout pointed bill; rounded wings; crested. Black foreparts; dark blue lower back, wings, and tail. Some races and immature have brownish tint on back.

Incubation, 16 to 18 days; young stay 18 to 21 days in nest.

Size of eggs, 1.2 x 0.9 in.; one brood per year.

SCRUB JAY (*Aphelocoma coerulescens*)

The oak and pine scrub of Florida and the dry sagebrush and chaparral hillsides of the West are the haunts of the scrub jay.

This uncrested blue and gray jay inhabits saw palmetto and rosemary in Florida and willows and chaparral in California and Oregon. The catchall botanical name of "chaparral" of the West embraces manzanita, buck-brush, juniper, mountain mahogany, wild plum, buckthorn (Ceanothus), and sagebrush. In the Rockies, scrub oak, pinyon, and juniper are the bird's customary haunts.

The behavior of the scrub jay varies somewhat in different parts of its range. In Florida and California it is tame, comes readily to feeders, often takes food from the hand, and may even perch on hat or shoulder. The Florida bird sometimes seems almost unnaturally tame, particularly when nesting, since it can be handled on the nest. The scrub jays of the Rocky Mountains and some other subspecies are more cautious, but all forms come readily to squeaking noises made by bird watchers.

Despite its tameness, on many occasions this species sometimes stays well hidden in the scrub and is hard to see unless "squeaked up." When perched and at ease, the bird lets its long tail hang down. When nervous, it jerks and twitches its tail and often rubs its bill on the branch of its perch.

This jay is frequently seen on road shoulders, where it may pick at the sand or earth with its bill. It does not walk, but takes long, buoyant.

hops. It also hops on branches. A peculiar trait is its liking for bright objects such as spoons, buttons, bottle tops, or bits of china or glass, which it steals and hoards.

Unlike many other jays, the Florida form is not particularly aggressive or domineering and seems to get along well with other birds such as quail, ground doves, meadowlarks, red-winged blackbirds, and grackles. But Bent says that the California subspecies is "cordially disliked and dreaded by all smaller birds." It quarrels particularly with the acorn woodpecker, often over acorns the other bird has or wants.

The short flights of the scrub jay appear slightly labored, with heavy flapping of its broad wings. Such flights are punctuated with tail jerking and glides on widespread wings. The bird can sail through scrub with great agility, without being seen. On long flights the wings beat steadily. In the West the jay often coasts down a slope with wings and tail outspread, then glides upward to its perch. On alighting, it may bow deeply several times and in different directions. Like the blue jay, a group will fly across an open space one at a time.

The scrub jay often lives in loose colonies and travels in small flocks, especially in winter. As do other jays, this one serves to some extent as a sentinel, warning other birds of approaching danger.

Special courtship performances seem to be unknown, but the birds appear to remain mated throughout the year. The nest is relatively small. In Florida it is flat and well built of sticks, plant stems, and leaves and lined with moss, rootlets, wool, or feathers. It is placed in a low bush or tree, vine or tangle, from 4 to 12 ft. up. In the West the structure is bulkier and often lined with horsehair. It is located amid sagebrush and chaparral, usually in a low bush but sometimes in a tree as high as 30 ft.

The three to five greenish eggs of the Florida and Rocky Mountain forms are irregularly blotched with brown or cinnamon, usually more heavily at the larger end of the egg. The four to six eggs of the California subspecies are noted for their variations in color and appearance. Two general types are recognized, the red and the green. In the red type the ground color varies from grayish to green and the fine markings are sepia and brown. In the green type, the green background carries dark green or olive markings. Both male and female incubate the eggs, through the female may sit longer while the male brings her food. The young often return to the nest after they are fledged, an unusual trait.

The notes of this bird are not generally considered quite so noisy as those of other jays. The California bird utters a flat, rapid *quay-quay-quay-quay-quay-quay-quay*, sometimes written *kwesh-kwesh, kwesh, kwesh, kwesh*; an emphatic *boy-ee, boy-ee*; an inquiring *quay-kee*; a high-pitched *queep-queep-queep-queep*; a harsh *tscheck, tscheck* (higher-pitched than that of Steller's jay); a harsh, rising shriek; and a harsh *ker-wheek*. Notes of the other subspecies are similar. The *churr* sound of the Florida bird reminded Howell of the boat-tailed grackle. Sprunt describes some of the jay's low notes as a "chuckle." The Paiute Indians called the Rocky Mountain form *wé-ahk* in imitation of its shrill screech.

The food of the scrub jay is both animal and vegetable in origin. The proportions vary with locality and the season. In Florida, animal food may be 60 percent of the total; in California, as low as 27 percent. Animal food includes crickets, grasshoppers, caterpillars, beetles, bugs, ants, wasps, spiders, and (particularly in California) birds' eggs and young birds. In Florida it is reported to have an unusual habit of eating ticks off cattle by perching on their backs and rumps or by jumping up from the ground to pick insects off their flanks and legs.

Vegetable food includes acorns, huckleberry seeds, palmetto seeds, fruit, planted peas and corn, grain, almonds, walnuts, pinyons, and other nuts. The bird is readily attracted to feeders where it especially loves bread, peanuts, and suet.

Description: Length, 12 in. Long and rounded tail; long, heavy bill. Mostly dull, blue-gray above and gray white below with reddish or brown patch on back and incomplete gray breast-band (obscure); note also pale superciliary; no crest. In southwest, the scrub jay might be confused with the gray-breasted (Arizona) jay, but that species is more uniformly colored above and below, lacks patch on back, breast-band, and superciliary.

Incubation, 16 days; young stay 18 days in nest.

Size of eggs, 1.1 x 0.9 in.; one to two broods per year.

GREEN JAY (*Cyanocorax yncas*)

The green jay is a resident species of southern Texas from Laredo to Norias, with a small colony at San Antonio. From Texas and northern Mexico it ranges south in the highlands to northern Honduras. The bird is not found again until reaching northern South America, where it occurs in the subtropical zone from Venezuela and Colombia to northern Bolivia. Such discontinuous distribution is attributed to two general causes, operating separately or in combination: physical changes in habitat or competitive pressure from more successful species.

The plumage of this well-named species is all green except for a blue cap, black throat, and yellow outer tail feathers. It has no crest. It is a bird of thickets and tangles, where it slinks through the underbrush with great ease, or flits through the confusion of branches and vines that barricade a subtropical jungle. It is seen also both in deep woods and around the habitations of man where, like other jays, it comes for handouts of food. Its habitat generally is lowlands and woodlands, but in Mexico it ranges to 6,000 ft. in the mountains.

The green jay is a rather shy and retiring species, lacking the bold aggressiveness of the blue jay or Steller's jay. It retains the natural inquisitiveness of its family, however, and is not afraid to visit ranches and houses. It has even been known to enter kitchens and take food from plates. It has lively curiosity and can readily be captured by baiting a trap with meat. In former days, before caging native birds was made illegal, the green jay was in demand as a cage bird on account of its gaudy plumage. In captivity and presumably in the wild, it is a voracious eater.

This species has little or no courtship display. Nesting in southern Texas starts in April. The rather large nest is 9 in. in diameter; it is composed of sticks and thorny twigs and is lined with smaller twigs, rootlets, and sometimes grass, moss, or hair. The eggs may sometimes be seen from below, as with the mourning dove. The green jay usually hides its nest in a thicket or on the branches of a tree, bush, or sapling from 5 to 10 (and sometimes 25) ft. above the ground.

The female lays from three to five eggs, but the normal clutch is four. They have a whitish, buff, or light greenish ground color and are boldly blotched with browns, grays, and lavender, with the markings often heaviest around the larger end.

The green jay, as are other jays, is a noisy bird. It has a wide variety of notes, most of them loud and harsh, although its repertoire includes some musical whistles. One sound is a distinctive froglike rattle.

Although the green jay has been charged with occasionally taking the eggs and young of other birds, by far the greatest part of its diet consists of insects, seeds, and fruits. Seeds of the ebony (Siderocarpus) are important to it in winter, as is the fruit of the palmetto; the bird is also partial to corn.

Description: Length, 12 in. Plumage, generally green; lighter or yellowish below. Blue crown; black throat; yellow outer tail feathers; black bill; brown feet. Young are similar but duller.

Incubation, 16 to 17 days; young stay 18 to 20 days in nest.

Size of eggs, 1.05 x .80 in.; two broods per year.

COMMON CROW (*Corvus brachyrhynchos*)

The common crow is one of the most abundant, widespread, conspicuous, adaptable, and well-known birds in North America, and also one of the most intelligent.

The fact that it has survived centuries of persecution by farmer and gunner speaks well for its intelligence and adaptability. But its survival and abundance are also an indication of the benefits the crow has gained from the settlement of North America. Man replaced the forest and prairie with grain fields that are far more useful to the crow.

The growth of cities has not wiped out the crow, and the bird is frequently found in the suburbs. It has been shot, poisoned, bombed, and subjected to organized "varmint hunts," but probably is just as common now as it ever was. It is almost certainly more abundant than it was before the landing of the Pilgrims.

The crow has long had a bad reputation for its eating of farmers' grain. But it also eats many insect pests and carrion. Ecologists, who study the relation of animals and man to their environment, oppose any general condemnation of the crow, and favor its control only in cases of direct damage where other deterrent measures have failed. One deterrent they recommend is treating grains of corn with creosote before planting. The creosote does not hurt the grain and crows do not like it.

The crow's range includes most of North America, but it is less common in the West than in the East. In the winter it retreats from the northern areas. Crows in some areas have extensive migrations; in other areas they move little. In the Great Plains, birds that summer in Canada may winter in Oklahoma, but banding records show that birds of the Atlantic coast may not migrate or wander more than 100 miles. There is also a shift toward the coast in the colder months, for food is easier to find along beach and estuary than in frozen or snow-covered countryside. When migrating, crows fly high and by day.

The crow is primarily a bird of fields and edges of woods, but it may be found almost everywhere except in deserts, deep forests, and high mountains. In Florida it frequents open pine forests, hummocks, prairies, and small cypress swamps.

Crows usually occur in small groups of three to eight. They attract attention by their calls. Prolonged cawing is usually a sign that they have found an owl or hawk. The discovery of either of these gives the local crows a field day. They will mob an owl in a tree by flying up to it, cawing loudly, feinting, and mocking it with what sounds like loud and derisive laughter.

They also will fly after a hawk to chase it across the sky, cawing loudly and feinting at it. Several species of hawks occasionally retaliate by including a crow in their diet.

In a fashion similar to its attacks on hawks, crows themselves are frequently badgered by eastern kingbirds or red-winged blackbirds. These birds will fly up with shrill cries to try to peck the crow. Sometimes they attempt to perch on the crow's back to get a better purchase. Invariably the crow retreats before the onslaught.

Crows make good pets. If one is taken from its nest within two weeks of hatching, it will adopt its captor as if it were its offspring. It will follow the new master around and, neglecting other crows, cling to its human guardian.

A pet crow can be taught to talk, or at least to say such words as "papa," "mama," and "hello." It can also imitate human laughter.

The crow is not a particularly early riser. Wright made a ten-year study of the waking habits of various birds in late spring, in the White Mountains of New Hampshire. He found the crow ranked twenty-fourth among common birds in giving voice in the morning. The average time of its first caw is 3:44 A.M.

COMMON CROW

When a crow is traveling a long distance, its flight is high and direct. Its strong, steady wingbeat has sometimes been described as "rowing through the air." For shorter distances the crow's flight is somewhat less even. On windy days, crows sometimes seem to be "blown about the skies," like Tennyson's rooks.

In courtship the male and female perch on a limb together. The male walks along the branch toward the apparently indifferent female. Facing her, he bows low, ruffles his body feathers, and slightly spreads his wings and tail. After bowing perhaps twice, he lifts his head straight up and then lowers it until it is below his feet. As he lowers it he utters his love song, a quick rattling succession of sharp notes that has been said to resemble grinding teeth. The male may repeat this performance several times. Mated or courting crows sometimes bill like doves, one caressing the head of the other with its beak. Sometimes the male utters his love rattle in flight.

The crow builds a large, bulky, cupshaped nest of sticks, lined with bark, vegetable fibers, rootlets, grass, and moss. Sometimes the nest includes corn stalks, feathers, or seaweed. It is usually placed in a relatively secluded tree about 30 ft. up, but heights range from 10 to 100 ft. The great horned owl often "highjacks" a nest of a crow for its own use, and the long-eared owl will frequently make use of an abandoned nest.

The three to six eggs have a greenish background blotched with brown and gray. They vary somewhat in shape, size, markings, and color. Incubation starts with the laying of the first egg. Hence the eggs hatch over a period of a few days, the first-laid presumably hatching first. Male and female both incubate the eggs and share in care of the young.

The common call of the crow is an open *caw, caw, caw,* into which the bird puts many subtle variations of pitch, emphasis, rhythm, intonation, and notes. Ernest Thompson Seton, the nature writer, recognized many different "words" in crow language, some of which he thought he could understand. He believed that the birds had a large vocabulary. Charles W. Townsend, who made a special study of the voice and courtship of the crow, reports an *orr, orr* and *ah, ah,* delivered "as with a great feeling of relief"; a nasal and taunting *gnaw, gnaw*; a rapidly repeated and wailing *kaa, wha, wha, wha, kaa, wha, wha, wha,* or an *ou, ahh, ahh, ahh*; a loud, cheerful, gull-like *ha, ha, ha*; a despairing *nevah, nevah*; and an occasional loud cluck. The call of the young crow is a *car, car,* much like the call of an adult fish crow.

The common crow is omnivorous. Department of Agriculture studies show that about one-quarter of its food is animal and three-quarters is vegetable in origin. The animal food includes carrion, insects, spiders, snails, snakes, salamanders, frogs, lizards, mice, some eggs and young birds, and occasionally fish, which it catches with its feet.

Among insects that constitute two-thirds of the animal food are a high proportion of beetles, grasshoppers, locusts, crickets, cutworms, angleworms, caterpillars, and May beetles. During outbreaks of insect pests, crows will add more of the pest species to their diet, in this way being of direct benefit to man.

Eggs and young birds constitute only one-third of 1 percent of the diet of adult crows, except when crows live near waterfowl-nesting concentrations or heron colonies. In such places crows often prey heavily on the eggs and young of the nesting species.

Along the seacoast crows eat clams and other mollusks. A crow will carry a clam aloft in its bill, as does a gull, and keep dropping it on a rock or other hard surface until the shell breaks and he can get at the meat inside. Crows often comb the beach for dead fish, shellfish, and other organic refuse.

Corn makes up about half of the crow's vegetable diet. This includes corn in the blade, in the milk, in the ear, and a great deal of waste corn. In areas where wheat or oats are grown, they replace corn in the crow's diet. Fruits and berries also are eaten, notably those of sumac, poison ivy, Virginia creeper, pokeberry, bayberry, dogwood, grape, and wild cherry. Favorite nut foods include acorns, beechnuts, and pecans. Crows also like salt. As do owls and hawks, they cast up as pellets the indigestible parts of their food such as fur, bones, fish scales, and hard seeds.

In one day, if food is available, a full-grown crow will eat about 1½ lbs. of food and a young crow will eat half its own weight. A crow digests its meal in 1½ hours and may eat eight to ten full meals a day.

Crows will come to feeders and to food that is put out for them on the ground. They particularly like bread. Young crows can be raised on a diet of vegetables, dogfood, table scraps, and vitamin D.

Judging from Audubon Christmas census counts, crows are one of the most common winter birds in North America. At this season they often gather from miles around and assemble in great roosts. One in Washington, D. C., in the 1920s, was estimated to contain 200,000 birds. A famous one at Pea Patch and Reedy Island in the Delaware River, was estimated in 1899 to contain 500,000 birds.

These are spectacular aggregations. From such a roost the birds may scour the surrounding countryside as far as 50 miles. They fly out in the morning at a low elevation, looking for food. In the afternoon they return usually at a greater height to an assembly point, where they wait for all to gather before entering the roost for the night.

Description: Length, 20 in.; all black; tail gently rounded; shorter than common raven (25 in.), which has wedgeshaped tail and says *c-r-r-r-u-u-k*. Fish crow is virtually identical in appearance, but is smaller, and says *car*, not *caw*.

Incubation, 18 days; young stay five weeks in nest.

Size of eggs, 1.8 x 1.2 in.; one brood per year in North and two in South.

CLARK'S NUTCRACKER (*Nucifraga columbiana*)

Where the air is rare and cool on the high evergreen slopes of our western mountains, there we find Clark's nutcracker. It loves the somber hillsides of uncut timber, where sunlight flecks a forest floor untrodden by the foot of man.

Clark's nutcracker occurs from the Black Hills to the Pacific and from Alaska to Lower California. It breeds in the United States at an altitude of 5,000 to 8,000 ft. in the zone of pine and spruce, but is also found at different seasons and latitudes at elevations ranging from 3,000 to 13,000 ft. It is one of the birds most often noticed in the Yellowstone National Park.

After nesting, the nutcracker may roam over the grassy and stony ridges above timber line in search of grasshoppers and other food. In autumn it will often gather in flocks of dozens to several hundred. Some wander down to the valleys and even to the Pacific coast, but many merely descend from the spruce belt to the yellow-pine belt and winter in the mountains, defiant of the heavy snow, bitter wind, and biting cold.

The nutcracker's plumage is conspicuous when the bird is perched in the open, but the plumage has a so-called ruptive pattern that often blends with its background.

Lewis and Clark, on their expedition to the mouth of the Columbia

River in 1804 to 1806, were the first to report the species. Its common name commemorates Captain William Clark.

The nest is frequently placed under an overhanging evergreen twig that serves as shelter from the weather. When the bird is incubating, there is often snow on the ground and the temperature may be below zero, creating the need for a warm, deep, and protected nest. The two to four pale greenish eggs are thinly spotted throughout or wreathed at the larger end with tiny dots of brown, drab, or olive.

CLARK'S NUTCRACKER

The protracted flight of a nutcracker is straight and rapid, made with vigorous and regular wingbeats somewhat faster than those of a crow. On shorter trips the flight undulates like that of a woodpecker (p. 39), with wings alternately open and closed.

The flight maneuvers of this species are most impressive. Sometimes above pine-clad mountainsides and even above crests of the Rockies and Sierras a group may soar like hawks with wings and tails outspread.

At other times, in precipitous dives with folded wings, they may plunge down the steep sides of the mountains. As they near creek and canyon below they open their wings with an explosive sound, check the fall, and glide gently to their perch. In late afternoon the birds fly from tree to tree up the mountainsides to keep above the shadows and take full advantage of the sunlight until it ceases to warm the ridges.

Nutcrackers have many jaylike traits. They are boisterous and aggressive. They quarrel with Douglas' squirrels over pine cones. With their inquisitiveness and noisy calls they serve as sentinels, just as jays do. When nutcrackers are acting up, the children of the wild will be on their guard.

Clark's nutcracker likes to perch on a commanding post at the top of a dead tree that affords an extensive view. Sometimes the bird hammers a limb and plays a tattoo like a woodpecker with its big strong beak. The nutcracker is also fearless. One has been seen driving away a golden eagle, and a group frequently will mob a hawk. The nutcracker can be lured by an imitation of the cry of an owl, particularly that of a pigmy owl or of a great horned owl; and a young nutcracker can be tamed just as a crow can.

This species is noisy, except in the breeding season or on the ground. Its most common notes are harsh and grating and are often heard in flight. They have been written as *chaar, char-r-r, churr-churr,* or *kr-a-a, kar-r-r-r-aah,* each note repeated several times. It also utters a strange, piercing, catlike *meack, mearrk.*

Two birds, acting in concert, sometimes produce a totally different sound:

hee hee   hee   hee hee
hoo   hoo   hoo, hoo

According to Leon Dawson, the California ornithologist, this resembles toy tin trumpets, pitched about a fifth apart. The bird is something of a mimic, and observers have reported hearing every call of the crow and magpie in the random reminiscences of old and young nutcrackers.

Like most other members of the crow family, Clark's nutcracker is omnivorous. Its animal food includes insects, notably ants, beetles, grasshoppers, caterpillars, and black crickets. Sometimes the bird catches insects in the manner of a flycatcher, darting out after them from an exposed perch. Sometimes it picks grubs from the bark of a tree by holding onto the trunk like a woodpecker. Sometimes it robs other birds' nests and takes their eggs or young.

The nutcracker is very fond of pinyon nuts and feeds these to its young while they are in the nest and afterwards, both by regurgitation and directly. When regurgitating, the parent puts its beak far down inside the young one's throat. The pinyons are hulled for the young, but the adults eat the shell as well as the kernel.

Seeds of the yellow pine also are a favorite food. In eating these from a plucked cone, the bird, perching on one foot, uses the other to grasp the cone firmly as it pecks out the seeds with its beak. When feeding on pine cones that are still on the tree, the bird often hangs head down like a chickadee or goldfinch.

Nutcracker diet also includes spruce and fir seeds, cedar and juniper berries, and acorns. When thirsty, the bird turns its head sideways and drinks from the side of its bill. When a flock feeds on the ground its members move slowly forward, with the birds at the rear of the flocks constantly flying over the others to the area ahead, in a kind of feathered leapfrog.

Clark's nutcracker, like the gray jay, has learned to frequent camp-fires and cabins of man. It, too, has been given the name "camp robber" and "meat bird." It also visits feeders, where it particularly likes bread, meat, and seeds. Often it takes large pieces of food to store them.

Description: Length, 12 in. Stout, pointed bill; rounded wings; pale gray body; black bill, wings, and tail; wing patch, white sides of tail and undertail are conspicuous in flight.

Incubation, 17 to 22 days; young stay 18 days to 4 weeks in nest.

Size of eggs, 1.3 x 0.9 in.; one, sometimes two broods per year.

TITMICE / *Paridae*

BLACK-CAPPED CHICKADEE (*Parus atricapillus*)

Throughout most of its range, the black-capped chickadee is the only small gray bird with a black cap and black bib. It is found all over northern North America from the Atlantic to the Pacific. It closely resembles and is closely related to the willow tit of the Old World. This chickadee can be found throughout the year in most of its range, but individuals seen in winter may not be the same ones seen in summer. There is a seasonal migration, and during the colder months some birds disappear from their most northerly haunts and others appear at places in the south where the species is unknown in summer.

The habitat of this chickadee is woods and the edges of woods, particularly conifers in the East and hardwoods in the West. It also likes second growth, willow thickets, poplar groves, and alder patches.

This species is found in pairs in the breeding season, but for the remainder of the year it travels in small groups. In late summer and autumn it roams the woods in loose flocks with warblers and vireos. In winter it often moves about with nuthatches (p. 91), downy woodpeckers (p. 49), kinglets, and brown creepers (p. 98). Whether alone or with other species, it keeps up a busy conversational chatter, which helps keep the flock together when individual birds are out of each other's sight.

In feeding, the black-capped chickadee often clings to outer twigs and branches, hanging head down, swinging acrobatically and frequently turning complete somersaults in search of food.

The black-capped chickadee is exceedingly alert and quick. If alarmed at a feeder, it disappears. Such a fast getaway is a lifesaver for a small bird with many enemies. The regular flight of this chickadee, however, is rather feeble and bouncy as it travels from tree to tree or feeder to tree; it often seems to flit, pause and flit, rather than fly. If you are nearby you will hear a faint rustling whir each time it flits its wing. In migration its flight is more sustained.

At night the bird roosts in a protected spot such as a cavity in a tree, an abandoned bird's nest, a leafy grapevine, or in dense evergreen branches. Chickadees often roost together. They will occupy the same roost night after night and will use a roosting box. When breeding, the female roosts in the nest cavity, while the male is nearby.

A bird bander, Lester W. Smith, found the black-capped chickadee more intelligent than juncos, tree sparrows, or purple finches in finding its way out of a sparrow trap, with an entrance under inward sloping wires. Other birds get hopelessly confused, but the chickadee quickly learned the exit. It would enter the trap, seize a sunflower seed, and then take it outside to eat it.

The migration of small birds is less conspicuous than that of large ones. For this reason, and because black-capped chickadees are present throughout the year in most of their range, we seldom think of them as migrants.

Before crossing large bodies of water, such as the Great Lakes, chickadees crowd points of land, filling the woods while waiting for fair wind and auspicious weather for launching their perilous adventure. W. E. Saunders, a Canadian student of bird migration, at Point Pelee, Ontario, reported that sometimes 300 to 400 chickadees would be waiting there to fly south across Lake Erie.

The black-capped chickadee's courtship is confined to a few loud *PHE-bee* songs by the male, a special twittering mating note, and some wing fluttering. The male helps the female excavate the nest hole and shares with her the care and feeding of the young. The actual nest, however, is constructed by the female alone. It is made of mosses, cottony vegetable fibers, cinnamon fern wool, cocoons, feathers, hair, fur, and wool. The female alone incubates. Excavating the hole takes seven to ten days; building the nest takes two to four days. There is some evidence that black-capped chickadees may remain mated for more than one nesting season, perhaps for life.

The typical nest of this species is a cavity about 6 in. deep, 3 to 15 ft. above the ground in a dead stub or branch of a tree, usually birch, pine, or poplar. The bird often uses a hole started by a woodpecker. This enables the chickadee to get through the resistant bark or hard outer wood. Inside, however, the chickadee itself excavates the rotten wood and, unlike a woodpecker, scatters the telltale chips some distance away. Natural cavities in other trees are also used, as are old woodpecker holes or nesting boxes.

The six to eight thin-shelled eggs are white, evenly marked or wreathed at the larger end with small red-brown dots. The incubating bird, if disturbed, will fluff out its wings and, with a wide-open mouth, will hiss and sway like a snake. The young are hatched naked and blind. Their eyes are not fully opened for 12 days.

The familiar call of a black-capped chickadee is a cheerful, sprightly *chick-a-dee-dee-dee-dee-dee* (one to ten *dees,* but usually four; sometimes with two *chick-a*'s). Often only the *dee dee dee* notes are uttered. The bird has many other notes. Some are almost as high as the insect-like *seep* of the golden-crowned kinglet. Others include a lisping *sth* or, in flight, a *stheep*; a pretty *sizzle-ee* or *sizzle-oo*; a rapid *si-si-si-si,* when alarmed; and a long jingling like distant sleighbells.

The song of this chickadee is a sweet whistled *PHE-bee, PHE-bee.* The first note is higher, the second sometimes has a quaver in the middle. It is sung by both male and female.

The black-capped chickadee is seven-tenths insectivorous and three-tenths vegetarian. Its chief animal foods include caterpillars, spiders, beetles, ants, sawflies, plant lice, scale insects, and insect eggs. Vegetable foods are principally wild fruits, mast from conifers, bayberries, poison ivy berries, and blueberries. At feeders, chickadees like suet, sunflower and pumpkin seeds, and nut kernels.

The annual cycle has been intensively studied for only a few species of birds. Eugene P. Odum did such a study of the black-capped chickadee on a 576-acre tract in Rensselaerville, New York, in 1939 to 1940. Individual birds were identified by the use of colored bands. Here are a few of the facts he uncovered.

During the year the total chickadee population varied. The peak was 30 birds per 100 acres in the fall. Winter flocks broke up gradually in the spring, with pairs splitting off one at a time. A new mate was readily accepted when the old one was lost. One female had three successive mates during the nesting season. Establishment and defense of a nesting territory began at about the time of cavity excavation and ended when the young left the nest. The male defended the territory by "vocal challenging," chasing, and (rarely) by actual fighting. Territories varied from 8.4 to 17.1 acres, averaging 13.2 acres.

The number of eggs varies from five to eight; most sets have seven. Eggs are laid one a day; the female starts incubating only when the clutch is complete. The average attentive period for the incubating female is 24 minutes; the average inattentive period is 8 minutes. During the inattentive period the female begs for food and is fed by the male.

After the eggs hatch, the male stops feeding the female and both feed the young. The feeding of advanced young places a great strain on the energy reserves of adults so that their survival time without food is sometimes as low as 16 hours. As with most land birds the nestlings are born cold-blooded. Temperature control begins to develop on the fourth day and the nestlings become warm-blooded by the twelfth. Fledglings can feed themselves ten days after leaving the nest. They remain with their parents three to four weeks.

Vocal activity is important in controlling the behavior of the flock; 16 clearly distinguishable notes are identifiable. Natural flocks in the woods are composed of seven or eight individuals; congregations around feeding stations are larger. Flocks move on the average 1,425 ft. per hour. The five main methods of feeding are foliage examination (summer), twig and bark examination (winter), seeds and fruit (autumn and winter), weed-top examination (autumn), and ground feeding (occasional).

Description: Length, 5 in. Small, plump, big-headed; short and straight bill; black and beady eyes; rounded wing; soft and fluffy plumage. Black cap and bib; gray underparts with white edges on wing feathers; white underparts with pale chestnut wash on flanks. White cheeks conspicuous.

Incubation, 11 to 13 days; young stay 16 to 17 days in nest.

Size of eggs, 0.6 x 0.5 in.; one, sometimes two broods per year.

CAROLINA CHICKADEE (*Parus carolinensis*)

This chickadee is smaller than the similar black-capped chickadee and its wings lack a white bar. These and other fine points described below are difficult to see well in the field, but since the ranges of the two chickadees overlap only in a narrow belt across the east-central United States, a very simple way to distinguish them is by range. The most obvious distinction between the two species, however, is the voice.

The Carolina chickadee replaces the black-capped in the southeastern United States. It ranges south and west from Kansas, southern Ohio, and central New Jersey to Texas. It is a resident species and has no migration.

The habitat of this chickadee includes open pine country, pine barrens, deciduous woods, edges of woods, coastal plain swamps, and residential areas. In the southern Appalachians, Carolina chickadees generally breed up to about 3,000 ft. in West Virginia and up to 4,000 ft. in the Great Smoky Mountains. Higher than that, the black-capped chickadee nests; but if the latter is absent, then the Carolina will nest to an altitude of 5,000 ft. Occasionally, however, there is some slight overlap of range, and the two species have been heard singing in the same tree. This close association, virtually without hybridization, shows that these two are distinct species and not subspecies differing by slight variations in plumage.

The Carolina's habits are much like those of the black-capped chickadee, but it sometimes seems to be more timid. It roams through the woods with woodpeckers, titmice, nuthatches, yellow-throated and pine warblers, and (in winter) with myrtle warblers (p. 156) and both king-

lets. In these mixed flocks the chickadees appear to be second in com-
mand after the tufted titmice.

Some species of hole-nesting birds, and this is one of them, emit a
snakelike hiss when their nesting tree is disturbed. It is thought by
some that this is an imitative defense mechanism meant to frighten
away predators about to investigate the cavity.

The nesting habits, including courtship feeding of the female by
the male, are generally similar to those of the black-capped chickadee.
The Carolina is a relatively early breeder, nest construction sometimes
starting in February. In the Great Smoky Mountains it breeds two to
three weeks earlier than does the black-capped. Fence posts and decayed
stubs of small saplings are favored nest sites. So are man-made bird
houses.

The nest, usually 6 to 15 ft. high, consists of a foundation of moss,
grass, bark shreds, lined with vegetable down, feathers, hair, and fur.
The bird has the interesting habit of building one side higher than
the other. This makes a flap with which the parent covers the eggs
when it is away from the nest. The six eggs are practically indistinguishable from those of the black-capped chickadee.

The Carolina's *chick-a-dee-dee-dee-dee* is higher pitched and faster
than that of the black-capped. Furthermore, its song is composed of four
notes rather than two. A short whispered sibilant *su* precedes or follows
each of the main whistled notes; thus *su-FEE, su-bee,* or *FEE-su, bee-su,*
the *su* being usually lower and softly whispered.

George Finlay Simmons, the authority on birds of the Austin region
of Texas, described at length the voice of this bird. Though he made
his studies in Texas, these observations also apply to the bird in other
portions of its range. He says its voice includes a:

chick-a-dee-dee-dee-dee-dee-dee-dee; tweesee-dee-dee-dee-dee; a clearly whistled *psee-a-dee*; a low plaintive *tswee-dee-tswee-dee,* of four tremulous whistled notes, in sharp contrast to the clear, ringing notes *te-derry,* of the
Northern birds; a low *sick-a-dee*; a short *chicka-a-da*; a clearer *my watcher
key, my watcher key*; a series of *day-day-day* or *dee-dee-dee-dee* notes.

Studies by Department of Agriculture biologists show that 72 percent of the Carolina chickadee's diet is animal in origin, and 28 percent

vegetable. Moths and caterpillars make up almost half its diet; next most important are bugs, stink bugs, shield bugs, leaf hoppers, tree hoppers and plant lice, and spiders. The chief vegetable food is poison ivy berries. The species also likes insect eggs, seeds, and acorns.

At the feeder the Carolina chickadee likes suet, sunflower seeds, pumpkin seeds, peanut butter, nut kernels, cheese, and bread crumbs. It also likes to pick at a bone with some meat and gristle attached.

CAROLINA
CHICKADEE

MOUNTAIN
CHICKADEE

Description: Length, 4½ in. Similar to black-capped chickadee, but usually lacks white on wing. Best distinguished by voice.

Incubation, 11 to 12 days; young stay 17 days in nest.

Size of eggs, 0.6 x 0.5 in.; one brood per year.

MOUNTAIN CHICKADEE (*Parus gambeli*)

If you visit western mountain parks you may be looking forward to seeing dippers in the mountain streams and white-tailed ptarmigan or gray-crowned rosy finches above timber line. But one of the first birds you will see is the mountain chickadee.

In the pines nearest your tent or cabin you may notice a small puff of black and white tumbling around the end of a branch and hear notes that remind you of your own backyard chickadee. But the voice is slightly different. The bird says *chick-a-dee-a-dee-a-dee*, not *chicka-dee-dee-dee*. It is a mountain chickadee, the high altitude chickadee of our western ranges and a new bird for the "life list" of the easterner and lowlander. It is found from the Rockies to the Pacific and from British Columbia to Lower California, except along the humid northwest coast.

In appearance the mountain chickadee differs from the black-capped chickadee (p. 74) in having a white line over the eye. When the bird "raises its eyebrows" this line is more conspicuous. But if it leans forward, the line may be hard to see. It may also be hard to see in the worn plumage of early summer.

The breeding habitat of this chickadee is the evergreen forest from 6,000 to 11,000 ft. It is found from the pinyon and juniper zone up through hemlocks, pines, and firs to the spruce zone. In fall the birds wander up to the tree line and beyond. In autumn and winter some of them descend to lower elevations, where they roam among the chaparral of the slopes, the deciduous trees of the valleys and the cottonwoods, alders, birches, and willows of the streamsides.

At all elevations the mountain chickadee is a familiar companion of man. It frequents the neighborhood of his camps, cabins, summer hotels, mountain villages, roadside restaurants, and isolated homesteads. It comes readily to bird feeding stations on the lower, more arid slopes, and if provided with water it is a particularly enthusiastic visitor.

The habits of the mountain chickadee are much like those of the black-capped chickadee. The female on the nest engages in a defensive performance that resembles the lunging and the hissing of a snake. A female at Mineral, California, once repeated this performance 19 times before flying from the nest at an intruder's close approach.

The nest of the mountain chickadee is placed in the cavity of a stump or branch, in an old woodpecker hole, or in a bird box. It is usually located at a height of 1 to 15 ft., but some have been found higher. The entrance hole, as a rule, is 1½ in. in diameter, and the cavity may be as much as 9 in. deep. The nest itself is made of grasses, mosses, plant down, shredded bark, rootlets, feathers, sheep's wool, cattle or deer hair, and squirrel or rabbit fur.

W. E. Griffee, who made a special study of chickadees, writes:

In my experience, the short-tailed chickadee always stays on the nest from the time the first egg is laid. Probably this is necessary because of the great abundance of chipmunks, which are small enough to run into a chickadee nesting hole and make a meal of the eggs. . . . The Oregon chickadee, which nests where chipmunks are much less common, and makes a smaller entrance to its nesting cavity, apparently is not so much bothered by chipmunks and . . . does not hesitate to leave its nest unguarded until incubation begins.

The clutch consists of 6 to 9 or sometimes 5 to 12 white eggs, some of which may bear fine red-brown spots, often concentrated around the larger end. Nestlings are said to be fed by regurgitation for the first four days; after that fresh food is given them directly. In one pair closely studied for a short time, the parents fed the young 11 times in half an hour.

Except when nesting, mountain chickadees roam through the woods in loose flocks with woodpeckers, black-capped chickadees, nuthatches, creepers, and kinglets, and in summer also with flycatchers, vireos, and warblers. In such flocks, nuthatches dominate chickadees, and the black-capped chickadee dominates the mountain chickadee.

The voice of the mountain chickadee is somewhat like that of the black-capped chickadee, but the mountain's notes are hoarser and more deliberate and, in addition to *chick-a-dee-a-dee-a-dee,* have been variously written as *chick-a chay chay chay* and *chuck-a-zee-zee-zee.* Ralph Hoffman, who wrote *Birds of the Pacific States,* points out that:

The sweet whistled call is more often made up of three (sometimes four) notes than that of the eastern bird. Sometimes the three notes come down

the scale to the tune of "Three Blind Mice." At other times the last two are
the same pitch *tee-dee-dee*. Occasionally the bird either leaves off the third
note or adds a fourth. As the chickadee gleans from twigs, it utters a hoarse
tsick tsick dee dee or a husky *tsee dee,* and other little gurgling or lisping
calls, and a sharp *tsik-a* when startled or excited.

Florence Merriam Bailey, author of several books on western birds,
thought the whistles of this chickadee to be "perhaps the commonest
notes heard in the forests of the Sierra Nevada" and noted occasionally
"a complicated guttural outburst suggesting *skit'tle-dee* or *skit-tle-little-
dee.*" Milton P. Skinner, who studied the birds at length in the Yellowstone National Park, describes the song there as *"phee, phe-e-e-e, phe,
phe,* with the second note accented and slightly prolonged, and the
whole having a dreamy and rather sorrowful tone."

The food of the mountain chickadee is substantially the same as
that of the black-capped, and includes spiders, insects, and their eggs,
young or pupae; also berries and seeds. At feeders it particularly likes
suet and pinyon nuts. It has been trained to eat from the hand.

Description: Length, 5½ in. Resembles black-capped chickadee, but
has black line through eye and white line over eye. In early summer,
white line may be hard to see, but at all seasons plumage is grayer than
in black-capped, and sides are brownish gray rather than buff.

Incubation, 14 days; young stay nearly three weeks in nest.

Size of eggs, 0.62 x 0.49 in.; often two broods per year.

BOREAL CHICKADEE (*Parus hudsonicus*)

It is obvious that the boreal or brown-capped chickadee is closely related to the black-capped chickadee, which it much resembles except
that the boreal's cap is brown and its voice has a husky drawl. Both are
also closely related to other chickadees and it is not hard to imagine a
common ancestor for all.

The boreal chickadee is a bird of the Great North Woods, whose vast
solitudes and occasional openings it shares with the gray jay (p. 53).
It also shares the jay's liking for the company, tables, and feeding trays

of man. This chickadee ranges north to the limit of trees and occasionally even wanders out of the barren lands in low birches and willows
along watercourses. It particularly likes thickets, swamps, and the neighborhood of bogs and muskegs.

The species is normally a permanent resident within its range, but
in periods of extreme weather it sometimes retreats from its most
northerly outposts or seeks lower elevations in mountains. At infrequent intervals in winter, for reasons presumably associated with
weather or food supply, numbers come south of their breeding range
and appear irregularly in the northern United States. These so-called
flight years usually coincide with heavy southward flights of the black-
capped chickadee. In Massachusetts, such years have been 1889–1890,
1913–1914, 1916–1917, 1941–1942, 1945–1946, 1954–1955. Alert bird
watchers in the United States, in the regions just south of the bird's
normal range, keep on the lookout through winter for this species, particularly at feeders.

The habits of the boreal chickadee are much like those of the black-
capped, although some observers find them more timid. When the two
species are together, the boreal may forage higher in the tree than will
the black-capped.

William Brewster, the famous Massachusetts ornithologist, watching
them in winter at Lake Umbagog, Maine, found that they:

differed from the black-caps as follows:—they were much less noisy (often
passing minutes at a time in absolute silence); they seldom hung head downward; they hopped and flitted among the branches more actively and cease-
lessly, spending less time in one place; their shorter tails were less in evidence; they flirted their wings much more with a more nervous, tremulous
motion very like that of kinglets.

In the face of danger when young are nearby, the parents may pre-
tend they are injured, sometimes falling over with fluttering wings in
order to try to lure the enemy away from the young. This seems to be
true of some other chickadees as well.

An unusual example of mid-air courtship feeding by the male has
been reported for this chickadee in Saskatchewan. Another courtship
scene has been described by Frederick H. Kennard as he saw it in late
May at Averill, Vermont:

... the male was very thoughtful and attentive to his little mate, whom he fed frequently. She kept up an almost continuous twittering call, and would flutter her little wings and ruffle her feathers on his near approach. We saw him give her several green cankerworms and many other small bugs; and I saw them copulate once.

The nest of the boreal chickadee is usually placed in a natural cavity or one excavated by the birds in a stump, perhaps 6 in. deep and from 1 to 10 ft. from the ground. Sometimes an old woodpecker hole is used or perhaps even the natural hollow in the top of a stump. The nest is made of moss, lichens, bark shreds, and fern down, and is lined with feathers or fur, often from deer or rabbit. The five to seven white eggs are unevenly sprinkled with tiny reddish brown dots.

The notes of the boreal chickadee have been variously described as more lisping, nasal, wheezy, or husky than those of the black-capped chickadee. They have been rendered by different authors as *atser-day-day-day*; *chicka-deer-deer*; *tsickaday-day-day*; *chee chee zay zay*; *chick, chee-dáy, dáy*. Brewster found the ordinary note "much louder and more petulant" than that of the black-capped chickadee. He said "another note frequently heard is a sharp *chip, chee-chee, chee* sometimes preluded by a sharp *che-chit* or *chee-chit-chit*."

There is dispute among bird students about its song. A. A. Saunders, the great bird-song expert, has never heard it. Neither did Brewster. But such a Massachusetts expert as C. W. Townsend heard in August on Cape Breton Island, Nova Scotia, "a low, bubbling, warbling song which began with a *pset* or *tsee,* followed by a sweet but short warble." And Francis H. Allen, another Massachusetts authority, in late September at Mount Moosilauke, New Hampshire, heard a warbling *wis-sipawiddlee* of which the final syllable was "sometimes trilled and sometimes pure."

The boreal chickadee is largely insectivorous. It consumes quantities of spiders, caterpillars, moths, beetles, and other insects and their eggs and pupae. The bird also likes seeds, especially pine and birch seeds, and cedar berries. At the feeder it comes to fatty foods such as suet and bacon grease. It also likes peanut butter and bread crumbs.

Description: Length, 5 in. Plump, big-headed; bill, short and straight; black and beady eyes; wings rounded. Brownish above, whitish below;

brown cap; black bib; chestnut flanks; no white on wing. *Note*: Black bib smaller, chestnut flanks brighter than in black-capped chickadee, and cheeks not so white.

Incubation, probably 14 days; young stay 14 to 16 days in nest. Size of eggs, 0.55 x 0.45 in.; probably one brood per year.

PLAIN TITMOUSE

TUFTED TITMOUSE (*Parus bicolor*)

The tufted titmouse is the only small gray bird in the eastern United States with a crest. It occurs as a year-round resident, west to the plains, and from Minnesota and New York to the Gulf. In recent years it has been gradually extending its range to the north, particularly in New York State. This is ascribed by some to an amelioration of the climate and by others to an increase in suitable habitat through the maturing of the forest on abandoned farm land on the Allegheny plateau. The plain titmouse occurs on the lower mountain slopes of the West.

The habitat of the tufted titmouse, in addition to the oak-beech, hickory woodlands already described, includes other deciduous woods, the edges of woods, bushy tracts, swamps, orchards, and trees in residential areas. In the Middle West it favors bottomland forests for breeding. In Florida and the Gulf states it is common in live oaks, hummocks, and cypress swamps.

In Maryland a maximum breeding population density of 13 pairs per 100 acres has been recorded in a well-drained flood-plain forest of mixed deciduous trees and also in an upland oak forest. The tufted titmouse is closely related to the chickadee (in the old days most chickadees were called titmice) and is similar in its habits. It seeks its insect food by carefully canvassing the bark, buds, twigs, and leaves of trees, and its search extends from the underbrush to the upper branches. It is active and vivacious and frequently hangs head down near the end of a twig or clings to the bark of branch or trunk. It is also excitable and inquisitive. It will come to investigate, sometimes at arm's length, an imitation of its whistle or the "squeaking" that a bird watcher uses to attract birds by kissing the back of his hand. If it disapproves of what is going on, it will scold the deceiver.

Titmice are usually seen in groups of two to six. Such a group will stay in one tree until its business there is completed, then fly on to another, gradually working its way through the woods. In fall and winter titmice often form part of a loose flock with woodpeckers, chickadees, nuthatches, creepers and sometimes sparrows, finches, kinglets, and Carolina wrens (p. 108). In late summer and fall migrating warblers and vireos for a time may join such a flock. Most of the year titmice are noisy and much in evidence, but in the breeding season they retire to secluded woodland retreats and are seen less often.

Tufted titmice seldom fly far. Their flight from tree to tree is light and "bouncy," somewhat like that of a chickadee. When a bird flies any distance, perhaps in crossing a stream, it reminds some observers of a miniature blue jay.

The limited amount of study that has been given the weight of birds has resulted in the enunciation of the so-called Bergmann rule that individuals of the same species tend to become larger in the cooler parts and smaller in the warmer parts of their range. The tufted titmouse bears this out. A study showed that the average weight in the cooler parts of its range was 24 grams and in the warmer parts of its range only 20 grams.

The courtship of this species has seldom been noted, although at least one case of courtship feeding of the female by the male is on record. Further observations during the spring months might show this to be a more common practice. Verna R. Johnston, who included a study of titmice in central Illinois in a Ph.D. thesis, thought the birds found mates by "calling and answering." Of the actual mating she writes:

Two titmice sat about one foot apart, fifteen feet up in a tree. The male, identified by his actions, began to utter a high, shrill buzz and to flutter his wings very rapidly at the same time. The female sat motionless. The male kept up his performance for about three minutes until finally the female began to give the same high buzz and to flutter her wings. The male then hopped onto her back and copulation took place.

The titmouse builds its nest in a natural crevice, cavity, or old woodpecker hole in a stump, stub, branch, pole or fence post. It is usually from 3 to 30 ft. above the ground, occasionally higher. One in Rosedale, Mississippi, was 97 ft. high in a black locust. The entrance hole is usually about 1½ in. wide. Inside the cavity both sexes help build a nest, which may include leaves, bark shreds, mosses, grasses, cotton, wool, feathers, hair, fur, and sloughed snake skins. Titmice also build in bird boxes.

The birds have several curious habits in nest building. They will, for example, take a damp leaf and hammer it together into a ball. They have been seen to pluck hair from a living dog, woodchuck, and red squirrel. Even humans are not immune from such attacks.

The five or six white eggs are marked with fine brown dots, sometimes concentrated in a wreath at the larger end. Oldtime egg collectors found that titmice were very close sitters and had to be lifted from the nest before they could be examined. (Egg collecting is now illegal.) If the nesting stump or stub is knocked on, a sitting bird will often give a hissing noise like the Carolina chickadee, perhaps in imitation of a snake.

Both male and female incubate the eggs and help feed the young. The male gives food to the female when she is brooding. After leaving the nest the young stay with the parents in a family group until joining the mixed flocks of other species. In summer months the tufted titmouse comes readily to a bird bath and in winter to a bird-feeding station. Judging from Audubon Society Christmas census records, the species is probably among the 20 most abundant winter birds in eastern North America.

The most familiar call of the tufted titmouse is a loud ringing *Peter, Peter, Peter,* or *peto, peto, peto,* which is uttered by both sexes from 3 to 11 times at a stretch. This is heard almost throughout the year, but less frequently in late summer. The first note is usually higher, but sometimes the order is reversed. A. A. Saunders, the bird-song expert, writes it variously as *peto, peto, wheedle, daytee, toolee,* or if the first note is short, *tleet* or *tlit.* He says: "sometimes a song begins or ends with notes unlike the rest, as *tidi, waytee, waytee, waytee,* etc., or *wheedle, wheedle, wheedle, whee, whee.*"

The call of the titmouse is often confused at a distance with the song of the Carolina wren, but near at hand the difference between the two syllables of the titmouse and the three of the wren is quite apparent. The titmouse also has a *dee-dee-dee* call and other chickadee-like notes; a scolding nasal *ya-ya-ya;* various whispers; a high, thin note of complaint like a blue-gray gnatcatcher; and a note like the fall warble of a blue-bird (*purity, purity*).

The food of this titmouse is about two-thirds animal matter and one-third vegetable. Caterpillars constitute one-half and wasps one-quarter of the animal food. The remainder includes beetles, various other insects, and their eggs and larvae. Acorns and beechnuts are the principal vegetable foods, but the birds also take seeds, wild fruits, and berries, especially mulberries and wax myrtle berries.

At the feeder the titmouse's favorite foods are sunflower seeds, honeysuckle berries, bread, doughnuts, and suet. According to some observers the tufted titmouse dominates the feeding tray, yielding place only to the blue jay; others assert that nuthatches are dominant over titmice.

Description: Length, 6 in. Crested head; short, thin, and straight bill; black and beady eyes; rounded wings. Forehead blackish; gray upperparts; whitish cheeks and underparts; chestnut wash on flanks. Female slightly smaller and duller. Plain titmouse similar but lacks black forehead.

Incubation, 12 days; young stay 15 or 16 days in nest.

Size or eggs, 0.7 x 0.5 in.; one brood per year.

NUTHATCHES / *Sittidae*

WHITE-BREASTED NUTHATCH (*Sitta carolinensis*)

The white-breasted nuthatch occurs from southern Canada to the mountains of southern Mexico. It is resident over almost all the United States throughout the year, although there is a shift southward from the northern parts of its range in fall, and some birds move a short distance from breeding grounds to winter-feeding territories. It is our only nuthatch with white cheeks. Its black cap, blue back, and clean white underparts give it an exceptionally trim and well-groomed appearance.

The habitat of the white-breasted nuthatch over much of its range is deciduous woodlands, groves, and shade trees. In the South it is also found in mixed woodlands or in pine woods. In the West its principal habitat is the coniferous forest up to timber line. In the East its favorite tree is white oak.

Nuthatches are acrobats of the bird world; they go head-first down a tree trunk as well as up. When going down, one will often stop and hold its head out horizontally. This species spends almost all its time on either trunk or limbs of a tree. It investigates the bark minutely for insects and their eggs, searching branches to their tips and often feeding from underneath like a fly on a ceiling. When flying from branch to branch or tree to tree, it has a characteristic, slightly undulating flight. It seldom flies far.

In mixed flocks and at feeding stations, nuthatches drive away chickadees. Among nuthatches, the white-breasted dominates the red-breasted. W. K. Butts, with the aid of colored bands, made an intensive study of this species around Ithaca, New York. He discovered:

(1) that each pair had a winter territory of 25 to 30 acres in wooded country and 50 acres in semiwooded country
(2) that a pair at breeding season had the same acreage, but not necessarily the same place as in winter
(3) that the nest was in or near the winter feeding territory
(4) that a pair might use the same nest hole in successive seasons
(5) that there was always a number of unmated birds about; in case a member of a mated pair disappeared, an unmated bird would take its place.

The white-breasted nuthatch appears to mate for life. The male engages in various forms of courtship activity. Winsor M. Tyler, who contributed the sketch of this species for Arthur Cleveland Bent's *Life Histories of North American Birds,* reports that with the advent of spring:

A real courtship begins: he carries food to her and places it in her bill, he stores bits of nut in crevices of bark for her convenience, and he often addresses his singing directly to her. Standing back to her, he bows slowly downward as he sings, then in the interval before another song he straightens up, then bows as he sings again. The songs come with perfect regularity over and over again and can thus be recognized even in the distance as the courtship song.

We may imagine what a changing color scheme is presented to the female bird, if, as his song invites her to do, she glances his way—the black of his crown and his rough raised mane, then the blue-gray of his back, then the variegated black and white pattern of his expanded tail, then, perhaps, at the end of his bow, a flash of ruddy brown. At other times he approaches the female more aggressively, strutting before her with stretched-out neck and flattened crown, a pose of intimidation.

The nesting site of the white-breasted nuthatch is a hole in a dead branch or stump from 2 to 60 ft. above the ground. It may be a natural cavity, an old woodpecker hole, or (rarely) it may even be excavated in old rotten wood by the bird itself. The hole may lead as much as 6 in. back into the wood and go down for 6 to 8 in. to the nesting cavity. The nest has a foundation of loose bark overlaid with grass, twigs, root-lets, bark shreds, and feathers. The lining is of hair or fur of squirrel, rabbit, skunk, cow, deer, or even bear. Sometimes this is shed hair found in the woods; sometimes it comes from a carcass. Sometimes the bird may try to pluck it from the living animal.

The white-breasted nuthatch nests in woods, orchards, and tree-lined streets. The female builds the nest; the male brings her material and feeds her while she is building. If you want to have nuthatches around your home, nesting places are as important as artificial feeding. You can put up nesting boxes, or better yet, you can leave dead stubs on your trees.

The eggs of this nuthatch are creamy white, sparingly speckled with red-brown dots, often most heavily around the larger end. The number varies from four to ten; the average differs in different parts of the country. The female alone incubates; the male feeds her while she is sitting (18 times in $1\frac{1}{4}$ hours, according to one observation). Both help feed the young.

After the breeding season these nuthatches roam the woods in loose flocks with chickadees, downy woodpeckers, titmice, kinglets, creepers, and migrating warblers. Members of the flocks keep up a loose con-versational chatter that has the effect of keeping the flock together as its members work their way from tree to tree through the woods.

The white-breasted nuthatch is one of our 25 most common winter species. During this season several birds may share a common roost at night. One observer saw 29 of these nuthatches slip into a crack in the trunk of an old, dead, yellow pine. When ice storms coat tree trunks and branches, the white-breast has trouble finding food.

The spring song of the white-breasted nuthatch is a pleasant, low, nasal series of woodsy whistles on the same pitch. Thoreau wrote them down as *to what what what what*. There is much charm in this simple lay, particularly when heard from streamside woods in March against a foreground of melting snowdrifts. The male sings repeatedly from

March through May, the rest of the year only occasionally at dawn. There is often a slight difference in dialect between the songs in different parts of the country.

The most common note of the species is a nasal *Yank, Yank, Yank,* sometimes *Yank, Yank, Yank-ee, Yank-ee, Yank, Yank, Yank.* The bird also has an abrupt, high, conversational *hit hit.* Ralph Hoffman describes the songs of the Pacific coast subspecies as a "sharp nasal *keer, keer*" and says:

When two birds are working together, they utter a low *quit quit.* A high *quer* is the alarm note about the nest. In early spring and summer the male repeats a mellow *too too too,* like the blowing of a little trumpet; this song is generally given from a twig, an unusual perch at any other time.

Half the yearly food of this species is insects and spiders and their eggs and pupae. The insects include scale insects, weevils, leaf beetles, plant lice, wood-boring beetles, ants, flies, caterpillars, grasshoppers, locusts, and moths, especially coddling moths. The stomach of one nuthatch was found to contain 1,629 eggs of the fall cankerworm. The other half of its yearly diet is beechnuts, hickory nuts, and acorns; waste grain and seeds, such as those of pine, fir, maple, and sunflower; berries of mountain ash and juniper, and fruit such as half-rotten apples. To get at the meat of a nut, the bird will push it into a crevice, then hammer away at it with its bill. Nuthatches, as do jays, often store food in crevices in bark or in other hiding places.

The favorite feeder food of this species is suet hung on a tree, but the bird also comes to window feeding trays. It takes sunflower seeds, bread crumbs, carrots, raw beef, and (when cut in half) the seeds of squash and pumpkins.

Description: Length, 6 in. Body, stout; bill, thin and sharp; tail, short and squared; legs and feet, strong; overall appearance somewhat flattened. Male: black cap, nape, and beady eye; white side face and underparts; gray back; chestnut undertail coverts; white markings on outer tail feathers; no dark line through eye. Female: paler, crown grayer.

Incubation, 12 to 13 days; young stay 14 days in nest.

Size of eggs, 0.7 x 0.6 in.; one brood per year.

RED-BREASTED NUTHATCH (*Sitta canadensis*)

The red-breasted nuthatch may be extraordinarily common in parts of its winter range one year and very rare the next. We presume that these winter "irruptions" are connected with the failure of its favorite food supply, but this has not been fully documented.

The species has a curious, disconnected range in the Northern Hemisphere. At one time it must have been widespread in both Old World and New, but the effects of the various ice ages or other geologic disturbances have scattered it widely and have broken it into three isolated groups—one on the island of Corsica, one in eastern Siberia and China, and one in North America.

In North America the red-breasted nuthatch breeds in coniferous forests of Canada and mountains of the United States. It winters from southern Canada erratically to the Gulf coast states and southern Arizona. Its fall migration starts early, sometimes even in July. The preferred habitat of this nuthatch is evergreen conifers, both in summer and winter, but it is also found in deciduous woods and sometimes, as in Oregon, on sagebrushes far from timber. In migration and particularly during great irruptions, it may be seen almost anywhere, such as the rocks of bare coasts and islands, about houses and buildings, along roadsides, on fences, bushes, weeds, and in other odd places.

The red-breasted nuthatch, like the white-breasted, is an "upside-down bird." It climbs around the trunks of trees either head up or head down, moving in short, jerky hops, searching the bark for insects and larvae. Most frequently it is seen clambering on the outer twigs of an evergreen, particularly a spruce. Occasionally it hops on the ground, searching for food, and enjoys bathing in a bird bath or natural pool. Sometimes it catches insects in the air. Its flight is undulating, with quick beats of short wings. Flights, except in migration, are usually very short.

It is a sociable species and frequently is found in small groups of three to six birds. In winter it roams the woods in loose flocks with other species of nuthatches as well as chickadees, titmice, downy woodpeckers, kinglets, creepers, and warblers. In the avian "peck order" this species at a feeder dominates the pigmy nuthatch and all chickadees, but in turn yields place to the larger white-breasted nuthatch.

In courtship the male struts before the female, flirting its wings and tail, and bowing. The male also has a courtship flight.

Witmer Stone, in his *Bird Studies at Old Cape May,* writes:

Several times I have seen a red-breasted nuthatch flying wildly round and round above the tops of the pines in an ellipse probably one hundred feet in length, covering exactly the same course several times before coming to rest. I could not guess at the meaning of this unless it is the recurrence of a flight song performance incidental to the mating time.

The nest of this nuthatch is a hole in a branch, stub, or stump. It may be a natural cavity or an old woodpecker hole, or excavated by the birds themselves in soft wood. Sometimes they use a man-made nesting box. The bird has an unusual habit of smearing pitch around its entrance hole. It carries the pitch in little round globules in its bill. The hole is 1 in. in diameter and goes several inches in and down to the nesting cavity. The nest is sometimes composed of wood chips alone, but often contains feathers, grasses, rootlets, and bark shreds.

The four to seven white eggs are variously marked with red-brown spots, generally less heavily, however, than the eggs of the white-breasted nuthatch. Most hole-nesting birds have immaculate white eggs, possibly because it is easier thus for the female to locate them in the semidarkness or maybe because the value of markings to make the eggs less conspicuous in an open nest no longer exists for eggs in a hidden cavity. In any case, the fact that nuthatches do not have pure white eggs suggests that the hole-nesting habits of these birds may be of recent origin.

Mated birds seem to stay together for more than one season. The female does most of the incubating; the male feeds her while she is sitting, and both parents feed the young. When entering the cavity the birds have an unusual habit of flying straight in without perching on the edge of the entrance hole.

The voice of this bird is more highly pitched than that of the white-breasted nuthatch. *Ink, ink, ink* it seems to say in high, nasal notes, like those of a tiny tin trumpet. It also utters short, high-pitched, conversational *hit hit* notes, similar to those of the white-breasted. Its rarely heard song reminds some observers of the white-breasted, but it is higher, faster, and reedier.

The favorite natural food of this nuthatch is seeds of spruce, fir, and maple, and in winter those of giant ragweed, dock, and other weeds that project above the snow. It also likes rotten apples and drinks sap from little holes in bark made by sapsuckers. Its animal diet includes spiders and insects, and their eggs and larvae. Insects include beetles, flies, pine-borers, caterpillars, moths, wasps, ants, leaf hoppers, and plant lice.

The red-breasted nuthatch stores food in crevices in the bark and in other woodland hiding places.

Favorite feeder foods include sunflower seeds, nut kernels, especially those of black walnuts, peanuts, and pecans. With some patience you may be able to teach the tame little bird to take food from your hand.

Description: Length, 4½ in. Body, stout; bill, thin and sharp; tail, short and squared; legs and feet, strong; overall appearance, somewhat flattened. Male: black cap and line through eye; white line over eye; dark blue-gray upperparts; reddish underparts. Female and young: slaty gray cap and eye strips; underparts are paler than in adult male.

Incubation, 12 days; young stay 21 days in nest.

Size of eggs, 0.7 x 0.6 in.; one brood per year.

CREEPERS / *Certhiidae*

BROWN CREEPER (*Certhia familiaris*)

Elfin minstrel of the tree trunk, the brown creeper is a bird with a very wide distribution. From tree-bordered gardens of England, through wilds of Siberia and Alaska, across coniferous forests of Canada, the range of this sprite encircles the northern part of the globe.

From boreal evergreen wilderness the bird ranges far south in mountains. It is at home on pine-clad slopes that overlook banana plantations of Nicaragua as well as on smoky summits that tower over tobacco fields of North Carolina. In its ancestral haunts it spirals up trees beside the paths of smugglers and refugees in the Pyrenees and Carpathians. It lisps to the tread of European explorer and Sherpa tramping new trails up Kanchenjunga and Everest. It gleans its way amid shell-scarred groves in Korea and in national parks of Japan. Over all these hundreds of thousands of square miles the birds are of the same species. Seven races in North America and several more in other parts of the world mark its geographical variations.

The creeper family is of Old World origin. Our species is a relatively recent immigrant to the New World. Members of the family are widely distributed and are found in every continent except South America.

98

The brown creeper is an inconspicuous bird. Seldom is more than one seen at a time. Half a dozen in a day, except in migration, would be a high count. While it is glad to visit and eat suet at the feeder, it never displays the confiding spirit of the chickadee or the boldness of the nuthatch. It is a bird of quiet dignity and gentle grace, born in a bark-shielded, pine-needle cradle, far in the forest primeval in a world of pattering rain, swirling mist, and soughing pines.

BROWN CREEPER

In North America the creeper breeds from Alaska, northern Canada, and Newfoundland south into the northern tier of states, farther south in the eastern mountains of Tennessee, and in the western mountains to Nicaragua. It winters from British Columbia, the northern states, Quebec, and Nova Scotia south to the Gulf.

In summer, in much of its range, the brown creeper is a bird of the Canadian and Hudsonian life-zones, of fir and spruce forests of the northern wilderness, and of the Appalachian, Rocky, and Sierra Nevada

Mountains. Along the humid Pacific coast, however, it is found near sea level; there and in other parts of California and the West it also occurs in the Transition zone. It is much at home in lofty aisles of the redwoods and in groves of incense cedar.

In New Mexico the creeper breeds from 7,500 to 9,000 ft.; after breeding it may ascend to 12,000 ft. In Arizona it is found from 6,000 ft. to timber line, but is more often seen amid spruce, fir, and aspen than lower down in the pines. In the Huachucas it is common from 8,000 ft. up. In the San Bernardino Mountains in California it ranges from 5,600 to 9,500 ft., but is most abundant in the incense cedar belt. Within its breeding range the bird is found in mature forests, wooded swamps, and the edges of bodies of water with flood-killed trees.

In fall and winter the bird descends to lower elevations and moves south to lower altitudes. It may then be seen in trees almost anywhere. Deciduous woodlands, pinelands of the South, and shade trees in gardens, parks, and villages are good places to find it.

The brown creeper follows a more monotonous routine than do other species. It spends most of the daylight hours spiraling in short hitches up and around the trunk of a tree. When it has reached a good altitude, it drops down, almost like a falling piece of bark, to the base of another tree and then spirals its way up that. In Massachusetts, C. E. Bailey once watched one for an hour, during which time it inspected 43 trees, principally white oaks, and worked its way about 100 yds. through the woods. It began about 2 ft. from the ground and ascended about 20 ft. before dropping to the next tree.

As the creeper hitches, it gleans its food—insects, spiders, and their eggs—from the crevices in the bark. Many insect eggs are minute and are overlooked by larger, grosser feeders such as woodpeckers. The creeper's sharp, delicately pointed bill is a fine tool for careful gleaning. Its stiff tail, composed of 12 stout elastic feathers, and its curved, sharp-clawed toes enable it to cling easily to the trunk. When it molts, its hitching and spiraling remain unaffected, for the long central tail feathers are not lost until all other tail feathers have been replaced.

So deeply ingrained is the instinctive habit of clinging and climbing that, in migration, if a creeper comes to an area where there are no trees, it will cling to a sand bank, rock, brick wall, fence post, telegraph pole, or amazing as it may seem, to a man's trouser leg or a cow's tail!

Florence Merriam Bailey, the well-known writer on western birds, describes its habits in the Sierras:

In the stillness of the high mountain forests your ear sometimes catches the thin, finely drawn pipe of the brown creeper, and if you watch patiently on the dark-shaded boles of the lofty trees you may discover the little dark-colored creatures—seeming small and weak in the great solemn fir forest—creeping up the trunks, examining the cracks with microscopic care as he goes. . . . On Mount Shasta, where the first are decorated with yellow moss, the Sierra creeper goes around its pads when he comes to them, but works carefully over the dark lichen-covered branches.

Of the courtship of the brown creeper, Arthur C. Bent, the great bird biographer, writes:

The creeper's courtship appears to consist of a display of agility in the air. Once in a while we see a bird launch out from a tree and at top speed twine around it close to the bark, then dart away and twist around another tree, or weave in and out among the surrounding trees and branches. He has thrown off his staid creeper habits and has become for the time a carefree aerial sprite, giving himself up, it seems to an orgy of speed, wild dashes, and twists and turns in the air. But after a round or two, back on the bark again, he resumes his conventional routine and becomes once more a brown creeper.

The early ornithologists, Audubon, Wilson, and Nuttall, were incorrect in their statements that creepers customarily nest in holes in trees. They rarely do so. It was not till late in the nineteenth century that the bird custom of nesting in the cosy dry space under a loose flake of bark, still joined to a standing tree trunk, was discovered.

The female alone builds the nest, but the male helps by bringing her material. Twigs that she fails to get into position fall down to the foot of the trunk and apparently are regarded as unsuitable for reuse, for the male never goes to this stockpile as a source for material.

When the nest is completed the female deposits in it five or six (sometimes four to nine) white eggs finely dotted with red-brown spots which are often wreathed about the larger end. The birds are thought to pair for life.

Brown creepers are night migrants and relatively early migrants. Some arrive in New England in the first half of September. Though we seldom notice more than isolated pairs on their breeding grounds or in winter, in migration we may see more. Fall and spring counts of 20 in a day are not uncommon.

In South Carolina, where the creeper occurs from mid-October to March, it is more common in severe winters. In Louisiana it stays from October to April. In the West in winter the birds descend to the pinyons and cedars of the foothills and spread out through the deciduous timber along lowland streams. In the northern part of their winter range they are thinly distributed in protected areas. At this season they are often seen with or near the loose flocks of chickadees, titmice, nuthatches, kinglets, and downy woodpeckers that roam winter woods. But they are incidental associates of these flocks rather than forming part of them.

The common call of the brown creeper is a thin, high *seeeee,* somewhat longer than the similar *see* of the golden-crowned kinglet with which note it is often confused. The creeper commonly utters only one note at a time, while the kinglet's *see-see-see* often comes in groups of three or more.

The bird-song authority, A. A. Saunders, describes the lay of the creeper as "weak, high-pitched, but pleasing, and of somewhat sibilant, musical quality." It consists of four to eight (most commonly five or six) notes, generally beginning with the long high-pitched note, followed by two short lower-pitched ones. The remaining notes vary somewhat, but are often a repetition of the first notes: *see to ti see ti seetsi seetse seetsay.* The high notes of the song resemble the *seeeeee* note of the call.

The diet of the brown creeper is almost entirely animal matter. Its natural foods are insects, spiders and their eggs, and cocoons that it finds hidden in the crevices of bark. Such insects include weevils, leaf beetles, flatbugs, jumping plant lice, leafhoppers, scale insects, katydids, wasps, ants, other small hymenopters, sawflies, caterpillars, codling moths, and other moths.

The creeper also takes a few small seeds. Sometimes it feeds on the ground or snow. When it does so, it hops with legs far apart and body seemingly resting on its tail. It sometimes eats snow.

The favorite feeder food of the brown creeper is beef suet; but it also likes chopped peanuts and peanut butter stuffed in holes in a stick.

In flying towards the feeder the bird does not hop on it from above, but just drops lower down and then glides up to the shelf.

Description: Length, 5 in. Female smaller than male. Thin, sharp, and curved bill; wings rather long but rounded; tail feathers stiffened. Brown upperparts with some streaks of gray; pale rufous rump; white underparts. The bird shows a pale wing stripe in flight.

Incubation, 11 to 12 days; young stay 13 to 14 days in nest.

Size of eggs, 0.6 x 0.5 in.; one or two broods per year.

WRENS / *Troglodytidae*

BEWICK'S WREN (*Thryomanes bewickii*)

Bewick's is a medium-sized wren with an unusually long tail. In size and habits it resembles the house wren, but the two species are usually intolerant of one another and are seldom found in the same habitat.

Bewick's wren breeds from southwestern British Columbia to central Pennsylvania, south into Mexico, and to the northern portions of the Gulf states. It is largely a sedentary species, one of the most characteristic birds of the Upper Austral and Upper Sonoran life-zones. There is, however, some movement in the fall, which brings the bird to the Gulf coast and southern Florida. It is a plastic species, varying in appearance with geography and climate. As a result, 13 subspecies are recognized within the United States.

John J. Audubon named this species for Thomas Bewick, the English woodcut artist.

The basic habitat is wood edges with convenient cover in farming country, villages, and near buildings. Where trees are scarce, bushes and chaparral suffice. George F. Simmons, a Texas bird authority, says that the bird's habitat around Austin consists of:

... broken country, almost always near civilization; ... old pastures dotted with brush heaps and lined with brush fences; cut-over woods; ... thickets

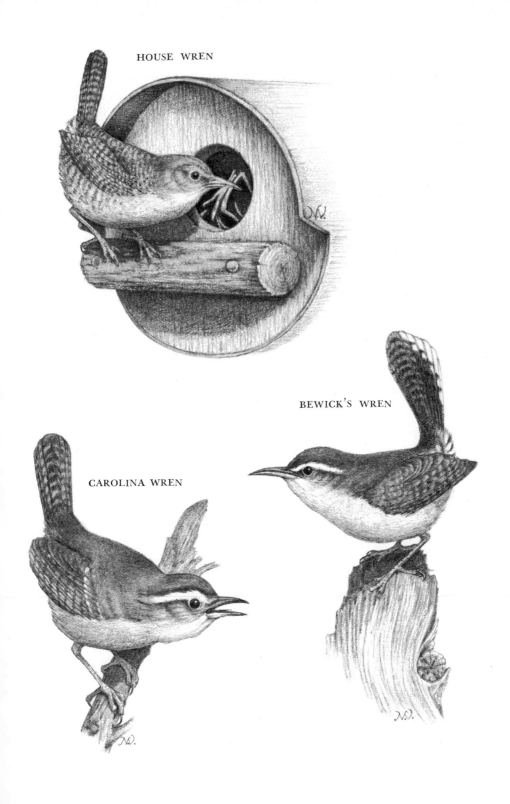

HOUSE WREN

BEWICK'S WREN

CAROLINA WREN

and beds of cactus in mesquite and cactus country; brush heaps and thickets along creeks; dense cedar brakes on the hills; along rather open creek valleys, on slopes and hills, and in semi-open country, but never in dense bottom woods or on extreme open country; about barns, deserted houses, wood piles and brush heaps. . . . The commonest local wren, a pair in nearly every garden.

W. Leon Dawson, in his *Birds of California,* notes that the species likes timber slashings, rocky hillsides, sunny arroyos, and chaparral, and is found from sea level up to 9,000 ft.

In the Upper Sonoran foothills of the Yosemite region, Grinnell and Storer point out that each of the four species of wrens there occupy a different habitat. The canyon wren inhabits steep canyons; the rock wren prefers rocky outcrops. The house wren is found about oak trees, while Bewick's wren lives amid small trees and scrub.

The most conspicuous habit of Bewick's wren is the way it manages its long, rounded tail, which seems loosely attached to the body. Dawson says, "With this expressive member the bird is able to converse in a vigorous sign language. It is cocked up in impudence, wagged in defiance, set aslant in coquetry or depressed in whimsical token of humility. Indeed, it is hardly too much to say that the bird makes faces with its tail." If there is a strong breeze, the wind may seem to control the tail more than the bird does.

This wren is a territorial breeder. Near Berkeley, California, Edwin Vance Miller made a study showing that each pair defends an area of 50 to 100 yds. Where both Bewick's and house wrens occur in summer, the resident and hardier Bewick's stake out their claims in spring before the migrant house wrens arrive. This gives them an advantage in the struggle for nesting territory.

Bewick's wren places its nest in almost any crevice or hiding place. In the past, the birds apparently built largely in knot holes, old woodpecker nests, brush heaps, or the root mass of fallen trees. With the coming of civilization, they find shelter in old automobiles, oil wells, sheds, stovepipes, old clothes, and a host of other artificial situations, including bird houses.

Dawson, referring to nesting sites in California, writes:

A cranny of suitable size is the *sine qua non,* and this may be in a rockpile, in a canyon-wall, in an old woodpecker-hole, in the mount of an old tunnel of a Rough-winged Swallow, under a root, behind a sprung bark-scale, in an old shoe or a tin can, or the pocket of a disused coat. It may even be, as frequently upon Santa Cruz Island, in the bedded leafage of the forest floor.

The nest is usually about 6 ft. off the ground, but may be as low as 3 or as high as 25 ft. Simmons, writing of the nest in Texas, gives details of its structure and ingredients that apply in many parts of the country. He says it is a:

. . . large, compact structure, top level and open above; composed of a mass of rubbish, principally cedar bark strips, small short sticks and twigs, dead leaves, bits of twine, and chicken feathers, with the occasional use of horse-hair, cowhair, grass, weed stems, rootlets, oak blossoms, cast-off snake skin, cotton waste, leaf skeletons, spider webs, cobwebs, caterpillar cocoons, paper, and bits of corn husks. Cedar bark and twigs are usually interlocked and moulded into a strong, symmetrical nest with deep, well constructed cup.

Unlike other wrens this species does not seem to build dummy or decoy nests. Ten days may be required for building.

The female lays five to seven white eggs dotted finely with red-brown spots, often wreathed around the larger end. According to Miller, the eggs are usually laid early in the morning. The female does all or almost all the incubating. This lasts for 14 days; the young stay in the nest 14 days; and the parents care for them outside the nest for another two weeks.

The male feeds the female on the nest. Both parents help feed the young.

In fall and winter there is some movement southward and to lower elevations. At such seasons in the West the Bewick's and house wrens may seem to share the same habitat with little friction, but close observation usually shows that each species has its own slightly different ecologic niche.

The male Bewick's wren has an unusually beautiful voice. Brewster found the song "sweet and exquisitely tender. . . ." The song of the Texas subspecies, however, reminded Simmons of the lark sparrow "with its buzzing quality." Singing is confined to the males. Birds in the West have a more beautiful and complex song than those in the East.

Ralph Hoffman, in his *Birds of the Pacific States,* speaks of the division of the song into three parts, "a high quick opening of two or more notes, then lower notes rather *burry* in quality, and in closing a very delicate fine trill." One of these trills, says Dawson, "after three preliminary notes, runs *tsu' tsu' tsu' tsu' tsu' tsu' tsu'*, like an exaggerated and beautified song of the towhee. Another song, which from its rollicking character deserves to be called a drinking song, terminates with a brilliant trill in descending scale, *rallentando et diminuendo*."

According to Hoffman the note is "a high-pitched energetic *chick chick* . . . (sometimes) varied to a throaty *kut, kut, kut*. Another characteristic note is a harsh *spee*." Some observers claim that Bewick's is a better mocker of other bird songs than the Carolina wren, the "mocking wren" of early writers. But others dispute the claim. Bewick's wren sings a great deal through much of the year. In Indiana its song period is from mid-March to the end of August; in Arkansas, from mid-March to mid-October. In many parts of the West it is the dominant voice in the avian chorus. The bird usually sings from an elevated perch, with the tail held either horizontal or drooping. It sings deliberately and without the haste of other wrens.

Bewick's wren is mostly insectivorous; food includes bugs, beetles, caterpillars and moths, wasps, ants, spiders, and grasshoppers.

Description: Length, 5½ in. Female smaller than male. Slender, brown above, light below, white line over eye and white tips to outer tail feathers (not always plainly visible). These white marks are lacking in the house wren, which is browner above and grayer below. The Carolina wren is larger, more reddish brown, and has no white tips to the outer tail feathers. The rock wren is grayer, has a finely streaked breast, and buff (not white) tips to the outer tail feathers.

Incubation, 14 days; young stay 14 days in nest.

Size of eggs, 1.0 x 0.75 in.; two broods per year; often three in the South.

CAROLINA WREN (*Thryothorus ludovicianus*)

This large wren is distinguished by a white line over its eye and reddish brown upperparts. It is a permanent resident of Upper and

Lower Austral life-zones and ranges north to Nebraska and Massachusetts, west to Texas, and south to the Gulf coast and northern Mexico. It is gradually spreading northward. The species winterkills easily, however, whenever a heavy blanket of snow keeps it from the normal source of insect food on the ground. Along the northern border of its range, populations oscillate in numbers with snowy winters.

Thickets, tangles, shrubbery, undergrowth, stream borders, alder swamps, brush piles, masses of logs, decaying timber, and old sheds are the favored habitats of the species. In the Deep South it also favors live-oak and palmetto hummocks, cypress swamps, bottomland thickets, and isolated clumps of trees in prairies and barrens. It is also found in farmyards and suburban gardens.

The Carolina wren is exceedingly restless, nimble, shy, timid, and wary, but it is also inquisitive. About feeders, however, it loses much of its wildness. It spends most of its time on or near the ground foraging in brush piles and thickets, although sometimes it climbs up or around tree trunks prying for food like a creeper.

Its flights are usually short and erratic; its short wings sometimes seem to buzz with the speed of a hummingbird's. On its occasional longer flights, however, it flies direct. When disturbed, it seeks safety in concealment and can dive and disappear into a tangle with amazing celerity, to flee on foot under cover of matted grasses or forest floor debris.

In the wild, the Carolina wren builds its nest in woods or near river banks, in a hole or cranny in or near the ground. Such a spot might be the root mass of an overturned tree, a hollow in a log, trunk, stump or limb, or a hideaway under an overhanging bank. The height above the ground, if any, is usually less than 10 ft. (though an extreme of 40 ft. has been reported). Sometimes a nest is placed in densely branched cedar or other conifer, or in thick undergrowth. A favorite location in the South is the "boot" of a palmetto, i.e., the area around the base of the trunk protected by the fallen fronds.

In civilization, this wren nests in orchard, farmyard and buildings, sawmills, and other structures. It uses a wide variety of nest sites: the inside of a tin can, coffee pot, old shirt, hat or old coat, child's boot, empty box, mail box, bird box, a hole in a sofa, or a mayonnaise jar on the back porch window sill.

The nest is a bulky affair of twigs, grasses, and leaves, lined with finer material. Mosses, rootlets, pine needles, weed stalks, bits of bark, hair, feathers, and perhaps an old snake skin may be used. If in the open, the nest, which may be as much as 6 in. deep, is usually roofed and provided with a side entrance.

A pair of Carolina wrens seems to mate for life. Both birds build the nest, which they may finish in a week or less; but if the weather is bad, it may take two weeks. The birds usually work for several hours in the morning, then rest for several hours or for a day or two.

The five (sometimes four to seven) creamy or pinkish white eggs are more heavily decorated with larger red-brown spots than the eggs of other wrens. These spots form a wreath around the larger end. Incubation is largely by the female; but the male joins in feeding the young while they are in the nest and afterwards until they are fledged. Frequently the male takes over the entire care of the young after they leave the nest, while the female lays again, often in a new nest.

In winter the species roosts in a protected space, such as behind ivy or in an old hornet's nest. Unusual sites have included a shirt pocket on a clothes line and the pocket of an old coat on a porch.

Suitable cover in winter is essential for survival. Consequently, near the northern limit of its range, it is found only where thickets and tangles are sufficiently dense to provide adequate shelter and bare ground. If you want to keep a Carolina wren in winter, supply it with a brush pile and food at the feeder.

The Carolina wren has a loud clear, ringing, three-syllable song commonly written *TEA-kettle TEA-kettle TEA-kettle*. Some listeners recognize it better as *Sweet WILLiam Sweet WILLiam Sweet WILLiam* or *COME to me COME to me COME to me*. It also has a two-syllable song, *TWEEdle TWEEdle TWEEdle* or *SWEETheart SWEETheart SWEETheart*. Any of these can be heard for a quarter-mile. Beginners find it hard to tell the songs of this species from the songs of the cardinal (p. 201) and tufted titmouse (p. 89). A. A. Saunders, the authority on bird song, admitting that it is hard to describe the difference in words, says he would describe the titmouse as having a clear whistle, the cardinal as having a reedy whistle, and the Carolina wren as having a rich whistle.

The song is usually delivered, with some squatting and jerking of the body, from the top of a tree, shrub, or other elevated perch. It is one of the characteristic sounds of the South. The Carolina wren is a mighty singer. Its loud-whistled, oft-repeated song rings through oak and pine, flat, and dingle every month of the year and in almost any kind of weather. We hear it most frequently in late winter and early spring at any time of day.

This bird has been called the "mocking wren." It has been reported to utter songs or sounds resembling those of the belted kingfisher, yellow-shafted flicker, catbird (p. 121), eastern bluebird, white-eyed vireo, pine warbler, tufted titmouse, red-winged blackbird (p. 168), eastern meadowlark, Baltimore oriole, common grackle, scarlet tanager, rufous-sided towhee, and song sparrow (p. 291). There is now some doubt as to whether these are real imitations or merely examples of the bird's versatility.

The calls of this wren include a great variety of clacks, rattles, and trills. A common alarm note is a long rolling trill *ch-r-r-r-r-r-r-r-r*, sometimes shortened to *CHEER-'p*.

Studies by government biologists, based on the contents of 291 stomachs, show that animal matter constitutes 94 percent of the food of this wren. Caterpillars and moths account for 21 percent; bugs, 19 percent; beetles, 14 percent; grasshoppers, crickets, and cockroaches, 13 percent; spiders, 11 percent; ants, bees, and wasps, 5 percent; and flies, 3 percent. The cotton-boll weevil, cucumber beetle, bean-leaf beetle, flea beetle, and chinch-bug are among pests included. The bird also likes bayberries and fruit of the sweet gum tree.

Favorite feeder foods are ground peanuts, walnut and pecan meats, suet, marrow, ground meat, and cottage cheese.

Description: Length, 6 in. Female smaller than male. Bill, slightly curved. Rich reddish brown above, buffy below; white throat and line over eye; wings, tail and undertail coverts barred with black. The house wren is smaller, grayer, and lacks the line over the eye; Bewick's is grayer brown, not reddish, has white line over the eye, but also has white tail corners. The long-billed marsh wren has a white line over eye, but a striped, not even-colored back.

Incubation, 12 to 14 days; young stay 12 to 14 days in nest.

Size of eggs, 0.8 x 0.6 in.; two, often three broods per year.

MOCKINGBIRDS, THRASHERS / *Mimidae*

MOCKINGBIRD (*Mimus polyglottos*)

The mockingbird is the most famous bird of the South. It has fascinated naturalists ever since Mark Catesby first wrote of it in his account of the "Mock-Bird of Carolina" in 1731.

Slim, gray, and white, it is a little longer than a robin. It has a long white-edged tail; the white patches on its wings are conspicuous in flight. The sexes are similar in appearance. The mockingbird is found from central California to Connecticut, south to southern Mexico and the Gulf. It is resident in the East, somewhat migratory in the West. It also occurs in Bermuda, where it was introduced in 1893. The family of mimic thrushes to which it belongs is believed to have originated in North America.

In recent years the mockingbird, like the cardinal (p. 199) and tufted titmouse (p. 86), has been extending its range northward and is now commonly seen in areas where it was unknown or rare 30 years ago. Some individuals wander widely and are likely to turn up—often in winter—in places north of its usual range, particularly along the coast.

Originally the mockingbird must have been a bird that frequented wood edges and clearings in the forest. Today it occurs most commonly near civilization. It likes parks, gardens, farmyards, ranches, orchards, orange groves, hedgerows, roadsides, towns, and villages. Ideal habitats are a lawn to forage over, brush to nest in, and trees to sing from. Such territory should be able to support one pair to an acre.

The species, however, is also found in upland cotton fields, coastal palmetto and magnolia jungles, and semiarid mesquite and brush. In the West its home is in the Sonoran life-zones, especially the Lower Sonoran where it breeds. In New Mexico it nests from an altitude of 3,800 to 7,500 ft. and, after the breeding season, ranges upward to 9,000 and 10,000 ft. It is generally believed to be more numerous now than it was before Europeans arrived in the New World. Bird watchers in cars look for it on roadside wires, housetop chimneys, and television aerials.

The actions of the species are vivacious and buoyant. On alighting it often raises its wings over its back before folding them, almost like a shore bird; it often hops, runs, and feeds on the ground with its tail raised. One characteristic action is a running hop on the ground, with head and tail high and wings dropping slightly. A bird feeding on the lawn sometimes stops and raises its wings over its back in an action called "wing flashing." Females and young practice this; males, rarely. Its purpose is unknown.

The mockingbird stands high on slender legs; its body often seems to vibrate. Its long, mobile tail is characteristic of a bird that hops a great deal from limb to limb and needs the support of such a tail in its short flights. When perched, the bird, like Newton's apple, often suddenly drops to the ground to catch an insect or glides down on set wings. Almost as quickly it flies back again, often swooping up to a landing.

The mocker's flight is well sustained but may seem labored in a heavy wind. Witmer Stone, the Cape May authority, compares it with an oarsman taking leisurely strokes in an old rowboat.

The species has a "dance," which Alice B. Harrington of Dallas, Texas, describes:

We saw the dance of the Mockingbird on two different days in June. . . . It was a curious and most interesting performance. The first time they danced exactly opposite each other. They faced each other about a foot apart, hopped up and down, moving gradually to one side, then back again, and so on. A second pair began their dance in the same position, but first one hopped twice to one side, then the other followed the first, which hopped again sideways and the other followed, always facing each other, then they moved back in the same manner to where they started and repeated the performance. After each dance was finished the birds flew off a short distance in opposite directions.

This dance has long been thought of as a nuptial performance. Amelia R. Lasker, however, who studied the bird at length in Tennessee, feels that it is a form of territorial defense behavior and has no such significance.

The mockingbird likes to play. It enjoys teasing a cat or dog. Sometimes the bird, while singing, flutters up from the top of a tree with legs dangling and wings flopping. Sometimes it turns an aerial somersault.

The mocker has a pugnacious disposition. It drives away virtually every other species except a kingbird and will often fight with others of its own kind. Alexander Sprunt, Jr., the Carolina Low Country authority, once saw 12 mockingbirds in a free-for-all. Its truculent disposition also leads it to engage in "reflection fighting," when a male (and sometimes a female) will attack its own image in a hubcap or cellar window. The bird is death on trespassing snakes, or at least it tries to be.

In former days, before keeping native birds in confinement was declared illegal, the mockingbird was a favorite cage bird. Some were caught, others raised by hand from the nest. Sometimes they were bred in captivity. Good singers commanded fancy prices.

Presumably because male and female are of the same general appearance, the male has trouble identifying the sex of another individual. Consequently he bristles on meeting another mockingbird, and if the other one bristles too, it is a male; if the bird appears submissive, it is a female.

Courtship among mockingbirds involves some form of wing stretching that may be similar in appearance to the territory guarding dance. The courting male runs, flirts by moving his outspread tail up and down, makes a soft cooing sound, and occasionally lifts both wings high above his back to spread them, revealing the conspicuous white wing patch. Sometimes he picks up a twig in his bill and runs back and forth with it in front of his mate. Monogamy is the rule in this species, but at least one case of bigamy (one male with two females on different nests) has been reported.

Frank F. Gander thus describes a mating he saw on June 21, 1929, at San Diego:

The male was singing from the top of a tall flagpole nearby. Suddenly he dropped from his perch. In full song, he shot down into the shrubbery about 15 feet beyond the female. As he sped past her, the female crouched a little and began to quiver her wings. She continued this as the male, singing excitedly and with tail and wings half spread, advanced toward her with dancing steps. As he neared her his excitement grew but his approach was stately and unhurried. As he came near he seemed to be floating along just over the ground and he rose gradually and settled upon her back. All this time he had been pouring forth impassioned melody. The act lasted several seconds and was accompanied by much fluttering of wings.

Originally the mockingbird built its nest in clearings in woods or along wood edges. It still does so, as it also does in pastures and prairies with occasional trees; but more frequently it nests near the buildings of man. For a nest site, it likes a thick low bush, tree, vine, or tangle from 3 to 10 ft. above the ground. Nests, however, have been found as low as 1 ft. and as high as 30 ft. Ornamental shrubs, porch vines, and garden borders are often chosen. Favorite nesting trees are apple, orange, holly, live oak, and magnolia; and, in the West, such plants as sagebrush, prickly pear, and cholla. The bird places the structure in a fork or crotch, among twigs, or on a branch. It sometimes nests on a stump, brush pile, fence post, or corner of a rail fence. Occasionally it picks an unusual nest site; one pair in Arkansas built in an old tin bucket someone left hanging on a barbed wire fence.

Both parents help build the nest, though the male may bring more material and the female put more of it into place. The bulky nest is made largely of twigs (often thorny), but leaves, grass, moss, weed stalks, bark strips, and rootlets are also used; so are string, rags, cotton, and paper, when available. The birds line the nest with fine grass, rootlets, plant down, and horsehair. Birds in a hurry have been known to build the nest in one day, but they usually take two or three days or longer.

The female lays three to six (usually four or five) greenish blue eggs spotted with red-brown and often wreathed around the larger end. Egg colors vary from pale to dark green, even to buffy gray. The colors of the markings may also be yellowish-, gray-, or chocolate-brown, or purple.

Incubation is largely by the female. When the eggs hatch, however, both parents share in bringing the young their food of green and brown slugs, cabbage worms, cutworms, various grubs and legless grasshoppers, and crickets. Both birds actively defend the nest and are very solicitous of their offspring.

Fall and winter in the East are times of wandering for certain individual birds. North of its customary range the species is usually seen only in these seasons, and then principally along the coast or at a feeder. In both cases, cedars or other thick cover nearby seem to be essential. Most of such off-season northern wanderers are males.

In the West, where the species is partially migratory, there is some movement from the Lower Sonoran to the Upper Sonoran zone in fall. Later in the season the birds forsake these elevations as well as the northern portions of their range and retreat southward. In the East some individuals may also move south; in fall and winter, mockingbirds become excessively common on the Florida Keys.

The extraordinary and mellifluous song of the mockingbird—one of the most remarkable in the world—is thrasherlike in quality, but each phrase is repeated, not twice as with the brown thrasher (p. 126), but three to six times. Intermingled with the beautiful phrases are various harsh calls, cries, and alarm notes.

The bird sings from an elevated perch, such as a telegraph pole, roadside wire, chimney, ridgepole, or television aerial. It often jumps up in the air while still singing, turns a somersault, and returns to its perch. Then and at other times it may fly up and descend again to its perch with dangling legs and loosely flopping wings. Its whole body, notably its wings, is often agitated as it sings.

The mocker gives voice by night as well as by day. Moonlit nights encourage its best efforts, but it is also heard in the dark of the moon. Its night song is often a flight song.

Near Chester, South Carolina, Leverett M. Loomis heard a mocker that in 10 minutes gave calls similar to those of 32 different birds. C. L. Whittle studied a wild bird that had wandered one winter to the Arnold Arboretum in Cambridge, Massachusetts. He heard it give the songs of 39 other species as well as the notes of a frog and cricket. The Massachusetts Audubon Society has issued a phonograph record with 50 different mocker songs. W. Leon Dawson, the California ornithologist, recognized similarities to 58 other species in a captive mocker. He heard it change its notes 87 times in 7 minutes. It imitated the songs of the wilderness, the pet shop, and the village.

The notion that the mockingbird imitates other species is commonly accepted as fact. Yet recent investigators point out that the bird's song is long and highly diversified; furthermore, the songs of individual mockers are never quite the same: each individual may have several variations on his own theme. Thus the doubters believe the number of purely coincidental similarities to songs of other birds accounts for the supposed mimicry. Whether deliberately uttered by the bird or freely interpreted by the listener, the extent and variation of these similarities are remarkable.

If all this is indeed deliberate mimicry, then the mocker must have an amazing memory for a bird; for on several occasions birds have been heard giving calls of migrants still in winter quarters outside the United States. These were notes that the mockers could not have heard for at least six months. Supposed mimicry is more prevalent in daylight singing than in night song; there seem to be wide variation among individual mockingbirds.

Some authorities claim the mockingbird sings all year; others, that it has a definite song season. In Georgia, it is said to sing from early February to late October, with time out for the midsummer molt. The truth is that the mockingbird in many parts of its range can be heard singing in virtually every month of the year, but not with equal frequency. Its season of exultant fervor lasts from February to July; considerable singing is heard again from late August to late October. During the rest of the year it performs less frequently. Nevertheless, the bird gives voice even in winter. The call of the species is a harsh *chack* or *smack,* and a grating *chair.*

The mockingbird's diet is half of animal and half of vegetable origin.

In spring and early summer its food is largely insects and spiders; in late summer and fall, largely wild fruits and berries. It also takes cultivated fruits and berries.

Insects eaten include flies, bugs, beetles, ants, wasps, caterpillars and grasshoppers, and the cotton boll weevil and boll-worm. In recent years it has eaten insects on radiators of parked cars.

Favorite fruits include those of holly, woodbine, sour gum, red cedar, sumac, grape, Virginia creeper, dogwood, palmetto, pepper tree, rose, smilax, mistletoe, cactus, and yucca; also blackberry, pokeberry, elderberry, serviceberry, mulberry, hackberry, raspberry, beautyberry, apple, persimmon, and manzanita. The bird sometimes gets drunk on berries of the nightshade, *Solanum seaforthianum*.

Favorite feeder foods include suet, nut meats, raisins, crumbs, sliced apples, chopped figs, currants, blueberries, small grains, and doughnuts. In addition to being attracted by food, mockers also come to water.

Description: Length, 11 in. Female smaller. Body slender; legs long; wings short and rounded; tail long and rounded. Gray upperparts; whitish underparts; no black mask on face (as in shrike); white outer tail feathers and wing bars; large white patches on wings, conspicuous in flight; yellowish iris. The female has less white on the wings and tail than the male. The young have spotted breasts, indicating perhaps that their ancestors looked like thrashers.

The mockingbird's colors somewhat resemble those of the logger-head shrike, but the shrike has a black mask, short legs, chunky body, and heavy head. It sits low on a perch with tail and head down, and flies with rapid wingbeats. Townsend's solitaire has a white eye ring, buffy wing patch, and is darker below. Mockingbirds sometimes show traces or cases of albinism.

Incubation, 12 to 14 days; young stay 7 to 13 days in nest.

Size of eggs, 1.0 x 0.75 in.; two or three broods per year.

CATBIRD (*Dumetella carolinensis*)

A thicket is a good place for catbirds. The species is found in summer throughout the United States and southern Canada, except in parts of the far West and Southwest; it breeds up to 8,000 ft. in the Rocky Mountains. It winters in the Gulf states, Mexico, and Central America, south to Panama, and in Atlantic coastal thickets from Massachusetts south.

The catbird is equally at home in bushes about the house or in the hurricane blowdown of the forest. It also likes cutover and burnedover tracts and is particularly fond of shrubby situations near water. The settlement of North America has increased the number and area of thickets, and the catbird is thought to be more common now than it was before 1609.

The maximum breeding density of this species in recent years in Maryland was 80 pairs per 100 acres in "shrub-swamp (alder, poison sumac, sweet pepper bush, swamp rose, etc.) in Prince George's County in 1945." Similar habitats in other parts of its range may also contain heavy catbird populations.

The catbird is alert, vivacious, and friendly. It is given to the flick of the wing and the flirt of the tail, is generally tame, and is relatively unafraid of man.

The flights of the bird are short and it seldom flies far from the security of its tangle. It forages on or near the ground, throwing leaves aside with its bill; it is fond of bathing in a bird bath. The average life of a catbird is reported to be about two and a half years.

Kissing your palm or squeaking an artificial bird call will soon call all the catbirds nearby; this species is one of the first to respond to the bird watcher's summons.

The catbird migrates by night. It arrives in summer quarters about the middle of spring migration, the bulk of the birds arriving about a week after the first. Most individuals leave the North in September and October. The species is generally quiet and inconspicuous. At migration funnel points, however, such as Cape May, New Jersey, concentrations of catbirds are sometimes seen.

Edward Howe Forbush, author of *Birds of Massachusetts*, writes of their courtship:

Not long after the males arrive in spring, the females appear, and then courtship begins. This is carried on largely in the seclusion of the thickets. There is much flight and pursuit, and an outpouring of song. The male with plumage raised and tail lowered bows until his bill touches the ground, and sidles about in a curious manner, or struts with lowered wings and tail erected, wheeling about and exhibiting the chestnut patch on his under tail-coverts.

The marital habits of the catbird are not distinguished for constancy. Some pairs remain mated for two seasons, perhaps longer. On the other hand, some birds change partners for successive years, and even for successive broods. A mated pair has a territory that it guards. For a second or third nesting in the same season the same mated pair may use the same nest and defend the same territory. A different combination of partners usually builds a new nest and defends a new territory. The new nest, however, may be close to the old one, and the new territory may include part of the old.

The catbird builds a fair-sized, scraggly, cupshaped nest of twigs, weed stems, leaves, and grasses, usually lined with rootlets. Sometimes paper is included. The nest is well concealed in a shrub, vine, thicket, or hedgerow, usually 2 to 4 ft. above the ground. It is often near a house. Occasionally nests have been found as high as 20 ft., and there is one report of a nest 60 ft. above the ground. Along the borders of swamps the catbird sometimes nests in bushes overhanging the water.

Both male and female bring material to the nest, but the actual nest building, which may take six days, is largely the work of the female. The four, glossy, greenish-blue eggs somewhat resemble those of a robin, but are greener in color, deeper in tone, and a trifle smaller in size. Sometimes a clutch contains three eggs or five. If a cowbird's egg is laid in its nest, the catbird customarily ejects it.

The female does most of or all the incubating and brooding. The nest is normally so deep that, while she is sitting, her tail projects upright and her head is thrown back.

Both parents feed the young. After each feeding they keep the nest clean by removing the fecal sacs of the young. Until the sixth day they swallow the sacs; thereafter they swallow some but pick up others in their bills and drop them some distance away. After the first young leave the nest the male feeds them until they can forage for themselves, while the female starts work on a new brood, often constructing another nest.

The catbird derives its name from its complaining, catlike mewing note of protest, a note that is also often sandwiched into its other vocalizations. The song is pleasing and highly varied, a thrasherlike or mockingbirdlike medley, delivered with much spreading of wings and tail and many contortions of body. The tail is often lowered and the body held close to the perch. Unlike the brown thrasher (p. 126), however, the phrases are not repeated. The Mimidae family's ability as songsters is attributed in part to its possessing seven pairs of intrinsic syringeal muscles, as compared with the single pair of such muscles possessed by many other species.

The male catbird sings from a perch 6 to 15 ft. above ground and is one of the first birds of the day to give voice, usually long before dawn. Indeed, he frequently sings at night.

Some catbirds appear to be accomplished mimics, although hardly the equal of mockingbirds. The catbird has been noted to give calls resembling those of the following species: red-shouldered hawk, bobwhite, killdeer, greater yellowlegs, belted kingfisher, flicker, eastern phoebe, least flycatcher, wood pewee, barn swallow, blue jay (p. 55), brown thrasher (p. 126), robin (p. 136), wood thrush (p. 140), veery, bluebird (p. 147); yellow-throated, solitary and red-eyed vireos; yellow, magnolia, black-throated blue, black-throated green, chestnut-sided, blackpoll, and prairie warblers; redstart, bobolink, western meadowlark, cowbird (p. 192), scarlet tanager, cardinal (p. 201), rose-breasted grosbeak (p. 205), goldfinch (p. 244), and towhee. (But see mockingbird, p. 117.)

The catbird often sings from a perch concealed in vines or bushes. Its very varied song consists of a series of nonrepeating phrases with pauses between, each with two to six notes. A. A. Saunders, the bird-song authority, once listened to one individual that had 74 different phrases all its own. He describes the special courtship song in these words:

The catbird during courtship sings a song that differs from the territory song chiefly in intensity. It is low and soft and almost in a whisper and is usually sung with the bill closed. One must be near the singer to hear the song. The bird closes its bill and sings the familiar carol so softly that it is audible only a short distance; at times the catbird accompanies it with a grotesque display, spreading the wings and tail and fluffing out the feathers.

It is not always certain, however, that peculiar songs at the height of
the mating season are stimulated by the presence of the female. At times
they may be due to the presence of a rival male, for bird song is used in
battle as well as in courtship.

This bird is a ventriloquist, and a song that seems to come from
some distance away in one direction may actually be coming from a
singer near at hand in another. The female sings quietly on the nest. So
does the male, at the infrequent times he shares the task of incubation.
In the north the male sings into late July or early August, but becomes
silent when the last young leave the nest. In the autumn a whisper
song, audible for only a few feet, is sometimes heard. So also at various
times is a series of chatlike phrases, hard to identify as belonging to a
catbird, that seem to represent a primitive ancestral song.

A common note is a low pleasant *chuck*. Another is a somewhat harsh
chatter, kak kak kak.

More than half of the catbird's food is of vegetable origin. Of this,
one-third may be cultivated fruit, two-thirds wild fruit; but these
proportions will vary, depending upon what is at hand. Where ample
wild fruit is made available, loss of cultivated fruit to catbirds is slight.

Favorite wild fruits include those of dogwood, sour gum, elderberry,
greenbriar, buckthorn, wild cherry, pokeberry, and honeysuckle. Favorite cultivated fruits include grapes, strawberries, and cherries.

The animal food includes beetles, ants, caterpillars, grasshoppers,
Japanese beetles, and plant lice. The proportion of animal to vegetable
food varies with the season. In spring and early summer insects are
a more important part of the diet than fruit. In late summer and fall
this is reversed. Almost all the food of the young is insects. Because
catbirds are virtually omnivorous, they often concentrate on areas of
infestations of insect pests and thus become especially valuable as-
sistants to the farmer and horticulturist.

Favorite feeder foods include raisins, cherries, currants, bread
crumbs, cheese, peanuts, soaked puffed wheat, apples, oranges, and
grapes. One operator of a feeding station taught her favorite catbird
visitor to catch raisins in mid-air.

Description: Length, 9 in. Wings, short and rounded; tail, long and rounded; slate gray plumage; black cap; chestnut undertail coverts; black bill, eye, legs, and feet.

Incubation, 12 to 13 days; young stay 10 days (9 to 16) in nest.

Size of eggs, 1.0 x 0.7 in.; two or three broods per year.

BROWN THRASHER (*Toxostoma rufum*)

Dead limbs and trees furnish food and homes for many kinds of insects and birds. They provide nesting sites for sparrow hawks, owls, woodpeckers, chickadees, titmice, and nuthatches, and cavorting grounds for brown thrashers. A dead tree near the house will provide exceptional views of numerous birds that perch on its leafless branches to glean insects from the exposed trunk.

The brown thrasher is our only big, streak-breasted, brownish song bird with a long tail occurring in the East. It is slim and longer than a robin. The rufous-brown upperparts are set off by yellow eyes and long curved beak. It is the only thrasher found east of the Rockies, and it is not found west of them.

In summer these birds breed from Florida and Louisiana north to southern Canada, and to an elevation of 7,500 ft. in Colorado. In winter the species retreats within the borders of the old Confederacy, but along the coast a few may linger north to Massachusetts in protected thickets or near feeders. Its numbers are sometimes subject to marked fluctuations.

The brown thrasher is primarily a bird of treetop and dry thicket. It sings from the former, and forages and breeds in the latter. Only after the nesting season is over is the bird commonly seen playing on low branches. It likes much the same kind of cover as does its cousin the catbird, but prefers dry situations. The thrasher seems to be less common around human habitations than does its relative.

Other favorite habitats of the thrasher include farming districts, brushy hillsides and pastures, second-growth sproutlands, the edges of woods, shrubbery about gardens or houses, and osage orange hedges.

In the South the species frequents tangles of cherry-laurel, blackberry, Cherokee roses, magnolias, holly, and mulberry. In the dense hummocks of Florida it is one of the commonest winter species.

Due to the replacement of primeval forest by gardens, suburbs, and second growth, there are more thickets now than there were before the landing of the Pilgrims. Hence there are more brown thrashers. This is one species that has benefited from European settlement of North America.

Like most thrashers this species is best distinguished by its skulking habits. It spends most of its time in dense tangles and underbrush and, while not difficult to locate, is not seen much in the open. When it is seen, it is usually flying low across the lawn or road on its way from one patch of low bushes to another. When about to give voice it mounts a tree from limb to limb to a lofty, exposed perch, where in the breeding season it sings for long periods. Its song may be heard for half a mile. If disturbed it dives into a thicket.

This thrasher is bold and aggressive. It is fearless in defense of nest and young, and tolerates no intruders around its breeding quarters. Audubon remarked that it chases cat and dog, teases fox and raccoon, and defies hawk and snake. It is well known for attacking humans, often aiming for the eyes.

The thrasher has various modes of progression. It runs, walks, or hops, as occasion demands. Sometimes it takes long, high hops; sometimes it partially spreads and flutters its wings when running. It is equally fond of dust and water baths. It forages on the lawn for earthworms and pulls them from the ground like the robin. Sometimes it follows the plow for exposed worms.

In foraging a thicket the thrasher uses its bill to turn leaves or to probe in soft ground and humus; less often it scratches away leaves with its feet. It chases insects on foot and leaps into the air to catch them. Its degree of sociability undoubtedly varies from place to place, but this probably depends on many factors, not geography alone.

The flight of the thrasher, usually near the ground, is even, steady, and moderately slow. Its flights are short. In piney, barren country the rufous coat of the species is frequently seen flashing low across the road in front of an approaching car. The birds migrate by night.

Males reach the North before females. After skulking in a thicket or reconnoitering the countryside for a few days, the male selects his territory and mounts to a treetop to summon a mate. In parks, campuses, or suburban areas the birds often use man-made structures such as buildings, driveways, and walks as territorial boundaries. Males fight for territory.

After females arrive, the male will sing a subdued song from inside a thicket, or will sing on the wing or strut before her, trailing his tail. William G. Erwin, who studied the species on the Peabody Campus in Nashville, Tennessee, describes its further courtship as follows:

April 29, 9:00 A.M., both male and female were observed under the shrubbery at the right of the exit. The female hopped out in the grass away from the shrubbery about 10 feet and began to dig in the ground with her bill. After about 5 minutes the male came out a distance of about a foot from the shrubbery. The female picked up a small twig in her bill and hopped back to the male, fluttering her wings as she went, after which she dropped her twig and fluttered her wings vigorously, giving soft chirps. No further activities were observed as they searched for food among the leaves for 8 minutes. Then the female hopped out on the grass, again secured a twig, and began to flutter her wings and give soft chirps as before. The male picked up two dead leaves and hopped toward her, whereupon she fluttered her wings even more vigorously and issued chirps a little louder. Both dropped the materials held in their bills and engaged in coitus. Both birds then hopped down the shrubbery row, the female gathering twigs and fluttering her wings several times, after which both went under the shrubbery.

These birds will often find new mates for a second brood.

The brown thrasher builds on the ground or near it, in a bush, shrub, hedge, vine, or low tree, seldom at a height more than 7 ft. It builds in wilderness tangles and in garden shrubbery, and in Florida orange groves. The bulky, twiggy-looking outer nest may contain three inner cups. The first is composed of dry leaves; the next of grass stems and small twigs; the third cup, or lining, is made largely of grass rootlets. The nest, which takes the pair six to ten days to build, is usually found near the base of the male's favorite singing tree.

The choice of the nest site, whether on the ground or above it, varies in different parts of the thrasher's range. In northern Michigan the bird generally builds on the ground, but in southern Michigan it nests in bushes.

The four or five whitish eggs, sometimes with a bluish or greenish tinge, are heavily spotted with fine dots of reddish brown. Both birds incubate, although the female does three times as much sitting. Both parents sing a whisper song while on the nest. The thrasher is a close sitter, hard to flush. Occasionally the female brown-headed cowbird (p. 191) puts its eggs in the brown thrasher's nest.

Both male and female feed and brood the young. They bring grubs, caterpillars, and earthworms. The parents eat the infants' fecal sacs until about the eighth day; after that they drop them away from the nest. After the first young leave the nest, the female builds a second one while the male cares for the fledglings. When these can forage for themselves, the male returns to help with the second brood.

The voice of the thrasher may be heard from April on. The species arrives in the van of the main spring migration, and within a few days to two weeks of its arrival starts its treetop singing. The song is typical of the mimic thrush family and suggests the mockingbird. The thrasher, however, is much less given to apparent mimicry; although different individuals from time to time have been reported mimicking the whip-poor-will, kingfisher, great crested flycatcher, blue jay (p. 55), Carolina wren (p. 110), robin (p. 136), common yellowthroat, bobolink, red-winged blackbird (p. 168), Baltimore oriole (p. 180), scarlet tanager, cardinal (p. 201), and goldfinch (p. 244). (See also mockingbird, p. 117.)

The song is unique in one outstanding respect. Almost every phrase is repeated twice. This characteristic distinguishes it from all other mimic thrushes and true thrushes. Not every phrase is repeated twice, but this is the impression given. An analysis made by a careful student of bird behavior found the phrases actually were repeated in this fashion: "2,1,2,3,2,1,2,2,2,1,1,1,1,1,1,2,3,3,1,2,2,2,3,1,3,4,2,3,1,3,4,2,3,2,2, 2,2,2,1."

The song frequently has been rendered into English. Thoreau thought the New England farmer heard it say as he was planting corn: *"drop it, drop it, cover it, cover it, I'll pull it up, I'll pull it up."*

Thrashers usually stop singing in New England by July 11. Individuals do not sing when nesting. In fall a whisper song is sometimes heard.

The call of the thrasher is a characteristic kissing *smaack,* which Witmer Stone, the expert on the birds of Cape May, describes as "almost exactly like that produced by sucking the tongue against the roof of the mouth and suddenly removing it." He also notes a peculiar ventriloquial *chuuurl,* given when parents are feeding young. The thrasher has a sharp click, a hissing sound, and a plaintive whistled *wheurrr* or *wheeu* which is a typical autumn sound in the South. There is also a series of loud harsh, slurred *teea teea*'s, repeated and rising in pitch.

The food of the brown thrasher throughout the year averages about two-thirds insects and one-third fruit, berries and grain. In the spring the percentage of insects is higher; in summer and fall there are more fruits and mast (acorns and beechnuts). The principal insect groups are beetles and caterpillars, but Gabrielson found that during a grasshopper infestation, the proportion of those insects in their diet rose considerably. Other favorite insects are white grubs, bollweevils, army-, canker-, cut-, and wireworms; tent caterpillars, grasshoppers, wasps, and leafhoppers.

The thrasher's vegetable diet is almost half fruit and mast. The bird prefers, in order, the fruit of blackberry, elderberry, dogwood, sumac, blueberry, grape, bayberry, strawberry, holly, hackberry, greenbriar, sour gum, and Virginia creeper.

Favorite feeder foods include white bread crumbs, walnut meats, and raisins.

Description: Length, 12 in. Female smaller than male. Wings, short and rounded; tail, long and rounded; reddish brown upperparts; whitish underparts with conspicuous brown streaks on the breast. Yellow eye; bill, long and curved; two white wing bars. The young are duller and have a gray iris. (Thrushes have brown eyes, lack wing bars, and are spotted, not streaked, below.) In winter and during migration the brown thrasher may be found together with sage and long-billed thrashers along the western edge of its range. Both are less rufous above (darker or grayer brown) and have black streaking below; sage, in addition, is smaller and more robinlike with shorter tail and bill.

Incubation, 11 to 14 days; young stay 11 (9 to 13) days in nest.

Size of eggs, 1.1 x 0.8 in.; two broods per year, possibly three in South.

CALIFORNIA THRASHER (*Toxostoma redivivum*)

The California thrasher is slightly larger than a robin. Gray-brown above, paler below, unstreaked, with rusty undertail coverts, it is readily distinguished by its sickle-shaped bill and long, rounded tail. It is a nonmigratory resident of California and northern Lower California, found west of the Sierras, from the head of Sacramento Valley south. Its home is the foothills of the Upper Sonoran life-zone up to an altitude of 5,000 ft. This is the chaparral zone of scrub oak and greasewood. Sometimes the species ventures into river valleys and the drier Lower Sonoran zone below, but seldom or never does it go higher up the mountains into the Transition zone.

The best-liked habitat of the species is chaparral-clothed hillsides with dense cover. There, where the ground is protected from above by a thick low canopy of spreading branches, the bird runs over bare ground or forages amid dry leaves. Its associates in this terrain are the brown towhee and wren-tit. The thrasher also likes river-bottom tangles. In foothill towns and villages it comes into shrubby areas of parks and residential gardens. It is fond of brush heaps and, where shelter is nearby, is seen about the dooryard. It is not a shy bird, but spotting it is difficult amid thick bushes and thorny shrubs.

This thrasher is a runner. Except for the space of a foot or two when it may walk or hop, the bird normally progresses by running, tail up. It flies reluctantly, with drooping head and tail. Its short wings make flight jerky and labored.

In foraging the California thrasher locates food with its beak, not its feet. It uncovers spiders, insects, and their larvae. Sometimes it thrusts its bill into the ground, hooking it in and out several times to build a little pile of dirt behind the boring. It may use its bill even more like a pick axe to excavate a wide hole 2 or 3 in. deep. The beak is a powerful tool. One observer noted that it could toss aside a 2-in. clod of dirt with ease. Among the bird's favorite foraging spots are flower beds and the leafy litter under buckthorn (Ceanothus) bushes.

The California thrasher is fond of water for drinking and bathing. The curved bill, however, is not so efficient for drinking from a shallow pan. The bird can secure only a drop of water at the tip of the beak and must take many short drinks to quench its thirst. It will drink like other birds if it can immerse its whole bill in water in a deep trough. Sometimes a thoughtful pause overtakes an individual at the edge of a water pan; there is a burp, and the bird ejects the hard pit of a manzanita berry before drinking.

This species—perhaps even more than the brown thrasher—is highly aggressive in defense of its nest. It dashes excitedly at an intruder to threaten his eyes or face with its sickle bill.

The California thrasher places its shallow nest near the ground in a bush well hidden by dense shrubbery. Scrub oaks and lemonadeberry bushes are favorite sites. Rough twigs compose the outside of the nest. The interior is lined with rootlets and grasses. The structure somewhat resembles that of a mockingbird (p. 115), but is larger and contains coarser twigs. Both male and female help in the building and in incubating the three or four brown-flecked, light greenish blue eggs. For security reasons a parent usually approaches the homesite from the ground and jumps into the nest from directly beneath it.

The species starts to build in February and March, but the rearing of a second brood may drag out the breeding season into July. Some pairs also build and lay in the fall, but such nestings seldom hatch. Nevertheless there is at least one record of young in November.

The young are fed by regurgitation until their fourth day, when their eyes open. After the young leave the nest, the parental feeding continues for a time. This task devolves on the male alone, once the female has started a second brood. The breeding territory of a pair varies between 5 and 10 acres. A pair may, or may not, remain together throughout the winter. If the two birds separate, each will defend a winter territory of its own.

In juveniles the bill is short and only slightly curved. In young adults the bill is longer, but its full growth is not attained for a long time. Indeed, some students suspect that the bill continues to grow throughout the life of the individual. The late summer molt puts the adult into a much more disheveled-looking condition than most birds.

The beautiful and spirited song of the California thrasher suggests that of other members of its family. Easterners sometimes find in it a resemblance to the brown thrasher. Each phrase is usually uttered two or three times. Structurally the song is composed of a series of separate phrases, some sweet, some harsh.

The male sings from the top of a small tree or bush, seldom more than 30 ft. high. Robert S. Woods considers the song "less fluent than that of the mockingbird, but deeper and richer." Others have described it as lower in pitch and more leisured than that of the mocker.

The song varies considerably, both between individual singers and between the same singer in different moods. The bird sings throughout the year, except during late summer molt; it delivers its song with the greatest vigor in winter and in early spring after the winter rains.

Though less of a mimic than the mockingbird, the California thrasher has been heard to imitate the red-tailed hawk, valley quail, red-shafted flicker, acorn woodpecker, olive-sided flycatcher, scrub jay (p. 63), plain titmouse, white-breasted nuthatch (p. 94), and the house wren; also the robin (p. 136), ruby-crowned kinglet, yellow-breasted chat, Bullock's oriole, black-headed grosbeak (p. 205), purple finch (p. 227), house finch (p. 231), and American goldfinch (p. 244). It imitates the wren-tit so successfully that the other species answers back. In imitating the robin it has even been seen to mimic a flirt of the wings characteristic of that species, but it might be noted that wing-flirting is also common among many Mimidae. The repertory of various individual thrashers has been known to include the note of a frog, the short wail of a coyote, and a postman's whistle! The passing of a truck or the noise of a low-flying plane are said to stimulate the species to song.

Other notes of the thrasher are a dry *tchak* or *tchup,* a sharp *wheek* or *hreek,* a liquid *g-lik,* and when alarmed, a purring, nasal *tchurrr.* The female also sings, but not so much as the male. Male and female sometimes sing together or in responsive alternation.

The food of the California thrasher, according to the studies of

Department of Agriculture scientists, consists of 59 percent vegetable matter and 41 percent animal. The vegetable portion includes various fruits such as those of elderberry, manzanita, toyon, redberry, firethorn, myrtle, privet, California pepper tree, poison sumac, and other sumacs. It also enjoys grapes, weed seeds, various berries, and mast. Animal food includes ants, wasps, bees, beetles, and their larvae. Termites, when they are starting to fly, are much sought after.

Favorite feeder foods include dry bread crumbs, kibbled dog-biscuit, peanut hearts, suet, seeds, raisins, currants, other berries, and grain. At the feeder this species will drive away the scrub jay.

Description: Length, 12 in. Bill, curved and longer than head; brown iris; tail, long and rounded. Plumage, unstreaked; no wing bars; grayish brown upperparts, paler underparts; throat whitish or buff; brownish breast and darker than buffy forebelly; rusty lower belly and undertail coverts; dark feet. This thrasher is longer, darker, and has a more curved bill than the desert-loving Leconte's. The crissal thrasher has more rufous undertail coverts; the sage thrasher is shorter and streaked. The brown towhee has a short, conical bill and a shorter, rounded tail (see p. 250).

Incubation, 14 days; young stay 12 to 14 days in nest.

Size of eggs, 1.18 x 0.84 in.; two broods per year.

THRUSHES / *Turdidae*

ROBIN (*Turdus migratorius*)

The robin may be found in spring and summer throughout North America, from the limit of trees almost to the Gulf coast and to northern Mexico. The bird winters from southern British Columbia, the Missouri, and Ohio Valleys, and Nova Scotia south to the Gulf and to southern Mexico.

Originally a bird of barrens, open woods, burned areas in the forest, and of forest edges, soon after settlement of North America the robin adapted itself to the artificial edges of human gardens. As pioneers settled the prairies and the plains, the robin moved west with them. It is now found from the seashore to timber line, particularly about lawns and gardens, farms, parks, golf courses, suburbs, swamps, and cutover areas. It breeds in all life-zones from the Upper Austral to the Hudsonian.

The robin is our largest North American thrush, robust and upstanding. In remote areas such as Alaska, northern Canada, and mountain wilds, it is apt to be shy and wary, but near civilization it is tame. It is always excitable and alert, however, and is quick to launch a loud and vigorous attack against man, snake, or other enemy that threatens its young. The robin's flight is steady, direct, and horizontal. It flaps its wings deeply, 2.3 times per second, and has a normal speed of 25 to 28 mph. When flying, the belly appears gently curved, and the white rear flanks can easily be seen. After landing, it will give one or two quick flirts with its tail.

The nesting territory has been variously reported as $\frac{3}{10}$ to $\frac{3}{4}$ acre. Beyond this area there is neutral foraging ground that may be shared with other robins.

The bird is fond of bathing, and providing a bird bath is a good way to attract it. On occasion the species has been seen anting, preening its feathers with an ant held in its bill (a curious habit described more fully in the sketch of the blue jay, p. 56).

Ten years is the maximum age reported for a robin in the wild. The life expectancy of a newly hatched robin is 14 months.

One of the characteristics of the thrush family is a "booted tarsus"; i.e., the leg is sheathed in one long scaly "boot," not covered with many scales, as is a chicken's. No other North American bird of the robin's size has booted tarsi.

Migrating northward principally by day, the robin keeps pace with the advance of spring. It follows the 37° F. isotherm, averaging about 38 miles a day. Those that breed in extreme northwestern Alaska take 78 days to fly there from their homes in Iowa. Joseph Hickey, author of *A Guide to Bird Watching*, made a study of 61 banded robins and found that about half the first generation returned to nest in the region of their birthplace, about a fifth nested within 10 miles, while the remainder scattered, even up to a distance of 400 miles away.

Males precede females by a week or ten days in their northward migration. When they arrive, they mount to treetops at dusk to deliver loud and pleasing song. When females arrive, there are battles between males and furious chases for the females' favors. Males will jump up in the air to claw and clash like gamecocks. The species is normally monogamous, but cases of sporadic polygamy have been known.

Courtship is the time of year when a male is sometimes seen pecking furiously at his own image in a hub cap or cellar window, and a bird will frequently return to the same object of attack several days in succession. Such a bird seems to think that he is attacking a rival. To help him avoid injury, one might try moving the car or putting a screen on the window.

The robin is catholic in choosing a nesting site. Originally most robins probably saddled sturdy nests in the forks of a horizontal branch or in crotches by the trunk of a tree or sapling. Today the use of man-made structures is widespread. These may be nesting shelves or nooks and crannies on porches; barns, sheds, and outhouses; under bridges, or in industrial structures. Sites have included a lamp bracket in a dance hall; a trolley wire; a wheel hub; smoke pipe; tire iron; old nests of hornets, catbirds, and orioles; a rotted-out woodpecker hole; and the inside of an eel trap.

The cupshaped nest is substantially made of twigs, cemented with mud and lined with fine grasses, rough on the outside, but smooth within. The female generally builds the nest alone, the male helping to bring materials. Nest-building takes four or five days, but it has been done in one day or, if the weather is bad, it may take 20. The bird brings mud with its beak, in the form of gummy pellets, from distances up to a quarter-mile. With her breast the female smooths the inside of the nest to fit the contour of her body. If the weather is dry, the bird may take dirt in its bill and wet it in water, or take water in its bill to bring to moisten the dry dirt. (If you want to help, sink an old cake tin in the ground and keep it full of moistened earth or clay for the birds to use. Some people also put out string for robins to use in building their nests. If you do, drape it over a branch out of reach of a wandering cat, and don't offer pieces more than a foot long, so the bird will not get tangled.)

The three to four eggs (rarely five) are, of course, robin's egg blue in color. Three seems to be the common number in the West, the Arctic, and Newfoundland; four is usual in the East and South. Eggs are usually laid one a day in late morning. Should a cowbird lay its egg in a robin's nest, the robin will eject it. Incubation, performed largely or wholly by the female, while the male guards the nest, takes 13 days; it starts on the evening following the laying of the second egg. Two and sometimes three broods are raised each season. The young are hatched naked, with a bright orange gape. They remain in the nest about two weeks.

To keep the brood clean, the parents swallow the fecal sacs. Both parents bring food to the young; the female brings more than the male. The last day in the nest, a young robin may eat 14 ft. of earthworms. In their two weeks of nest life a brood of robins will eat 3.2 lbs. of food. After they leave the nest the male takes charge and feeds the fledglings for the 14 days until they can forage for themselves. This leaves the female free for her second brood, which she sometimes starts incubating within six days of the first young's leaving the nest.

More than half the later broods are raised in a different site from the first. The female may rush a second nest to completion in two or three days. When she does not move, she refurbishes and repairs the old nest. Although the first nest is likely to be in an evergreen tree, later ones are often in a deciduous tree. The next year the pair may repair an old nest or build a new one on the foundation of the old; cases are on record where six nests have been built on top of each other.

While first nesting is in process, males fly in loose flocks to roost for the night. When the first fledglings fly they join the nightly gatherings. After the second or third broods are awing the females and new young also join the assemblages.

In late summer and fall, individuals tend to wander. In mountains they are more likely to be seen at the timber line or above; in the Arctic they will be on the tundra. But with the advent of colder weather, robins move down the mountains to lower altitudes.

In southward migration, robins collect at such famous gathering points as Cape May, New Jersey, where (late October or early November) 10,000 in one morning have been reported swinging around the Point to head northwest up the shore preparatory to flying across Delaware Bay. In fall, robins tend to frequent woods where there are berries. In spring they are more likely to be seen on fields, as worms and insects stir with new life.

In the northern parts of its range the winter robin seems to be a bird different from the spring robin. Indeed, it may be a different bird, for the population as a whole shifts southward with the advent of cold weather. Those that patroled the croquet court in summer are patroling croquet courts 400 or 500 miles farther south in winter, while winter shrubbery provides shelter for new visitors from several hundred miles to the north. Some individuals seem to be content with shorter migrations, and may leave the lawn in fall for a protected swamp or cedar grove nearby. To see a robin in winter, one need only look in a nearby swamp.

In winter quarters, robins often collect in large roosts. One in Florida was reputed to have 50,000 birds. Balander, in 1932, reported 165,000 robins in an assemblage in Lakeside Park, Oakland, California. Such roosts are often shared with other species such as red-winged blackbirds and common grackles; at dusk the robin is usually the last species to roost.

The robin makes at least ten different kinds of sounds. Many of us consciously recognize the song, the *tuk-tuk-tuk* alarm note, and the shriek the bird makes when we near its nest. Winsor Marrett Tyler gives us this list:

1. *Seech-ook*; an exclamatory note which the young robin utters soon after leaving the nest.
2. *Pleent, tut-tut-tut*; the first note, which might be written *plint,* and sometimes sounds more like *week,* is usually single, but may be repeated once or twice, and may be given without the *tut* notes. It is a sort of gasp, accented, higher in pitch than the succeeding, more rapid *tuts.* The latter (*huh* suggests the aspirated quality) may be likened to the interjection commonly written *humph,* representing a low-spoken exclamation.
3. *Sss, tut-tut-tut*; a sibilant variation of the above, a tremulous, sibilant sound, a shaky squeal, followed by troubled sobbing.
4. *Skeet, skeet*; two or three high screams, uttered as if in haste.
5. *Seech, each-each-each*; a screaming variant of 2 and 3. It may be given *see-seech* with the second note accented and on a higher pitch. A common note, suggesting unrest.
6. *He-he-he-he-he*; a rapid, laughing giggle, suggesting sometimes a note of the red-winged blackbird, or in lighter, more musical form it may run quickly up and down the scale. This is the note which reminded Schuyler Mathews (1921) of the once popular song "Hiawatha."
7. *Chill-ill-ill*; varying from 3 to 8 notes, given in a tinkling voice, the *chill* struck firmly, the *ills* successively lowering force and dropping slightly in pitch to the final *ill.* The rhythm strongly suggests the ringing of the kind of bell formerly used on ambulances and police wagons. In tone of voice and in pitch this note resembles the song but differs from it in phrasing.
8. *Hisselly-hisselly*; sibilant, whispered phrases arranged as in song. It

is associated with courtship apparently. The hiss may also be given
in one long syllable, repeated slowly with downward inflection.

9. *Sssp*; a faint, trembling hiss, a refinement of the shriek (4) often
given when a bird starts away in flight, and at the close of the day
as it flies to its roost.

10. A low, sobbing note with a deep undertone; a note of trouble. A
modification of the *tut* or *huh,* but clearly recognizable in quality
and slow delivery as an entity. It is given when a cat is prowling near.

In most regions the robin is the earliest bird of the day to sing, often
starting an hour or more before dawn. The well-sustained song averages two phrases per second, with an almost imperceptible pause every
few phrases. Careful listening will identify slightly different songs of
individual birds. During the period of courtship the male sometimes
sings with its bill closed, and can be heard only at a short distance. In
Wisconsin, Hickey found that the robin's lowest acceptable singing
perch was about 12 ft. from the ground.

The robin sings longest in early morning. It has a rebirth of song
late in the afternoon, but during the day it is seldom heard. If the
sky is heavily overcast, the robin will often tune up, as it will before
rain and on the rare occasion of an eclipse of the sun. In New England
it stops singing for the season between July 31 and August 15, about
five days before the hermit thrush.

In addition to earthworms, the robin likes fruit. The land owner
sometimes complains of the bird's depredations of his cherries, grapes,
or strawberries. The birds can normally be diverted from eating cultivated fruit by the provision of earlier ripening, wild varieties or mulberries. They enjoy a variety of fruits. In the West they like berries
of madrone, cascara, pepper tree, Russian olive, and buckthorn; in the
South they like fruits of cabbage palm, yaupon, persimmon, camphor
tree, gallberry, and mangrove.

Research by Department of Agriculture biologists has shown that
about 58 percent of the robin's food is of vegetable origin and 42 percent of animal origin. The latter, in addition to earthworms, includes
flies, caterpillars, crickets, grasshoppers, locusts, beetles, wireworms,
weevils, borers, cutworms, leaf-runners, ants, cankerworms, army
worms, cicadas, and spiders. On occasion a "fishing robin" has been
known to take trout fry from newly stocked streams.

Sometimes robins get drunk on mountain ash berries or on umbrella chinatree berries; on such occasions Frank Bralliar, a writer on birds, says: "They fall to the ground and lie on their side, occasionally feebly fluttering, apparently as happy as any drunkard in his cups."

Description: Length, 10 in. Yellow bill; black head and tail; slaty back; reddish breast; belly, and in some races, tips of outer tail feathers, white; female much paler than male; young has black spots on buffy breast.

Incubation, 13 days; young stay about two weeks (10 to 16 days) in nest.

Size of eggs, 1.1 x 0.8 in.; two or three broods per year.

WOOD THRUSH (*Hylocichla mustelina*)

The wood thrush, slightly smaller than its cousin the robin, is reddish brown above, brightest on its head, with a creamy white breast decorated with large round spots of brown. It was called the "wood thrush" or "wood robin" by early settlers because it was originally found in moist deep hardwoods, particularly those with dense understory, and in mountain ravines.

Today the wood thrush also inhabits shade tree, lawn, garden, park, and suburb. Adaptation to man-made habitats seems to have been particularly rapid during the years 1890 to 1910. However, the densest breeding population in recent years, in Maryland, was still in "virgin central hardwood deciduous forest" (white oak, tulip, poplar). The wood thrush is not so conspicuous a lawn promenader as the robin. The bird is tame, fearless, and independent. It brooks the presence of man with equanimity, perhaps pleasure; we must assume that the breaking up of the Great Forest into farms and suburbs has rendered some benefit to the species. It apparently always has liked the edges of woods, which the progress of civilization has vastly multiplied. Strips along parkways, patches of irregular undeveloped tracts, and groves of shade trees have furnished the wood thrush with many nesting sites and plentiful food.

This thrush is essentially one of shade and lower branches, for its large eyes are not well adapted to bright sunlight. It likes to bathe in bird baths or under the artificial rain of a lawn sprinkler.

The wood thrush arrives in the latitude of New York about April 28. From winter quarters in Mexico and Central America it migrates by night up the east coast of Mexico and across the Gulf. It reaches the United States in the Southeast in March; progress up the Mississippi Valley, where it arrives later, is more rapid than up the Atlantic coast. It arrives in Pennsylvania and New Jersey by mid-April, St. Louis by April 20, New York by late April, and London, Ontario, by May 10.

Although the species has varied considerably in numbers in New England over the past 100 years, it seems to be extending its range northward all over the country, particularly since 1935. In New Hampshire, in many places in the White Mountains, it is now common where 50 years ago it was virtually unknown.

Males arrive on the breeding grounds before females, to stake out nesting territories, which range from $\frac{1}{5}$ to 2 acres. A male may occupy the same territory for several consecutive years, possibly for life. Although the male chooses the territory, the female selects the nest site.

Courtship in this species is largely a matter of males chasing females through the forest trees, twisting, turning, and circling through the lower branches at breakneck speed.

The wood thrush builds a nest somewhat like the robin's, large and cupshaped, constructed of grasses, leaves, weed stalks, and sometimes moss; held together with rotted damp leaves or mud; lightly lined with fine grasses or rootlets. The thrush's nest is saddled in the fork of a horizontal branch or the crotch of tree or shrub, from 3 to 12 (rarely 50) ft. up. The thrush likes to put something white in the outer wall, a piece of paper or rag.

The three or four eggs of the wood thrush resemble a robin's, but they are a little smaller and more pointed at the smaller end. The female lays one egg a day. She develops a bare, blood-red brood patch on her stomach and does all the incubating, which she commences when the second or third egg is laid. She also does the brooding.

Both male and female feed the young and swallow or remove the fecal sacs. The young start to forage for themselves at the age of 20 days, but will still beg for food up to 32 days. The wood thrush starts a second brood almost immediately after the first is fledged.

In September the fall migration starts. By late October it is over. The birds have retreated to winter homes in Central America. Alexander F. Skutch, an authority on birds of that area, wrote:

The wood thrush winters in Central America throughout the length of the Caribbean lowlands; but I have found it far from abundant in Guatemala and Honduras, and exceedingly rare in Costa Rica and Panama. During the winter months it does not form flocks, but leads a solitary life, in the undergrowth of the forest, in low moist thickets, or even in banana plantations. On March 21, 1935, I heard a wood thrush sing in the undergrowth of the forest on Barro Colorado Island, Canal Zone. His song was subdued but perfectly distinct, and beautiful as always. The single thrush was in company with antbirds of several kinds.

Mathews translates the song of the wood thrush into: *Come to me, I am here, sweetest singer, warbling cheerily, tra-la-la-la-z-z-z.* Saunders reduces it to these syllables: *eechlay—ayolee—ahleelee—ayleahlohah—ilolilee.* He goes on to say:

Each phrase may have three parts, an introduction of two or three short notes, usually low in pitch and not especially musical; a central phrase of two to five notes, most commonly three, loud, clear, flute-like and extremely musical; and a termination of three or four notes, usually high-pitched, not so loud, and generally the least musical part of the song.

In recording 115 songs he found the pitch ranged from D″ to D″″. A tone or two over an octave was the range of the average bird. The song contains chords, and a person with good ears can detect four tones at the same time. The introductory *tuck, tuck,* occasional harsh interpolations, and a final trill or sputter may be recognized, but they in no way mar the song.

Early in the season the male sings his loudest, most variable, and most complete song from the top of the tallest trees in his territory; but after a week or so he is satisfied with a less elevated perch. The first males usually start singing half an hour before sunrise. As the season progresses, dawn songs become less conspicuous; but the evening singing, which, for this species, is always the most important and is all that is heard after the young leave the nest, keeps on until the end of July. The average date of the last song at Ithaca, New York, is July 29.

The alarm note of the species is a trilling *trrrrrrr*; when more upset, a nervous *putt, putt, putt*; and when really alarmed, a loud, agitated *quit quit quit*. Both male and female give a squeaky whistle with the mouth full when coming to the nest with food. This whistle is also given by the female on the nest.

The food of the wood thrush is about 62 percent animal in origin. This consists of spiders, caterpillars, worms, beetles, including the Colorado potato bug beetle, weevils, grasshoppers, and crickets. The vegetable food includes mulberries, elderberries, dogwood berries, blackberries, raspberries, strawberries, and other fruit, mostly wild.

Description: Length, 8 in. Body, plump; dark, shiny eyes; bright cinnamon brown upperparts; bright reddish brown head, nape, and upper back; creamy white underparts with large dark round spots on breast and sides. (The brown thrasher is larger, has longer, reddish brown uniformly colored tail and upperparts; curved bill; yellow eye; and streaks, not spots, on its breast.)

Incubation, 13 to 14 days; young stay 12 to 13 days in nest.

Size of eggs, 1.1 x 0.7 in.; one or two broods per year, possibly three in South.

HERMIT THRUSH (*Hylocichla guttata*)

The hermit thrush is russet brown above, with red-brown tail and wedgeshaped brown spots on its whitish breast. It breeds from central Alaska and southern Labrador south to southern California and western Maryland. It winters from southern British Columbia, northern Arizona, southern Illinois, and New Jersey south to Lower California, Guatemala, southern Florida, and the Gulf. In mild winters a few birds are found farther north.

The preferred habitats of this thrush are the northern and mountain forests of evergreens, mixed evergreens, and hardwoods. It also likes burned or cutover areas, second growth, tamarack, and balsam swamps and pine barrens, as on Cape Cod and Long Island. In winter it is a bird of underbrush, thicket, canyon, chaparral, and brushy areas near water.

Like many birds, this thrush forages on the ground but sings from treetops. One outstanding characteristic is a habit of pumping its tail. This consists of raising the tail on alighting on a branch and then slowly lowering it. The bird repeats this at intervals. It is the only one of our thrushes that habitually does it. Oddly enough, this habit is not so well developed in western as in eastern subspecies.

The hermit thrush is shy and inconspicuous, usually found alone, as its name suggests. You flush it from the forest floor or a low branch as you walk through the woods. The bird flies quietly ahead of you to perch motionless on a low branch where it seems to eye your continued approach with mild trepidation. Notice its relatively long, slender legs and, when perched, the statuelike immobility it maintains for considerable time. If you try to follow it, the bird flies off a short distance to another branch. The process can go on for some time. The thrush seldom flies out of sight, but it also seldom flies onto a perch where you can get a really good view of it.

W. Leon Dawson, author of *Birds of California*, describes its wing flitting habit as follows:

Perhaps the most prominent characteristic of the hermit thrush, and the one which does most to remove it from the commonplace, is the incessant twinkling of the wings—the action is so rapid and the return to the state of repose so incalculably quick that the general impression or silhouette is not thereby disturbed; but we have an added feeling of mobility of tensity on the part of the bird which gives one the impression of spiritual alertness, a certain high readiness. I tried on a time to count these twinkles, with the compensatory flirt of the tail, as the bird was hopping about on the ground in my rose garden. The movements occurred about once per second, yet oftenest in groups, and so rapidly, that not a twentieth part of the bird's time seemed so consumed. . . .

In one station which the bird occupied, being not over seven feet from me, I could, by closing one eye and focussing the other upon a closely placed background of greenery, note the extreme limit of the wing-motion. The tip, in each instance, travelled at least two inches from the body; yet the return was so instant and the dress so quickly composed that no detail of the readjustment could be traced.

The hermit thrush has the habit of anting, picking up ants and rubbing them over its wings and body feathers (a practice discussed under blue jay, p. 56). Though hardy, this thrush dislikes snow and in winter keeps south of the snow line. Unseasonable early or late snows and lighthouses that bewildered migrants lay a heavy toll on the species.

April brings the hermit thrush migration up the Mississippi Valley. By the first week of May the bird has reached the northern limits of its breeding range. Fall migrants start south in September, and most individuals have left their summer homes by the end of October. The species migrates by night. The morning after a flight often finds city parks and churchyards, tiny urban gardens, and indeed any patch of green in the concrete desert, alive with hermit thrushes. They are tired, hungry, and tame, and will often stay several days until strength is restored.

The nest of the hermit is usually found on the ground in damp, cool woods, often near a bog or stream, or the edge of a woods road or pasture. Often it is under a small evergreen, the lower branches of which form a canopy over it. On Long Island and Cape Cod the nest may be located amid bearberries on the hottest pine barrens. In the West, the bird frequently builds in a tree or shrub, 3 to 10 ft. above the ground. Occasionally it nests about buildings. The nest is a compact cup, often with bulky exterior. It is composed of twigs, grasses, bark fibers, weed stalks and ferns, sometimes with moss on the outside, and is lined with pine needles, fine rootlets, and occasionally with porcupine hair.

Four plain greenish blue eggs constitute the normal clutch. There may be three or five eggs, and very occasionally an egg will be found with fine dark spots. The female incubates alone. According to one investigator a single egg is deposited daily at about 10 A.M. Incubation starts at noon the day the last egg is laid. The male feeds the female while she is sitting, guards the nest, and sings from a perch nearby. Sometimes instead of food he brings nesting material to his sitting mate in a curious behavior pattern retained after it is no longer needed. This material the female graciously accepts, then tosses aside. She will desert the nest if it is disturbed.

Life is hazardous for ground-nesting birds. Gross gives the following details of the first few days of the young:

After the eggs are pipped hatching proceeds rapidly. The struggling embryo breaks the shell in two parts, the crack taking place near the greatest diameter. In the course of a few minutes the embryo is entirely free. . . .

Both parents flit about nervously and seem most anxious to serve their off-spring. They now exhibit less caution and more daring in approaching the nest. A small green larva was delivered and fed to the young in less than five minutes after it had come into the world.

At the time of hatching the young are nearly naked. . . . Though the eyes are closed during the first two or three days, the young birds are most responsive to the approach of the adults at the very start. In fact, a mere touch of the rim of the nest is sufficient to initiate the feeding response—uplifting their heads, extending their gape, and displaying the bright colors lining the mouth. Both parents take an active part in the feeding of the young and at all times take meticulous care of the sanitation of the nest. The excrement is received in their beaks as soon as it is emitted. The young are carefully examined and even stimulated by a stroke of their bills after each feeding until the fecal sac appears. During the first few days it is eaten, but thereafter it may be carried away and dropped at some distance from the nest.

Of 15 nests that Gross studied, 4 were parasitized by the brown-headed cowbird.

The hermit thrush is our hardiest thrush, the first to come north in spring and the last to go south in fall. A few linger into winter in the north, sometimes at feeding stations. It is normally silent in winter quarters and in migration. Neither Wilson nor Audubon ever heard or recognized its song, it is said, because they knew it only in winter or migration.

In the height of the song season the hermit thrush starts singing an hour before sunrise and may be heard half an hour after sunset. It sings from arrival on its breeding grounds until late August. F. S. Mathews, author of a *Field Guide of Wild Birds and Their Music,* collected in 40 years 150 different songs of this thrush, each "absolutely distinct in musical composition." The song is sometimes ventriloquial. In fall a "whisper song," a pale echo of spring song, escapes the bird through a closed bill and is audible for a distance of only a few feet.

In addition to song, the hermit thrush also has a scolding *tuk-tuk* note, a soft *chuck* and a *quirt* or *quoit* that indicates suspicion. The alarm note is a meowing catlike *pay.* There is also a lisp like a cedar waxwing, and in winter in southern California, a *chreeeeeeeee* is given with a slightly rising pitch. The parents utter a soft *wee* sound when they come to the nest with food. Occasionally there is an "indescribable explosive twitter of ecstacy made with fluttering wings."

The food of the hermit thrush over the nation as a whole is about 60 percent animal matter and 40 percent vegetable. The animal food includes spiders and such insects as caterpillars, beetles, weevils, ants, grasshoppers, crickets, earthworms, bees, wasps, and flies. The vegetable food consists largely of wild fruits and berries, among which are numbered those of staghorn sumac, mountain ash, barberry, poison ivy, privet, wild grape, black gum, pokeberry, holly, greenbrier, Virginia creeper, bayberry, hackberry, blueberry, and serviceberry.

Grinnell and Storer, in *Animal Life in the Yosemite,* describe its manner of feeding:

> The demeanor of the hermit thrust is quiet and deliberate. When foraging on the ground it acts in much the same manner as a robin, hopping several times in quick succession and then halting upright and immobile for a few seconds to scan the immediate vicinity before going forward again. There is this important difference, however: the hermit thrust seldom forages out in the open, and if it does it never goes far away from cover, to which it can flee in case of need. When foraging on shaded ground strewn with dead leaves its characteristic performance is to seize a leaf in its bill and throw it to one side with a very quick movement of the head, following this with an intent gaze at the spot uncovered. A thrush will flick over leaf after leaf in this manner, every now and then finding some insect which is swallowed, as is a berry, at one gulp. Hermit thrushes thus make use of a source of food not sought after by other birds; fox sparrows may forage over the same ground, but they are after seeds, which they get at by scratching. The thrushes do not use their feet at all for uncovering food. The thrushes' legs are relatively long, so that the birds stand high, and have consequently an increased scope of vision.

A captive was once observed to eat half its weight in raw meat, daily.

Description: Length, 6½ to 7½ in. Bill, thin, pointed; hazel eyes; russet brown upperparts; rufous rump and tail; some suggestion of rufous in primaries; whitish underparts with small dark arrow-shaped marks on breast. (The fox sparrow has a short, thick bill; its entire upperparts, not just tail and rump, are bright reddish brown.)

Incubation, 12 days; young stay 12 days in nest.

Size of eggs, 0.9 x 0.7 in.; one to three broods per year.

EASTERN BLUEBIRD (*Sialia sialis*)

The original habitat of the bluebird was scattered clumps of trees in open areas; farmland proved a perfect substitute. In the East, in place of unbroken forest, orchards and woodlots dotted the countryside. In the prairie states, where formerly trees occurred only along water-courses, windbreaks and shade trees provided suitable new habitat over hundreds of square miles of former grassland. A tame and confiding species, the bluebird adapted to the presence of man who, responding to its beauty and charm, fostered it by providing nesting boxes and protecting it from harm. Commenting on this relationship, George Gladden wrote:

Like the Robin, the Bluebird shows a decided fondness for human society. Orchards are favorite resorts of the bird, and furnish plenty of home sites in the shape of hollow trunks or limbs of trees, for this bird always prefers a cavity of some kind wherein to place its nest. The wise owner of such trees will do his utmost to encourage this tenancy. Indeed, if he will scatter through his orchard a goodly supply of Bluebird homes, in the form of short sections of hollow limbs, covered at the top and bottom, and with an auger-hole doorway, he will soon have plenty of tenants, who will pay their rent many times over by destroying injurious insects and worms. For, with the possible exceptions of the House Wren and the Purple Martin, the Bluebird is as willing as any bird to set up housekeeping in a dwelling for him made and provided.

Today the bluebird is a generally common, widespread species, though there was some decline in its numbers a few years ago, especially in the more populous sections of the northeast. Usurpation of its nesting places by starlings and house sparrows is one of the most frequently cited reasons for this decline. Moreover, the conversion of farmland into housing developments and industrial parks, for instance, had destroyed large tracts of suitable bluebird habitat.

The range of the bluebird is eastern and central North America, south to Florida and the Gulf coast, and west to the Rocky Mountains. They winter in the southern part of the range, chiefly from Maryland and the Ohio Valley southward, with a small number appearing northward to southern New York and southern Michigan in mild winters. The southward migration occurs chiefly in October, though bluebirds are seen with fair regularity in the North well into November. They are one of the earliest spring migrants, returning in early March, often before the last heavy snow storms of the season. The sight of these beautiful, delicate birds braving the gales of late winter has traditionally had a strong symbolic meaning for northerners, especially in New England, where the reappearance of the bluebird is one of the first signs of the passing of the long, bleak winter. There are limits to the bluebird's heartiness, however, and a protracted spell of freezing weather will exact a toll, as it does to all early migrants. At infrequent intervals these losses are severe.

Normally an occurrence of this sort has no lasting effect on the status of the species as a whole. A great reduction in numbers makes available to the survivors a greater than normal amount of suitable habitat and food; survival becomes easier for them. Because of this, not only are birds more likely to raise more broods per season, but a greater than normal percentage of young are likely to reach maturity. Numbers again begin to increase and in due time the population is back to its former level.

The male bluebird is a small, delicately formed, bright blue bird with a rusty-red breast and white abdomen. The female resembles the male but is somewhat duller. Young birds are mottled gray with blue-edged wings and tail and speckled on the breast.

Arriving on the nesting grounds a few days before the females, the male establishes a territory from which he drives any later-arriving males by singing a warbled warning from a succession of perches outlining the borders of his claim.

It is through such associations of gentle good nature, that the song of the bluebird has won human listeners. For though warm and quietly cheerful, the musical qualities of the song itself are limited, compared to the virtuoso performances of most other thrushes. To most observers, the song of the bluebird sounds as a soft caroling, mellow but muted.

With the arrival of the females, the pairs are formed and the birds begin their search for a nesting site. Selecting a suitably placed birdbox, an abandoned woodpecker hole, or a hollow formed by decay in a fence post or limb, they construct a nest of grass, weeds, and bits of bark, lining it with softer grass. In any locality the potential number of nesting sites is always limited and there is considerable competition for them. The starling, because of its formidable aggressiveness, and the house sparrow, by virtue of its numbers, exert especially heavy pressure on the bluebird. In these circumstances an adequate supply of birdboxes can be a great help. In many communities bird clubs have greatly increased the local bluebird population by setting out nesting boxes along several miles of country roads. Fence posts are admirably suited for this purpose, since house sparrows generally refuse to occupy a site located so near the ground. Starlings can be effectively discouraged also, if the diameter of the entrance hole is slightly less than 1½ in. The houses should be placed 100 yds. apart.

The female bluebird lays from four to six bluish-white eggs, which hatch in about 12 days. The young remain in the nest two to three weeks and are cared for by both parents, though the female seems to do the majority of the feeding while the male flits from fence post to phone pole, singing his territorial rights. The nesting season lasts from mid-March to early August; there are two, often three broods a season.

Few birds are so completely without fault as the bluebird. Even in the matter of food the bluebird preserves its immaculate reputation. The young are fed entirely on insects, mainly destructive forms such as cutworms, grasshoppers, and crickets. The adults are almost entirely insectivorous during the warmer months, feeding mostly on terrestrial insects, which they capture by suddenly dropping to the ground from the vantage point of a fence post, power line, or low limb. They seldom remain on the ground for any length of time, preferring to return to a perch before swallowing their catch. Flying insects are also taken occasionally. The bluebird, however, is not adept at aerial maneuvering and such agile prey forms only an insignificant part of its diet. During the winter, when insect food is scarce, the bluebird feeds mostly on wild berries. In a Department of Interior bulletin on the feeding habits of the bluebird, F. E. L. Beal wrote:

It is evident that in the selection of its food the bluebird is governed more by abundance than by choice. Predacious beetles are eaten in spring, as they are among the first insects to appear; but in early summer cater-pillars form an important part of the diet, and these are later replaced by grasshoppers. Beetles are eaten at all times, except when grasshoppers are more easily obtained.

So far as vegetable food is concerned the bluebird is positively harmless. The only trace of any useful product in the stomachs consisted of a few blackberry seeds, and even these probably belonged to wild rather than cul-tivated varieties. Following is a list of the various seeds which were found: Blackberry, chokeberry, juniperberry, pokeberry, partridgeberry, greenbrier, Virginia creeper, bittersweet, holly, strawberry bush, false spikenard, wild sarsaparilla, sumac (several species), rose haws, sorrel, ragweed, grass, and asparagus. This list shows how little the bluebird depends upon the farm or garden to supply its needs and how easily, by encouraging the growth of some of these plants many of which are highly ornamental, the bird may be induced to make its home on the premises.

Bluebirds remain in the general vicinity of their nesting place for some time after the breeding season is over. They are usually found in small flocks, probably representing family groups. As the season advances, flocking occurs more and more often. With the first sharp frosts of October, bluebirds, in groups of 12 to 70 or more, begin drifting south to their wintering grounds in the southern states. Blue-birds often migrate by day; the clear, plaintive *chur-wee* of their call-note overhead is a characteristic sound of crisp fall days. By December the migration is over, though each year a few individuals remain behind to spend the winter in some favorable spot with an abundant food supply and shelter from the wind and weather.

These northern wintering individuals seldom visit feeding stations. The usual offerings of seeds and suet are not particularly attractive to them and will seldom tempt them away from the berry bushes and tangles of sunny wooded hollows that are their usual winter refuge. In the milder climate of the southern states, though still preferring sheltered woodland, they are more likely to occur around the yard and garden, especially where there are plantings of red cedar, farkleberry, inkberry, or other growths that bear fruit throughout the winter.

Description: Length, 7 in. Bill, short and slight; wings, rather long; appears "round-shouldered" when perched. Blue back; bright rusty-red breast; white abdomen. Female duller than male. Young: mottled gray with bluish cast to wings and tail; speckled breast. Flight is slow, with slight undulation or "dipping." Blue jay is much larger, crested; Indigo bunting and blue grosbeak are entirely blue; none of these birds shows reddish below.

Incubation, 12 to 15 days; young stay 14 to 16 days in nest.

Size of eggs, 0.82 x 0.64 in.; two, sometimes three broods per year.

SPOTTED DOVE [I]

MOURNING DOVE

INCA DOVE

GROUND DOVE (female)   GROUND DOVE (male)

[II]   ANNA'S HUMMINGBIRD (female)   RUFOUS HUMMINGBIRD (male)

ANNA'S HUMMINGBIRD (male) ALLEN'S HUMMINGBIRD (male) RUFOUS HUMMINGBIRD (fen

BLACK-CHINNED HUMMINGBIRD (male)

RUBY-THROATED HUMMINGBIRD (female)   RUBY-THROATED HUMMINGBIRD (mal

RED-BELLIED WOODPECKER (adult)   HAIRY WOODPECKER (male)   [III]

RED-BELLIED WOODPECKER (immature)

DOWNY WOODPECKER (male)

YELLOW-SHAFTED FLICKER (male)

STELLER'S JAY   BLUE JAY

GRAY JAY

GREEN JAY   SCRUB JAY

BOREAL CHICKADEE

BLACK-CAPPED CHICKADEE

TUFTED TITMOUSE

WHITE-BREASTED NUTHATCH

RED-BREASTED NUTHATCH

[VI]

MOCKINGBIRD

CATBIRD

BROWN THRASHER

CALIFORNIA THRASHER

EASTERN BLUEBIRD (immature)   EASTERN BLUEBIRD   [VII]

WOOD THRUSH

HERMIT THRUSH

ROBIN   ROBIN (immature)

MYRTLE WARBLER (male)   AMERICAN GOLDFINCH (winter male)   [IX]
MYRTLE WARBLER (female and winter male)   AMERICAN GOLDFINCH (female)
                                         AMERICAN GOLDFINCH (male)

BALTIMORE ORIOLE (male)
        BALTIMORE ORIOLE (female)   ORCHARD ORIOLE (male)
                                         ORCHARD ORIOLE (female)

[X]   SUMMER TANAGER (male)   SUMMER TANAGER (female)

ROSE-BREASTED GROSBEAK (female)

WESTERN TANAGER (male)   ROSE-BREASTED GROSBEAK (male)

WESTERN TANAGER (female)

PAINTED BUNTING (female)   PAINTED BUNTING (male)   [XI]

    INDIGO BUNTING (female)

                                   CARDINAL (female)

INDIGO BUNTING (male)

                          DICKCISSEL (immature)

    CARDINAL (male)   DICKCISSEL (adult male)

[XII] EVENING GROSBEAK (male) PURPLE FINCH (male)
HOUSE FINCH (male)
REDPOLL (female)
REDPOLL (male) EVENING GROSBEAK (female) PINE SISKIN
PURPLE FINCH (female) HOUSE FINCH (female)

STARLINGS / *Sturnidae*

STARLING (*Sturnus vulgaris*)

Together with the house sparrow and rock dove, the starling is one of the three commonest urban birds, occurring in large numbers even in the heart of great cities. It is equally at home in the suburbs and in farming country, but does not occur in heavy woodland or forest. In its native home the starling is highly migratory, nesting in the temperate areas of Europe and western Asia and wintering in Africa and India. In the New World it has changed its habits and is mostly a permanent resident, though individual flocks wander erratically during the winter. During the westward expansion of the starling, the first appearance of this species in a new locality would occur at that season, when a wandering flock would settle down in some favorable locality to spend the winter and, with the coming of spring, form the nucleus of a new breeding population.

Though still increasing in the West, the starling population of eastern North America is now stabilized, and some objective assessment of this species' impact on its environment is now possible.

The starling has a generally bad reputation, especially with New York City policemen whose call box is under the viaduct at 125th

Street, where 125,000 starlings roost; the orchardman whose cherry crop is ripening just at the season when the first post-breeding season flocks are roaming the countryside; the suburban housewife hoping to attract bluebirds to a newly erected birdhouse.

Yet, here, after all, is a species that from original stock of less than 100 birds has, in 72 years, colonized a continent and now numbers in the millions. The starling is tough, intelligent, amazingly adaptable species. A. L. Goodman in describing the starling in Kansas in 1945, says:

Wildlife enthusiasts have felt that these strongly adaptive birds ultimately will preempt many of all natural sites for hole-nesting species, and thus result in the gradual elimination of many of our highly desirable native birds. Perhaps the time since their introduction in 1890 has been insufficient to reveal the full impact of their presence upon native species. It seems hardly just, however, that the people of the United States, in whom "Yankee ingenuity" is such a desirable trait, should grudge this same trait to a newer colonist in our midst.

This trait of usurping nesting sites is one of the most frequently cited claims against the starling. Starlings mate in early April, and by the middle of the month, the pairs are ready to begin nesting in some natural cavity, woodpecker hole, or birdbox. In cities, several pairs will often nest together in a loose colony among the eaves and crevices of a building. Starlings are highly aggressive, pugnacious birds at this season, and there is no doubt that they are inclined to seize upon the first attractive site available, regardless of whether it is currently occupied.

Having by one means or another obtained a suitable site, the starling builds a nest of fibrous grass lined with softer, finer grass. In rural areas, a few corn husks may be woven into the cup, and feathers of domestic fowl used for lining. The female lays three to six pale greenish or bluish white eggs, which hatch in about 12 days. The young remain in the nest two or three weeks and are fed by both parent birds. There are often two and sometimes three broods a year.

Commenting on the food habits of nestling starlings, E. R. Kalmbach in a Department of Agriculture bulletin, wrote:

Few birds are more voracious than young Starlings, and it requires the most strenuous efforts of the naturally active parents to supply the constant needs of their offspring when there are from four to six to be fed. Observations made on a brood of five young starlings revealed that they had been fed, on the average, once every 6.1 minutes during the nestling life. On the assumption that the young were fed 12 hours a day, which is conservative, a record of 118 feedings a day would be established. As this brood left the nest on the sixteenth day, probably several days short of the normal nestling period of the starling, for the birds were disturbed considerably during the latter period of nestling life, a total of 1,888 feedings would have been given to this brood of five, or 377.6 feedings for each nestling. One may get some idea of the quantity of food required to develop a brood of young starlings from the fact that the parent birds would often bring in three or four cutworms, earthworms, or grasshoppers, or an equal bulk of miscellaneous insect food at a single trip.

A detailed study of the food of nestling starlings gives striking evidence of the great influence they exert for good. More than 95 per cent of the nestling's food is animal matter, largely insects. Cutworms are especially attractive to the young birds, caterpillars as a group forming more than 38 per cent of their diet. The character of their beetle food is economically more favorable than that of the adults, and, though the nestling period is too early in the year to permit extensive feeding on grasshoppers, crickets in large quantities supply their orthopterous food.

As the young leave the nest they gather in flocks, which gradually increase in size through the summer. By the end of the nesting season in late summer, adults and young are gathered together in large flocks that forage across the countryside just at the time when crops are ripening. They often associate with red-winged blackbirds, grackles, and cowbirds at this season, and like those species, forage mostly on the ground.

Starlings are also fond of fruit, especially apples and cherries, and often do considerable damage in orchards. To offset this, however, starlings eat an enormous quantity of harmful insects during other times of the year. Over half the annual diet consists of animal food, including large quantities of imported pests like the cloverleaf weevil and Japanese beetle, seldom touched by native birds.

As winter approaches, the foraging flocks reach maximum size and begin using communal roosts, flocking in from all directions at evening to some grove of tall trees or large building. The habit of roosting on man-made structures is the third major cause of criticism of the starling. A large number of starlings create a large amount of mess; the defacement of buildings by their droppings is a serious problem in some large cities. Constant battle is waged between civic authorities and starlings, with screening, fireworks, klaxons, stuffed owls, and recordings of starling distress-calls on one side, and numbers and supreme indifference on the other.

Troublesome as these roosts may be, they do offer a splendid opportunity for observing the one beautiful aspect of the starling; its mastery of flight. In the air, a flock of starlings seems a single, connected unit, each individual turning, banking, and twisting in the same direction at the same moment through any number of intricate maneuvers, all without any apparent leader or perceptible signal. One of the finest places to view this sight is on the upper west side of Manhattan Island where every winter evening 125,000 starlings roost under the Riverside Drive viaduct along the Hudson River. Leaving the 400-ft. Palisades along the New Jersey shore, flocks of 1,000 or more birds sweep in magnificent synchronous movement high across the river, swooping down to the roadway crossing the viaduct, and at the last moment bursting into a thousand randomly swirling black flakes as they scatter to their perches.

The starling's aggressive behavior is confined to the breeding season. During the winter it is quite sociable, and its appearance at a feeding station is not likely to cause a disturbance. It is not a particularly colorful bird, and appears rather cumbersome and awkward on the ground. It has a variety of whistles and shrieking notes, some harsh, others quite melodic. The starling belongs to the same family (Sturnidae) as the famous talking mynah and is a clever mimic, though with a somewhat limited range. It is best at imitating high whistling or plaintive notes like those of the killdeer, wood pewee, and the flight call of the bluebird.

At the feeder, they show a decided preference for animal food; suet or meat scraps from the table are eagerly devoured; they are also fond of peanut butter, raisins, sunflower seeds, and apples. They will eat various small seeds, but will not seriously compete with small finches for them if food more to their preference is available.

Description: Length, 8 to 9 in. Stocky and short-tailed; bill, long and sharply pointed. Adult: in summer, black, glossy green and purple; yellow bill; in winter, brown bill, body speckled buffy-white. Young: brownish-gray with brownish bill. In flight, wings broad at base, sharply pointed at tip, giving triangular effect; tail short. Flight is swift and straight, without dipping characteristic of blackbirds.

Incubation, 12 days; young stay 16 to 21 days in nest.

Size of eggs, 1.20 x 0.86 in.; often two, sometimes three, broods per year.

WOOD WARBLERS / *Parulidae*

MYRTLE WARBLER (*Dendroica coronata*)

From time to time authorities have attempted to estimate the total number of individual birds inhabiting the North American continent. Various methods of tabulation have been used; in most cases they are based on the average number of individuals per acre from sample sections of the various major habitats of the continent. Most estimates place the number between 12 and 20 million, depending on the season of the year. To date no reliable species-by-species breakdown is available; no one knows with any degree of certainty whether robins, for instance, outnumber song sparrows, or even which is the more common species. The information to date, however, indicates that the most familiar and widely known species are not necessarily the most numerically abundant; in many cases it is simply that these species are noticed more frequently because of more conspicuous behavior or a tendency to live in close proximity to humans. Actually some of our most abundant birds go unnoticed by the casual observer and may not even be recognized by name. One such bird is the myrtle warbler.

The factors determining the abundance of a species are quite complex, involving availability of suitable habitat, presence of competitors and enemies, and the adaptability and resiliency of the species itself. Seldom do two closely related species of similar habits inhabit the same area; if they do, one will almost always lose out in the competition and become relatively rare. Usually the various members of a family of birds tend to follow diverse ways of life. Each occupies an environmental niche different from that of its close relatives of the same geographical area and becomes the representative or "dominant" species of its family for its particular habitat. When a species becomes firmly established in a habitat that offers an unusual opportunity for expansion, that species is likely to become remarkably abundant. This is strikingly evident in the case of the myrtle warbler, whose summer home is the "Great North Woods," extending along the northern border of the United States, from Maine to Minnesota, north and west to the limit of trees in northern Canada and Alaska.

The myrtle is not only our most abundant warbler; it is also somewhat of a maverick. During a large part of the year its way of life is quite different from other members of its family. It is an active, spritely bird, smaller than a sparrow, with a thin, sharply pointed bill and fanshaped tail. In spring the male is bright slate-blue with white, dark-streaked breast and conspicuous yellow patches on the rump, crown, and sides of the chest. The female is similar, but dull gray-brown replaces the slate-blue. Immatures and males in winter resemble the female. Male individuals in this plumage are quite nondescript. Look for the yellow rump-patch and listen for the call note, a full, throaty *check*.

During the breeding season, which begins in late May, the myrtle's way of life does not differ appreciably from several other members of its family. The nest is placed in a young spruce or fir, usually within a few feet of the ground but occasionally as high as 30 ft. It is made from dried grass, weeds, and strips of bark, bound together with spider webs and lined with hair or plant down. Construction takes about a week and is done almost entirely by the female, though the male will occasionally bring her bits of material to weave into the structure. The eggs are white, speckled brown, and purple, and are three to five in a clutch. The incubation period takes about two weeks, and again it is the female who does most of the work. The male spends most of his time singing to ward off unmated rivals from the nesting site.

The male myrtle sings a simple liquid rattle that at the height of the breeding season is sometimes intensified to a two-phrased trill with a lowering of pitch in mid-song.

After hatching, the young myrtles remain in the nest another two weeks. They are fed the same insect food taken by the adult birds during the summer: aphids, plant lice, and a variety of small flying insects forming the bulk of the diet. The myrtle is an active, restless feeder, constantly flicking its fanlike tail and fluttering from twig to twig as it gleans its food from the leaves and needles of the outer branches of the forest trees. It is also an adept fly catcher, cartwheeling in mid-air to snap up some passing insect while incidentally displaying to full advantage its flashing yellow, black, and blue pattern.

There is only one brood a year. Shortly after the young leave the nest, the family group disbands. The young birds molt their juvenile plumage while the male, his period of song over, begins the gradual transformation into the dull plumage of winter. Dispersed through the forest, the myrtle becomes relatively inconspicuous for a month or so until the coming of autumn when, from out of their 2 million square miles of breeding territory, myrtle warblers pour southward across central and eastern United States in incredible numbers. In most years the first individuals reach the vicinity of New York and southern New England in late August, but the bulk of the migrants generally arrive later than other species of warblers. They arrive between mid-September and the end of October and are still passing through in considerable numbers throughout November. All through the autumn, myrtle warblers are everywhere in woodlands, parks, gardens, and along tree-lined streets. But it is along the coast that the truly impressive flights are seen. At the peak of the flight, observers in particularly favorable localities have estimated as many as 10,000 birds in a single morning. By December the myrtle is rare in inland localities, but in coastal areas it is still one of the commonest birds and remains so throughout the winter along the entire Atlantic, Gulf, and Caribbean coasts of North America from Cape Cod to Panama.

The myrtle is the only warbler wintering regularly in numbers in the northern United States. While myrtles that winter in tropical areas forage in much the same manner as they do in summer, birds remaining in the north, departing from the insectivorous diet characteristic of warblers, depend entirely on seeds and berries as their main source of food. All along the barrier beaches of the Atlantic coast, from New England to Georgia, the chief winter food of the myrtle warbler is the bayberry or wax myrtle, the plant from which it derives its name. The number of myrtle warblers concentrated in any one place depends to a great extent on the size of the bayberry crop, which varies locally from year to year. Thus myrtles may be abundant in an area one winter and relatively scarce the next. They are never really rare in any year, however, for when the bayberry crop is poor, the myrtle turns to a variety of other plants of the coastal beaches, including red cedar, poison ivy, sumac, and goldenrod. Hibernating insects and the eggs of plant lice are always available to some extent.

In company with sparrows and juncos they search about on the ground among moldering leaves in brushy tangles and woodlots, and forage for seeds on open lawns and grass plots. They can also be seen, especially on calm sunny days, hopping about the tidal wrack of salt marshes and beaches, searching for tiny insects and minute marine life. In mid-fall and again in early spring when there are a few large ground insects about, the myrtle often adopts the hunting method of its principal winter enemy the shrike. Perched quietly on a low limb or plant stalk, it will suddenly pounce down on a beetle or spider on the ground below.

In the North the myrtle takes advantage of opportunities offered by feeding stations to supplement its diet, but will seldom depend on one as its main source of food. Feeders in coastal areas, close to a stand of the myrtle's winter staple, the bayberry, are visited regularly. But the presence of a feeder is seldom sufficient inducement in itself to entice a myrtle warbler to winter in the area. Thus myrtles are only rare winter visitors to feeders in most inland localities, except in late fall and early spring when small groups of migrants will spend a few days at a feeder before continuing their journey. In the southern states, where it is not so closely tied to the bayberry, the myrtle is more likely to be seen in the garden in winter.

At the feeder they will take seeds of sunflower, melons, and squash. They are especially fond of foods with high fat content, such as suet, doughnut crumbs, cake and bread crumbs fried in grease, chopped peanuts, and peanut butter.

In early spring myrtle warblers pass through southern states in late March, reaching New York and New England in late April. By mid-May, peak of the migratory period for other species of warblers, the majority of myrtles has already reached its northern breeding grounds and is ready for the new breeding cycle.

Description: Length, 5 to 6 in. Thin and sharply pointed bill, long and fanshaped tail. Male in spring is slate-blue with yellow patches on rump, crown, sides. Females, immatures, and winter males are similar, but are brown-gray rather than slate-blue. Their yellow crowns and sides are sometimes obscure, but rump patches are always obvious. Magnolia, palm, and Cape May warblers also show a yellow rump patch, at least to some extent, but these species all show yellowish coloration below. The myrtle has white underparts with blackish streaks.

Incubation, 12 to 13 days; young stay 12 to 14 days in nest.

Size of eggs, 0.70 x 0.52 in.; one brood per year.

WEAVER FINCHES / *Ploceidae*

HOUSE SPARROW (*Passer domesticus*)

No other bird has become so thoroughly a part of civilization as has the house sparrow. Like the brown rat, the bedbug, and the cockroach it has become a permanent adjunct of western man. It follows him to all parts of the world, living almost exclusively off his enterprises, but still maintaining an independence that in the end will doubtlessly enable it to transfer with complete ease to whatever follows man.

The male house sparrow is easily recognized by his gray cap, black bib, ashy cheeks, and chestnut-brown back. In new spring plumage he is decidedly more handsome than many of our native sparrows, but natural wear and tear together with city grime quickly obscure this freshness and he becomes quite dingy.

The female is streaky brown above and dingy white below, with a broad, pale eye line and grayish rump. Though rather nondescript, she does not particularly resemble any native species except certain individuals of the immature female dickcissel (see p. 216).

The most common notes of the house sparrow are a loud harsh *chirp* or *cher-eep* and a variety of chattering and grating calls. In the spring, the male combines several of these notes in a short, gurgling song, and

161

occasionally sings a very soft clear warble. Apparently they are physically capable of more intricate vocalizations, for there are records of captive birds learning to imitate the songs of canaries and other species.

The house sparrow, or English sparrow as it is commonly called in North America, belongs to the family Ploceidae, or weavers, a very large, widespread Old World family that includes the Java sparrow, strawberry finch, and other familiar cage birds. None is native to the New World, but a few species have been introduced to North America and the West Indies.

The native home of the house sparrow is Palaearctic Eurasia and North Africa, from the British Isles east through most of Europe, to central Siberia, India, and Ceylon. From here it has spread by introduction throughout the temperate regions of the world and now

female

male

HOUSE SPARROW

inhabits Australia, New Zealand, Hawaii, North America, and the temperate parts of southern South America and South Africa.

In North America it is a permanent resident from British Columbia, northern Manitoba, and northern Quebec south to Baja California, northern Mexico, and Key West.

The first North American house sparrows were introduced in the early 1850s at several localities between New York and Maine. During the next 25 years, introductions were made in additional places across the country as far west as Salt Lake City. By 1910 the house sparrow had spread over all its present North American range and had attained an amazing numerical abundance. According to A. C. Bent in *Life Histories of North American Birds*:

At the peak of its abundance, during the early part of this century, the English Sparrow was undoubtedly the most abundant bird in the United States, except in heavily forested, alpine, and desert regions. Within its favorite haunts one could easily see twice as many sparrows as all other birds combined.

From this high population, the numbers of house sparrows slowly began to decline as the natural forces of disease, predation, and weather began to overcome the initial impetus afforded by the opportunity of unlimited expansion into a new habitat—the city streets, yet unexploited by native species.

But there is some evidence that the leveling-off of the sparrow population was not accomplished by nature alone. The internal combustion engine may have played a part. With the disappearance of the horse, loose grain, which was the staple diet of the house sparrow, also disappeared from our city streets. Bent commented: "It is significant that the decrease in the Sparrow population in urban and suburban areas coincides very closely with the increased use of motor vehicles and the decrease in the number of horses that formerly spread a bountiful food supply along our streets and highways." Whatever the causes, the population of house sparrows was substantially reduced and now seems to be stabilized.

A great deal has been written about the house sparrow, almost all of which is severely critical. In reading about its life and habits one must always expect to find "bully," "belligerent," and "usurping" replacing the "bold," "fearless," and "resourceful" used to describe similar traits of native birds.

There is no doubt that the house sparrow competes very successfully with native species. But it is silly to consider it the prime cause of driving away native birds from areas in which man himself has effected such devastating changes that these areas become fit for nothing but house sparrows. In places where their habitat has not been destroyed or too badly altered, most native birds seem able to hold their own against the sparrow.

The real misfortune arising from the introduction of the house sparrow, it would seem, is not that it drives native species from their old haunts but that it effectively blocks them from exploiting new ones. The development of our cities was too rapid for more than one or two of our native species concurrently to adapt to them. It seems likely that many more would have eventually, but in the interim the house sparrow and starling, both fully pre-adapted to the city environment, became firmly entrenched. Between them, these two aggressive and resourceful species just about blanket all the possible ecological niches available in a city. In the face of such opposition, it does not seem likely that many native birds can accomplish the task of establishing themselves in this new environment.

The nesting season begins in March in the south and in early May in northern Canada. Elsewhere the average date is mid-April. There are two and occasionally three broods a year.

The courtship of the house sparrow is vigorous and straightforward. The male, calling loudly and with wings outstretched, bobs about in a curious crouch while the female remains quite still except to give him an occasional vicious peck. Sometimes several males form a dancing ring around one female; in these cases brief tumbling battles are inevitable until the female makes her choice.

Nests are usually located about the eaves, rafters, and drains of buildings, on ivy-covered walls and in birdboxes or natural hollows. But they have been found in bank swallow burrows, in the sides of ospreys nests, and even in a deserted hornet's nest. Though generally preferring cavities, they also nest among the branches of trees, especially in rural and suburban areas. As Bent commented: "The resourceful and adaptable English Sparrow will build its bulky, unkempt, and loosely constructed nest in almost any conceivable spot that will give it support, some security, and a reasonable degree of concealment, though some of the locations seem to lack even those requirements." The nest, built entirely by the female, is made mostly of grass, straw, and weeds supplemented with whatever material is handy. Newspapers, rags, string, gum wrappers, cellophane, hair, and feathers are only a few items that have been found in sparrow nests.

When completed, the nest is a loose shaggy mass containing in the center a more carefully woven compact pocket of softer material. The size of the nest varies, since the bird always attempts to fill a hole or cavity regardless of its dimensions; some nests may be as tall as 20 in. Nests on rafters and on other flat surfaces tend to be flat and broad, while nests in trees are large, well-made balls with an entrance on one side leading to the soft inner pocket.

Often house sparrows do not even bother to build, but usurp the nest of some other species, destroying the eggs or young that are present and altering construction to suit themselves. Nest raiding in order to steal the site, to feed on eggs and young, or simply to reduce the number of neighbors is so widespread among birds as to be commonplace. Many species, including wrens and the jays and many of the Icterids indulge in it for one reason or another, but the house sparrow, because it is considered generally undesirable in other aspects, is far more often condemned for this practice.

The eggs of the house sparrow are white, greenish, or bluish with tiny gray or brown spots, mostly on the larger end. Clutches vary from three to nine; the usual number is four or five. Incubation is entirely by the female and lasts 10 to 12 days. Both parents feed and brood the young.

Two-thirds of the nestlings' diet is animal matter, mostly weevils, grasshoppers, and other large insects; the remainder is soft vegetable matter. They are fed by regurgitation for the first several days, and then receive raw food.

Adults are 90 percent vegetarian. They have a special fondness for grain, and in rural areas do considerable damage to wheat, oats, and other cereal crops. They also attack newly sprouted garden crops, fruit, grapes, and berries. In the suburbs their food habits are considerably more beneficial. Crabgrass seed is one of their favorite foods, and they also eat considerable quantities of chickwood, dandelion, and ragweed seed.

Though only 10 percent of their annual diet is animal matter, house sparrows are of considerable help in combating sudden irruptions of harmful insects, especially in places where no other bird is particularly abundant. A serious outbreak of aphids, Japanese beetle, inchworms, or locusts is sure to attract a swarm of sparrows. For as long as the outbreak lasts the sparrows feed exclusively on insects and are remarkably adept at improvising methods of feeding that are most efficient for seeking out the particular prey in question. They will hang upside down like titmice to pick aphids off the undersides of leaves, cling to tree trunks like nuthatches, flutter in the air to snap up hanging inchworms, and even pursue and capture locusts and grasshoppers in flight.

Most people are probably more interested in keeping house sparrows away from feeders than in attracting them but, if so, they are tackling a very crafty and resourceful foe. Sparrows quickly learn to avoid traps and poison. Only by destroying every nest and shooting every individual that appears have sparrows been kept at bay, and then only as long as the violence remains unremitting. At the first lapse in persecution they will invariably return.

Such tactics may be worth while in defense of a crop field, but are quite unnecessary, not to mention highly impractical, with regard to a feeding station. Sparrows eat a good deal of food intended for species considered more desirable and do a fair bit of bullying and shoving, but they seldom appear at the average suburban feeder in such numbers as to be truly oppressive.

Sparrows are interested mostly in grain and seeds, and as a rule prefer feeding on the ground or a stable platform close to it. So it is best not to concentrate all the food on a single large tray where the sparrows are better able to take over by sheer weight of numbers and remain for long periods. Instead, offer a variety of foods in an assortment of feeding devices. The sparrows, preferring to feed on food fallen to the ground, are then more likely to visit the feeders in small numbers and for short intervals. Other species can hold their own against them under these circumstances.

Description: Length, 6⅓ in. Stocky and proportionately shorter-tailed than native sparrows. Bill, thick and conical. Male easily recognized by gray cap, black bib, ashy cheeks. No similar native bird. European tree sparrow, another introduced weaver, occurs in vicinity of St. Louis, has a chestnut crown, and black ear patch. Female resembles some dickcissels, but lacks rusty wing patch or any trace of yellow below; bill brownish, not blue-gray as in dickcissel.

Incubation, 10 to 12 days; young stay 15 to 16 days in nest.

Size of eggs, 0.88 x 0.60 in.; two to three broods per year.

BLACKBIRDS / *Icteridae*

RED-WINGED BLACKBIRD (*Agelaius phoeniceus*)

In order to obtain a better understanding of the relationship and present distribution of bird families, ornithologists have attempted to determine the original ancestral home of each so as to trace its progress to other parts of the world.

Very few families of North American birds, for instance, appear to have originated on this continent. They reached us either from Eurasia by way of the vast coniferous forests girdling the Northern Hemisphere, or from tropical America. Among those from the latter area are tyrant-flycatchers, tanagers, and the highly successful members of Icteridae, the family of the red-winged blackbirds (also called redwing).

This exclusively New World family is found throughout the Americas, the various members occupying a variety of different habitats and ecological niches. To the casual observer many of its members seem dissimilar. There seems little in common among meadowlarks, orioles, and blackbirds. But more careful study reveals many familial resemblances. The criteria used to determine which species of birds belong in the same family are based on similarity in skeletal structure, musculature, feather arrangement, and other anatomical characteristics.

When the first human settlers reached North America, the redwing was still a marsh bird, breeding in cattails, tules, and similar reed beds in fresh and salt marshes, and along the borders of lakes and streams. Today it is still most abundant in such locations, but has also spread out in great numbers into pastures, fallow fields, and practically any other open location affording a few weed stalks on which to hang a nest. Naturally the clearing of the land has been a great boon to the redwing, but its aggressive and opportunistic nature has played no small part in its rapid spread. Its present range is from coast to coast throughout North America from Alaska and northern Canada south to Florida and central Mexico.

The redwing is a medium-sized bird with a fairly long tail and sharply pointed bill. The male is unmistakable; jet black with brilliant red, yellow-bordered shoulder patches, or epaulets. The female is dull gray-brown, heavily streaked sooty-black above and below. No other female blackbird is streaked in this manner. The female is sometimes confused with the starling, but that species is much shorter-tailed and longer-billed, and is spotted, not streaked. Young redwings resemble females except that in late fall many young males show signs of the red shoulder patch, making identification of these individuals very simple.

The redwing is partially migratory, leaving the northern part of its range in October and November to winter in the southern states. By late February the return flight has begun, and by March, male redwings have become a familiar sight about the northern marshes, establishing their territories with their reedy, squeaky, bubbling song, *Ok-la-reeee* or *Kong-ka-reeee*. The vocalization of the redwing is, by any objective standards, a pretty poor bit of music, and if the birds did not begin singing so early it would certainly be given little attention.

For a week or two the males are alone on the nesting grounds, and though by day they usually remain about the one spot in the marsh they have chosen for their territory, they roost communally by night and generally show little animosity toward one another. But with the return of the females, activity quickens. The males accompany their reedy song with a visual display, fanning wings and tail, and ruffling feathers of the neck and back. At the height of display the epaulet, forming a brilliant patch of scarlet, seems spread to half again its normal size against the glistening blue-black wings and back. The female meanwhile selects a spot within the male's territory for the site of the nest, fluttering back and forth among the weed stalks while the male perches overhead singing and displaying.

Most Icterids are at least partially colonial and the redwing is no exception, nesting in aggregations that range in size from a few pairs to several hundred. But despite its gregariousness it is still decidedly territorial once nesting begins, defending from its neighbors with great vigor the few cubic yards immediately surrounding its nest. Against intruders of other species, avian or mammal, its fury is unparalleled. Several pairs often join in concerted action to drive away an intruding predatory mammal or large bird; even humans are not exempt from their attacks. Though many species of birds will flutter and dive at a human intruder, the redwing is one of the very few that will actually strike and, it might be added, strike with considerable force and vigor.

A redwing colony is a noisy, active place. The birds have a variety of chattering and piping calls in addition to their song. The two most common of these are a thin, high whine followed by a staccato chatter and a low, throaty *chuck*. The first is usually evidence of excitement or alarm; it is the note heard when birds are attacking an intruder. The *chuck* note is a conversational note between individuals. It is heard the year round when the birds are flocking and is the typical flight call of the species.

In most cases a pair of redwings remains mated throughout the nesting season, though many observers have found evidence of polygamy, especially in the larger colonies where the number of nesting females often outnumbers the males. Polyandry is also not unknown. Despite the vigorous efforts of the male to defend his territory, the crowded conditions of a large colony often make it impossible for him to drive off every intruding male; several incidences have been observed of the same female mating with more than one male.

The cupshaped nest of the redwing is built entirely by the female in about six days. In marshes it is usually suspended between reed stalks about a foot above the water, though occasionally it may be placed flat on a tussock, in a shrub such as buttonbush, which grows out of the water or even on the ground in some dry spot. In upland locations, alfalfa, goldenrod, and other sturdy-stemmed plants are used, though there are numerous records of redwing nests in trees, sometimes as high as 30 ft. In coastal areas nests are often found in bayberry bushes. The nest is woven from long strands of reeds and grass, which are bound round and about the supporting stalks. The interstices are filled with moss and mud and the interior is lined with soft grass.

The eggs are bluish white, spotted and streaked brown and dark purple. The normal clutch is four eggs, but may vary from three to five. Incubation is entirely by the female and takes, on the average, 11 days. The young remain in the nest 10 or 11 days and are fed by both parents. Their diet consists entirely of insects, mostly mayflies and caterpillars and also such harmful forms as weevils, grasshoppers, and crickets. There are usually two, sometimes three, broods per year.

Besides insects, summer food of the adults includes a great variety and volume of weed seed, some grain, and an occasional small snail, newt, or salamander. Though most of the food is gathered in the vicinity of the nesting marsh, redwings do considerable foraging in surrounding uplands, sometimes traveling a mile or two to favorite feeding grounds. Almost all the food is gathered on the ground, though an occasional redwing will make an awkward attempt at aerial flycatching, usually with indifferent results. There are some records of redwings feeding in trees, usually when there is an outbreak of caterpillars or other insect larvae, though they have also been observed feeding on the seeds of ash, pine, and maple.

At the end of the breeding season in late summer, redwings begin to gather in large flocks that scour the countryside by day and rest in communal roosts by night.

In coastal areas of Louisiana and other rice-growing areas the redwing has proved itself to be something of a menace. Bent wrote:

In the Southern states, it does great damage to the rice crop by pulling up the seedling rice plants in the spring and by eating the soft grain as it ripens. In this respect the redwing is almost as bad as the bobolink. It does some good, however, by destroying the seeds of the so-called "volunteer" rice, which, if allowed to grow, would injure the value of the crop.

As cold weather approaches, flocks grow in size until in some places they number in the thousands. Often, equally large flocks of grackles, starlings (in the East) and Brewer's blackbirds (in the West) join the roving flocks of redwings.

At night all the foraging flocks from miles around converge on a communal roost in a grove of trees or extensive reed bed. In southern states the largest of these roosts can contain as many as 4 to 6 million redwings, perhaps as many grackles, plus tens of thousands of other companion species. To spend twilight in the vicinity of one of these roosts is an unforgettable experience.

Counting the number of birds in a great roost would seem a staggering feat, but bird watchers have worked out methods that enable them to make fairly accurate approximations. The usual method is to establish the average number of individuals flying past a given point in 1 second and multiply it by the total number of seconds of the flight. If the birds come in from several directions, a number of observers are used, each with a predesignated sector.

Determining the actual composition of the flocks, i.e., the percentage of each species represented, is somewhat more difficult. One group of observers has recently hit upon a plan utilizing the natural mortality incident to any huge aggregation of birds. They count the number of dead birds of each species found under the trees each morning. If redwings account for, say, 75 percent of the total dead birds, they are then considered to comprise 75 percent of the total birds in roost.

In northern states redwings are much less numerous in winter, though roosts of a few thousand birds are not unusual. During the day they usually frequent marshes and coastal areas, feeding mostly on weed seed. They visit feeding stations regularly and are especially fond of smaller seeds such as hemp, millet, and cracked corn. They also take suet and other high-fat content foods such as doughnut crumbs, peanuts, and cheese. Raisins and bits of apple are popular; in fact, just about any of the food normally set out at feeders is acceptable to the redwing. The striking colored males are a handsome sight about the yard, but anyone attempting to attract a large variety of species to his feeder might feel the redwing's presence a bit trying. They are aggressive creatures with prodigious appetites and often appear in large numbers, especially at feeders near a roost. Like many other large birds, however, a flock of redwings seldom remains around the feeder for the entire day, but rather includes it in the foraging itinerary, perhaps visiting it three or four times a day for an hour or two.

Description: Length, 9½ in. Male: glossy black with red, yellow-edged shoulders. Female: gray-brown above and paler below; sometimes an orange throat, entirely streaked, sooty. Tail, fairly long; bill, long and sharply pointed. Flies in shallow undulations; usually found in flocks.

Incubation, 11 days; Young stay 10 to 11 days in nest.

Size of eggs, 1.00 x 0.70 in.; two, sometimes three, broods per year.

ORCHARD ORIOLE (*Icterus spurius*)

The orchard oriole occupies much the same geographic range and habitat as the Baltimore oriole (p. 180), and in many localities is equally abundant. Yet it is not nearly so well known, for as often happens when two similar-appearing species occur together, casual observers know only the more conspicuous by name. The Baltimore is familiar to everyone; the orchard is passed over as an individual variant or is not differentiated at all.

This confusion is understandable, for at first glance the orchard oriole would seem to be merely a duller, less flamboyant version of the Baltimore oriole. The males of the two species have similar patterns, but the back and breast of the orchard are deep chestnut rather than bright orange; the tail is wholly black and there is less white in the wing.

Females are olive above and dull, greenish yellow below with white wing bars. The female Baltimore is larger, more robust, and with a decidedly orange cast to the plumage, especially below. Female scarlet and summer tanagers (p. 198), which somewhat resemble female orchard orioles, do not have wing bars. In addition, their bills are heavy and finchlike and quite unlike the slim curved bill of the oriole.

Young male orchard orioles resemble the female but have black throats. No similar appearing species occurs in eastern North America. Unlike other songbirds, which assume adult plumage a few months after hatching, the young male orchard oriole retains this first plumage for an entire year.

Despite the superficial resemblances, the orchard oriole is not merely the duller-colored alter ego of the Baltimore. To those who know it, it is a distinctive species in its own right, with habits and history fully as interesting as its better known relative.

The family Icteridae is much more diverse in tropical America than it is in the north. Only a handful of species, representing a random sampling of the family, have managed to penetrate to temperate areas, and then only after a considerable amount of evolutionary modification.

As a result, many of the Icterids of North America seem so different from one another that a casual observer would hardly consider placing them in the same family. The orchard oriole, for example, certainly does not seem to be a relative of the red-winged blackbird. But studies of the birdlife of the American tropics show that there are a whole group of species which in habits and appearance represent various intermediate stages between the two.

This does not mean that there is a clear-cut, step-by-step progression from redwing to orchard oriole. This differentiation has taken place over enormous periods of time. Many of the connecting links are gone—some perhaps abruptly, through extinction, most by the more subtle process of having themselves evolved into a form different from that which served as a connecting link. Nevertheless enough evidence remains to demonstrate that the orioles, through a chain of marsh-dwelling Icterids, are directly linked to the blackbirds.

There is some question concerning the sequence of this development. Some ornithologists conceive of the orioles as deriving in a single line from the marsh blackbirds, with the Baltimore types as the more differentiated and the orchard types at some intermediate stage. Others think that two separate but parallel genera of orioles arose from opposite ends of the blackbird group: genus Icterus, large birds like the Baltimore oriole, with heavy, powerful bills adapted for piercing and gaping-open fruit; and genus Bananivorus, smaller birds like the orchard oriole, with slender, curved bills adapted for probing among blossoms and feeding on nectar.

If the latter theory is correct, the orchard oriole is not closely related to the Baltimore. The similarity in appearance between the two would be a result of "convergence," the precept of evolutionary theory that dictates that species subject to the same environment often tend toward similar morphological (outer appearance) adaptation to that environment and come to resemble one another.

Whichever the case, though the two are similar in appearance, the Baltimore orioles and orchard orioles differ considerably in habits, the orchard retaining many more of the traits typical of its ancestors.

During the summer months the orchard oriole is found from southern New England, west to southern Manitoba, and south to northern Mexico, the Gulf coast, and northern Florida. It is somewhat uncommon in the northern portion of its range, but becomes more numerous from central New Jersey and the Ohio Valley southward. It is abundant in the Gulf states and lower Mississippi Valley where it far outnumbers the Baltimore as a breeding bird.

In the northern portion of its range, the orchard oriole is inflexible with regard to nesting requirements, probably because it may not be fully adapted to the generally harsher conditions that prevail there. Like the Baltimore, it inhabits fairly open areas, frequenting farmlands, villages, and roadsides, and avoiding extensive stands of forest. In general, it prefers shorter, more bushy trees; the commonest nesting site is a hardwood 10 to 40 ft. high. The height and spacing of trees in a typical orchard apparently comes close to its optimum requirements, for as its name implies, orchards are one of its favorite nesting places. Other acceptable sites are second-growth trees springing up in abandoned fields, short ornamental or shade trees, and streamside thickets of willows, alders, and similar growth.

In the south, where it is more numerous and better adapted to its environment, the orchard oriole shows more latitude in its choice of nesting places. Short hardwood trees continue to be a favorite choice, but it will also nest among the lower branches of much taller trees or in conifers. In the marshlands of the Gulf coast, orchard orioles even nest among the reeds, suspending their nests between reed stalks in the manner of red-winged blackbirds.

Another blackbirdlike trait of the orchard oriole is its tendency toward colonial nesting. Even in places where extensive tracts of suitable habitat would allow them all the territory they wished, nesting pairs are often concentrated in a single small area. Where the species is especially abundant, it is not unusual to find several nests in the same tree.

In fact, the orchard oriole shows even less territorial instinct than the redwing. Not only does it nest in close proximity with its own kind, it is also quite tolerant of other species, often sharing the same nesting tree with them. Bent comments: "The Orchard Oriole is a friendly, sociable bird and is often found nesting in orchards with kingbirds, robins, chipping sparrows and other species, with all of which it seems to be on good terms. The eastern kingbird seems to be a favorite companion, from which it may gain some protection."

The orchard oriole winters entirely south of the United States, from central Mexico to northwestern South America. The northward flight in spring apparently follows two routes: one through the mainland of Mexico to southern Texas, the other from Yucatan straight across the Gulf of Mexico to Louisiana. There is also evidence of a light movement through the West Indies; these may be birds that avoid the mainland altogether, following instead the chain of islands from Venezuela to the Florida Keys. The first returning residents reach northern Florida by late March, Texas and the Gulf coast by mid-April, and the northern states by early May.

Courtship begins immediately. The males display in the typical Icterid manner, bowing before the female and singing vigorously from a conspicuous perch or while fluttering in the air. The song is a rapid, rolling outburst of caroled notes, quite variable, but usually ending in a distinctive downslurring note. The total effect is much closer to the bobolink than to the Baltimore oriole.

Commenting on this song, Bent wrote:

The orchard oriole sings from the time of its arrival to the earliest part of July. . . . The vivacious attractive song has been compared to the rollicking outburst of the bobolink, the rich spring song of the fox sparrow, and the warbling songs of the purple finch or the warbling vireo. It is not as loud, or as rich as that of the Baltimore oriole and is quite unlike it, but it is equally pleasing.

Young males, still in their green, black-throated plumage, but otherwise fully adult, also sing vigorously and show every other indication that they are actively seeking mates. Occasionally they succeed, and over the years there have been many records of birds in this plumage nesting successfully. Usually, however, they remain unmated during their first spring, probably because the older full-plumaged males are better able to attract the available females of the vicinity.

In appearance and method of construction, the nest of the orchard oriole is intermediate between the deep cup of the redwing and the pendulant sack of the Baltimore oriole. Carefully weaving together long strands of weed stalks, fibers, and dried grass, the female constructs a large, rounded structure with a constricted rim; when completed it resembles a somewhat mishapen goldfish bowl or a squat, neckless vase. Though unsupported below, it does not swing free, but is securely saddled in a fork or between stout reed stalks.

The eggs are bluish white, heavily blotched on the larger end with brown, purple, and lavender. The average clutch is four to six eggs. Incubation takes about 12 days and is usually done entirely by the female. Though there is some indication that the male occasionally shares this task, his usual duty is to gather food for the female, who during the time of incubation remains almost constantly on the nest. The young remain in the nest 12 to 15 days after hatching and are fed by both parents. There is only one brood a year.

The orchard oriole is almost entirely insectivorous; over 90 percent of its food consists of caterpillars, weevils, grasshoppers, mayflies and similar insects gleaned from the leaves and blossoms of trees and shrubbery. Cherries, grapes, peas, and other valuable crops attractive to the Baltimore oriole are almost never touched by the orchard oriole; the only fruit that seems to attract them are mulberries. These, and the nectar, stamen, and petals of flowers make up the small amount of vegetable food taken.

The orchard oriole, or the form from which it is derived, probably moved into temperate North America only in comparatively recent times, spreading north to occupy territory not yet inhabited by closely related and therefore ecologically competitive species, but unable because of the severity of the climate to remain there permanently.

This may in part account for the development of the migratory habit not only in the orchard oriole but also in other species of tropical origin, which take the opportunity afforded by the brief northern summer to raise their young in relatively uncrowded circumstances.

Whatever the case, the orchard oriole remains in the north only as long as it takes to raise its brood. The southward movement begins immediately after the end of the nesting cycle in mid-July. By late July, orchard orioles have disappeared almost entirely from the northern states, though in the south they linger in some numbers through August. There are a scattering of records from September and October, but these represent only lingering individuals. The average time spent on the breeding grounds is only about ten weeks.

There are no winter records of the orchard oriole north of the Rio Grande, though it is quite possible that occasionally an individual may linger into the winter season. There is no information available on just what foods would attract them, though studies of their diet in zoological gardens indicate that the food usually set out at a feeding station would be of little use to an orchard oriole. They eat no grain or seed, and very little fruit, subsisting almost entirely on meal worms and scraps of meat.

Description: Length, 7 in. Long, thin, sharply pointed, slightly curved bill. Adult male: unmistakable; chestnut and black. Adult and immature female: greenish above, greenish yellow below (see Baltimore, below). Immature male: same as female, but black throat. No similar bird occurs in east. Occurs in pairs or small colonies; usually gone from the United States by mid-August.

Incubation, 12 to 14 days; young stay 12 to 14 days in nest.

Size of eggs, 0.82 x 0.57 in.; one brood per year.

BALTIMORE ORIOLE (*Icterus galbula*)

Most of the common species of eastern North American birds had well-established names long before ornithologists began the task of placing each species in its proper place in a scientific classification.

The first English-speaking colonists simply chose names they thought fitting, often repeating names applied to Old World species of similar appearance or habits. Sometimes they happened to be correct and placed a bird in its proper grouping. But often, especially in the case of species from families unknown in the Old World, they were not. Nevertheless, these erroneous names, once established, remained in use and are current today.

female

male

BULLOCK'S ORIOLE

Our orioles, for instance, are not orioles at all, but members of the family Icteridae that just happen to resemble the true orioles of the Old World. And "Baltimore," incidentally, is not a geographic designation but was bestowed in honor of Lord Baltimore, founder of the Catholic settlements in Maryland. Orange and black, the colors of the Baltimore oriole, were Lord Baltimore's personal colors.

All this fine disregard of phylogenetic dogma has occasionally proved to be disturbing to tidy-minded perfectionists who feel perhaps *Icterus galbula* should better be named Lord Baltimore's pseudo-oriole or even Lord Baltimore's *Xanthosparine Icterid*. But Baltimore oriole it will undoubtedly remain, a trace of nostalgia combined with a bit of history which is unscientific but colorful.

A glance at the Plate IX is sufficient to learn the pattern of the distinctive male Baltimore oriole. In the east, he might possibly be confused with the male orchard oriole, but that species is smaller, with deep chestnut back and breast and an all-black tail. The Baltimore is bright orange on back and breast and has a two-toned black and orange tail. Along the western edge of its range the Baltimore sometimes occurs together with the very similar Bullock's oriole. Males of the two species are best distinguished by the pattern of the head. The Baltimore has an all-black head; Bullock's has orange cheeks crossed by a dark line.

The female Baltimore is much more plainly colored than the male; mostly dull olive above with dull orange-yellow throat and breast and two white wing bars. The female orchard oriole is a smaller, decidedly greener bird with mostly yellow and gray underparts and no trace of orange in the plumage. The female Bullock's is much more difficult to distinguish. Though generally grayer than the female Baltimore and with more decidedly whitish lower underparts, there is a great deal of individual variation in the plumage of both species, and the two cannot always be told apart with certainty.

The Baltimore oriole is one of the many species that have benefited from the presence of man in North America. It prefers locations in which tall trees, either singly or in small groves, are separated by intervals of open terrain, for the tree in which the nest is located must have a stretch of open land or water on at least one side. Neither the heavily forested east nor the prairies of the central portion of the continent offered much habitat of this type, and in pre-Columbian times the oriole was undoubtedly less common or at least of more local occurrence than it is today. Only along watercourses could any great extent of suitable habitat be found, and it was probably only in such locations that the oriole occurred in numbers.

But the advent of man changed this situation considerably. Tall trees left standing in pastures as shade for livestock, miles of tree-lined

city streets and country roads, the windbreaks planted across the prairies, all helped produce new tracts of suitable habitat.

The present summer range of the Baltimore oriole is from Nova
Scotia west to central Alberta and south to northern Georgia, central
Louisiana, and southeastern Texas. Its normal wintering grounds are
entirely south of the United States, from southern Mexico to northern
South America.

The first spring migrants return to the southern States in the last
days of April and usually reach the northern limit of their range in
southern Canada by the end of the first week of May. The male birds
return first, take possession of a nesting tree, and await the arrival of
the females, due a few days later.

The chosen tree is usually a hardwood, though there are a few records
of orioles nesting in conifers. Through the northern states the graceful
spraying branches of the American elm offer perfect sites for a hanging
nest, and this tree is decidedly the favorite of the oriole. Other choices
include poplars, birches, apple trees, and less frequently oaks. Cottonwoods in the west and pecans in the south are also favorite sites.

The male defends his chosen tree from later-arriving males by warning them away with his vigorous singing; an emphatic series of six
or seven loud, liquid piping whistles that seems to vary with each individual bird. Bent, in his *Life Histories of North American Birds*,
commented:

> Another feature of the song which attracts our interest is its infinite
> variety: no two orioles, we say, sing the same tune, but each bird, in the
> main, sticks to its own theme. It is one of the songs which, if you note it
> down, you must punctuate at the end with a period; the bird has said his
> say and stops; he has finished, for the moment, anyway.

Another note heard frequently at this season is a loud harsh chatter.
It is given by both sexes and is used chiefly as an alarm note, though
the male frequently intersperses it between the notes of his song.

With the arrival of the females, the singing of the males intensifies
and courtship begins. All Icterids display in essentially the same manner, and the resplendent oriole is no exception; he courts his mate in
very much the same way as his homely relatives the cowbird and grackle.
While the female looks on quietly, he droops his wings and tail, then

slowly fans them open while simultaneously bowing his head toward her and whistling a special courting call. Occasionally there are short aerial displays in which the male sings while fluttering in the air. Within a few days the pairing bond is formed and nesting begins.

Surveying the tree staked out by the male, the female oriole chooses the site for the nest. In pre-Colonial times the commonest location of a nest was apparently from a branch overhanging a stream. Suspended from the very tip of the branch, high over water, the nestlings were relatively safe from predation. Behavior patterns built up over long periods of evolution are not quickly abandoned even when they seem no longer of any particular benefit, for the oriole still persists in hanging its nest over a cleared spot. Nests in roadside trees, for example, are almost invariably located in a branch overhanging the road. This settled, she now begins building the famous hanging nest that is the hallmark of the Baltimore oriole.

Selecting a horizontal fork at the very tip of a high branch, she begins by winding a few long strands around one of the twigs. From this anchorage she suspends a blanket-like shaggy mass that will eventually form one side of the completed nest. The materials used are strips of weed stalk and inner bark. She is also quick to utilize bits of string and floss and can often be attracted to one's lawn if quantities of these materials are set out for her.

When the mass of material is the proper length, the oriole forms the outline of the rest of the nest with a few long strands strung to the opposite prong of the fork. Now working mostly from what will be the inside of the nest, she begins adding more and more strands, and at the same time binding and tucking the material already present. Working more and more rapidly, her bill often moving faster than the eye can follow, she weaves the amazingly tight even fabric that forms the shell of the nest. While there is apparently no conscious effort to tie knots or to work consistently with one strand until it is completely woven in, the hundreds of random tugging and tucking motions nevertheless produce knots and eventually weave in all the loose ends.

The outer shell is now complete, but two steps remain. First, the bottom of the pocket is filled with a pad of plant down or hair as a protective cushion for the young birds. Finally, working from inside the nest, the female, with much energetic bouncing, uses the round of her breast to mold the shell into its final shape.

The result of all this labor, which takes five or six days to complete, is a free-hanging, gourdshaped structure about 5 in. long, with a wide cushioned bottom to protect the nestlings, and a narrowly tapering neck to prevent their being thrown out when the nest is tossed about by summer storms.

It is not surprising that this intricately woven, skillfully engineered structure should excite the admiration of all who have seen it, or better, watched it being built. Too often, however, in popular literature this admiration gives rise to a tendency to extrapolate from the observed phenomenon signs of superior intelligence and parental solicitude or similar concepts. Yet the sole function of a nest is, after all, to serve as a shelter for the young birds until they are ready to shift for themselves. Does the oriole's nest really accomplish this end better than, say, the helter-skelter platform of sticks of the mourning dove? Are a greater percentage of young orioles raised successfully than are young doves? Probably not. Involved or specialized patterns of behavior are not in themselves signs of higher development, nor do they necessarily assure the species an advantage over others. They simply indicate that the species is, or was at some time in its evolutionary history, hard-pressed enough by its environment to force it to such extremes in order to safeguard its survival. An elaborate nest is, or was, necessary for the oriole; it is not for the dove.

The eggs of the Baltimore oriole are grayish white, irregularly blotched, and speckled brown, black, or lavender. The normal clutch is four to six and hatches in 12 to 14 days. There is only one brood a year.

The young remain in the nest about two weeks. They are much quieter than is usual for nestlings, at least up until a day or two before they are ready to fly; then they make up for lost time. Commenting on this sudden outburst of noisiness, Bent wrote:

On a certain day, over a whole township we hear it, over and over all day long, . . . a monotonous series of five or six notes, falling in pitch a little, with a ringing or resonant quality. It is a pathetic little childish cry or complaint, beseeching, yet insistent, halfway between entreaty and demand, *dee-dee-dee-dee*. The pitch is about F sharp, on the top line of the musical staff. This note has given the fledgling oriole the epithet "cry baby."

The young orioles are fed almost exclusively on animal matter; this is also the main food of the adults at this season. Caterpillars of various sorts constitute over one-third of the diet, including such notorious pests as tent and elm caterpillars and the larvae of the gypsy moth. Other insect food includes leafbeetles, plant lice, grasshoppers, weevils, and wood borers.

For the first few days after they hatch, the young orioles are fed by regurgitation; the adult birds crushing and partially digesting the food before passing it to them. As the young birds grow stronger this step is eliminated and they receive soft-bodied insects whole. When tougher prey is offered them, the adult oriole usually first removes hard or brittle parts such as wings or legs. Both sexes participate in feeding the young, sharing the job about equally.

For a few days after they leave the nest, the young birds still rely mostly on the adults for food, though they begin almost immediately to do some foraging on their own, and it is not long before they are completely self-reliant.

Immediately after the duties of the nesting season are over, the adult male leaves the family group, and for the rest of the summer wanders independently. Though a number of males may occasionally be found together in some spot where an abundance of food is temporarily available, they show no inclination to form a flock but continue to come and go individually. The females and young of the immediate neighborhood, on the other hand, collect into loose aggregations, which remain more or less intact until the fall migration.

During the nesting season, when they feed heavily on insects, orioles forage mostly among the leaves of tall trees. In late summer, while insects continue to be an important food source, there is a noticeable increase in the amount of vegetable matter consumed and a consequent widening of their scope of foraging activity. Orioles are especially fond of soft pulpy fruits and berries, and any sort of vegetation offering this food, even low bushes and vines, will attract them.

Orioles also visit orchards and vineyards and are quite fond of green peas. But the slight amount of crop damage done is insignificant compared with the enormous number of insects destroyed.

Later in the season orioles are willing to come quite close to the ground in order to feed on the ripening seeds of sunflowers, hollyhocks, and similar tall flowers.

In early September the small bands of females and young coalesce into more definite flocks, are rejoined by the adult males, and the fall migration begins. Flocks of southbound orioles giving their musical *heeep* flight call are found everywhere, from inland woods to the tangled growth of the outer beaches. By early October the majority of the population has reached its tropical wintering grounds, even though scattered individuals may still be present as far north as southern Canada.

During its winter visit to the tropics, the Baltimore oriole behaves in essentially the same manner it did during late summer in the north. Individually or in small, loose flocks, orioles are found in all the varied habitats of the tropics from desert scrub to lush mountain forest.

Because the Baltimore oriole is not normally found in the north during the winter, it is not usually figured among the species expected at a feeding station. On the other hand, most of the few winter records are from feeders, for when an individual does winter in the north, it will invariably seek out a feeder if one is available. There they have some chance of survival, for apparently severe weather in itself is not lethal to the oriole. Rather it seems that scarcity of food and the short amount of daylight available in which to seek it are the factors limiting its ability to winter in the north. When these factors are mitigated by the artificial concentration of food available at a feeder, orioles seem able to withstand the cold of an average northern winter.

Should an oriole appear at your feeder, remember that such a special visitor deserves a special diet. While it may seem content to peck at the seeds set out for more hardy species, it will require more suitable food for survival. Raw ground beef is one of the best. Grapes have often proved successful and are usually obtainable in winter. Slices of oranges or apples may be tried also, or berries of whatever sort can be obtained. The idea is to try to duplicate the balance of animal and vegetable food that constitutes the bird's normal diet. With such feeding, if the bird is in reasonably good health at the time it finds the feeder, provided there is no prolonged stretch of especially severe weather, it is very likely to live through to spring.

Description: Length, 7½ in. Long, stout, sharply pointed bill. Male: only orange North American oriole with combination of all-black head and two-toned tail. Bullock's oriole (western United States) has orange cheeks; Scott's oriole (southwestern United States), similar, but yellow. Female: in East, distinguished from female orchard by larger size, stouter bill, general orange tone; in West, east of Rockies, distinguished from female Bullock's by more olive (less gray) back, orange-yellow underparts. Females of various southwestern species resemble female orchard orioles.

Incubation, 13 to 14 days; young stay 13 to 14 days in nest.

Size of eggs, 0.92 x 0.61 in.; one brood per year.

COMMON GRACKLE (*Quiscalis quiscula*)

There are two general ways in which animals adjust to their environments. Some become more and more specialized, utilizing a single, very narrowly restricted niche. Others "generalize," inhabiting a variety of habitats, feeding on a variety of foods, doing well at some times in some places, and poorly in other circumstances.

Highly specialized forms, though they have the advantage of facing very little competition, require absolute stability of environment; the slightest change in their surroundings may, directly or through a chain of reactions, deprive them of their niche and leave them helpless.

It is not surprising, therefore, that it has been the generalized species that have held their own and even flourished under the rapid, often violent, changes wrought in the North American continent during the past 300 years, while the species that have dwindled are for the most part those that were too specialized.

Among the more resilient species that have survived the impact of human civilization is the common grackle and its sub-species *Q.q. stonei* (purple) and *Q.q. versicolor* (bronzed). The grackle is a large, long-tailed, long-billed, glossy-black bird, showing in good light iridescent purple, green, bronze, and blue reflections. The long tail has a longitudinal crease or "keel," a distinctive mark at any distance. The common grackle might be confused with the boat-tailed or great-tailed grackles of the south and west, but both those species are much larger, show less iridescent reflections, and have proportionately much longer tails. The Brewer's and rusty blackbirds are decidedly smaller than the common grackle and have proportionately shorter, unkeeled tails.

The grackle is found throughout eastern and central North America from southern Mackenzie and Newfoundland to southeastern Texas

BREWER'S BLACKBIRD

male

female

and southern Florida. It is partially migratory, withdrawing from the northern portion of its range in October and November and returning early in March.

Unlike more favored species such as the bluebird and the swallows, the grackle has survived the advance of civilization without the helping hand of man. Like other widespread birds it takes its food where it can find it and is large and powerful enough to take a great deal. To some extent the enmity of man toward the grackle is justified.

Though it is at home in a variety of habitats, the grackle has not completely broken its ties with the marshes that were the ancestral home of its family, the Icteridae. Its predilection for wet and swampy places is especially noticeable in early spring, when the first returning migrants, finding other forms of food scarce, resort to swamps and marshes or exposed mud flats along lakes and streams, where they search for snails, water insects, and any edible material that may have been exposed by the melting ice. As the weather warms, and insect and plant life becomes more evident, the grackle spreads out into the uplands.

It is at this season that the grackle does much to offset any crop damage it may have committed the previous autumn. Along with black-birds, meadowlarks, and certain species of gulls, it is likely to be found in recently plowed fields, searching through the freshly turned earth for grubs, cutworms, and other insects. When the first green shoots appear, the grackles are still to be seen probing among the growth and are frequently accused of pulling up young plants. Careful studies have shown, however, that they are actually feeding on cutworms that attack the roots of new plants.

By mid-April the courtship of the grackle is well under way. The spring song of the male is a squeaky, shrill wheeze with rising inflection. It is usually delivered from a perch in a low tree, but sometimes is given from the ground. Like its relatives the redwing and the cowbird, the grackle accompanies its vocal effort with a visual display, fanning wings and tail and erecting the rufflike feathers of the neck and upper back while drooping the head. In this position the iridescent feathers glisten brightly in the sunlight, though on dull days they do not show to full advantage because the gloss is not due to pigmentation, but is the result of refraction of light from the scalelike surface of the feathers.

Grackles are somewhat colonial in their nesting habits, several pairs usually nesting in close proximity. Pines and other evergreens are a favorite choice, but the grackle frequents a variety of sites, including orchards and tangles of vines suspended from tall trees. Occasionally the nest is hung between stalks of marsh grass like the nest of the red-wing. They have also been known to nest in natural cavities in trees and under the eaves of barns. The most striking location chosen by grackles, however, is among the cracks and crevices of the osprey's nest. These huge structures, built upon year after year, often reach a height of several feet, affording nooks and crannies enough for several pairs of grackles. The osprey, or fish hawk, feeds exclusively on fish and is no threat to the grackle.

The nest of the grackle is a large well-made structure of twigs and coarse grass or seaweed, sometimes cemented with mud. It is lined with softer grass.

The eggs are greenish white or pale brown, blotched and streaked dark brown, four to six in a clutch. Bent states that among the grackles of the eastern and southern states, both parents incubate the eggs in turn, but in his account of the bird nesting west of the Alleghenies, formerly known as the bronzed grackle, he states that only the female incubates. These eastern and western birds are the same species; *i.e.*, they will freely interbreed in areas where nesting ranges overlap, but are sufficiently distinct in minor taxonomic characteristics to be considered different subspecies. Perhaps this behavioral variation is also a subspecific character. In either case, the young remain in the nest about 14 days after hatching and are fed by both parents on a diet consisting exclusively of insects.

The grackle is not confined to rural areas; it has become quite acclimated to suburban areas and city parks, nesting in ornamental evergreens and deciduous shade trees. In company with robins and starlings, grackles are a familiar sight on suburban lawns, where they feed extensively on grubs of the Japanese beetle. The grackle, in fact, eats more of these pests than does any other species.

To be successful in a rapidly changing environment, a bird must be endowed with the proper physical equipment. The long, powerful bill of the grackle is not only useful for probing for grubs, but—true to the generalized development of the species—is also a fine, all-purpose tool admirably suited for a variety of uses, and undoubtedly is the key to the grackle's rapid adaptation. Very large forms of life easily fall prey to this powerful bird. Though insects are its principal early summer food, minnows, salamanders, snails, and even an occasional mouse form a regular part of its diet. Grackles have been known to catch small goldfish from ornamental ponds and crayfish and tadpoles from creeks and brooks. Aquatic food is taken either by wading and spearing like a heron or by plunging into the water like a kingfisher. Nestlings and eggs of other species are also taken, but apparently to no great extent.

By July and August, grackles descend on the grain fields; corn and wheat are their favorite grains. These raids continue until harvesting, at which time the grackle turns again to a diet of weed seeds, waste grain, and animal matter. During the fall they feed extensively on acorns, beechnuts, and chestnuts. Grackles do not, incidentally, need to hammer open the shells as jays do; they can easily crack them open by the pressure of their powerful bills.

As the season advances, grackles begin drifting southward to their wintering grounds in the southern states. Here they spend the winter gleaning fields for waste grain and weed seed, and flocking in great numbers in barnyards and stables to steal the fodder set out for domestic animals. At night they resort to communal roosts of many thousands of birds, usually in company with redwings (see p. 171).

A few grackles remain in northern states during the winter, mostly in coastal areas, and can be expected at feeders in these localities anytime during the winter. Their inland visits to feeders are mostly in late fall and early spring. Suet is a special favorite, but like the redwing, grackles will eat almost anything offered.

Description: Length, 12 in. Long and pointed bill; very long tail, often creased longitudinally. Males are glossed purple, green blue, and bronze. Young birds just out of the nest are rusty brown, but resemble adults by autumn. Flight even and direct, not slightly undulating as with redwing or cowbird.

Incubation, 14 days; young stay 14 days in nest.

Size of eggs, 1.14 x 0.82 in.; usually one brood per year.

BROWN-HEADED COWBIRD (*Molothrus ater*)

Strictly speaking, a parasite is an organism that lives and feeds upon another living organism without immediately destroying it. The cowbird, because it lays its eggs in the nests of other birds, is considered parasitic.

Slipping stealthily through the foliage, the female cowbird locates the nest of some small songbird, a chipping sparrow's perhaps, and waiting for a time when the sparrow is absent, deposits her egg in the sparrow's nest. She then flys off to rejoin her mate, leaving the task of hatching and rearing the young cowbird to its foster parents. Because it is larger than its nestmates and grows at a faster rate, the young cowbird usually destroys them, either by forcing them from the nest or by monopolizing the food.

The female cowbird is entirely dull gray, a coloration well adapted to her need to remain inconspicuous. The black-plumaged male is slightly more colorful; he has a brown head and shows bottle-green reflections on the back and wings in strong sunlight. Either sex is distinguished from similar blackbirds by the thick, finchlike bill.

Early settlers knew the cowbird as the "buffalo bird." Its original home was the prairies and high grasslands of central and western North America, where it attended the great herds of American bison, riding their backs to pick ticks (parasite preying on parasite), and feeding on insects stirred from the grass by the movement of the herd. With the clearing of most of the eastern North American forest for farmland and the irrigation of vast stretches of western desert, the cowbird greatly extended its range. At the same time it acquired a new name, since it now attended the herds of domestic cattle, which had replaced the vanished bison. Today the cowbird is found throughout most of the United States, southern Canada, and northern Mexico. It occurs most frequently around farms and pastures and in open woodlands, avoiding stands of heavy forest and desert areas.

The cowbirds are partially migratory, withdrawing from the northern part of their range in October and November and returning in March and April. The normal winter range is from Maryland, the Ohio Valley, and central California southward, but small flocks regularly winter farther north, especially in areas with abundant food supply.

Like most of its family, the cowbird is a gregarious species, and except for a short period during the breeding season, ranges the countryside in flocks varying from fewer than a dozen to several hundred. They feed almost entirely on the ground, strutting about, with head held high, in a ridiculous waddle. The roving flocks consume an enormous quantity of noxious insects and weed seeds and, if it were not for its parasitic habits, the cowbird would be considered an unqualified economic asset to man. More than 50 percent of its diet consists of weed seeds, and another 20 percent of insects such as grasshoppers, locusts, and beetles. Waste grain is also an important food item; fruit is practically never touched.

Early ornithologists thought the cowbird to be entirely promiscuous in its sexual relations. Later investigations, however, have proved it to be monogamous. In late March the male cowbird establishes a territory, where, perched on a conspicuous limb or fence post, he fans wings and tail wide, raises the rufflike feathers on neck and throat, rises to full height, and with a spasm of effort emits the wheezy squeak that female cowbirds find irresistible. Soon after, the pairing bond is formed, lasting for the length of the breeding season, as with most passerine birds.

Friedmann lists over 150 species in whose nests cowbird eggs have been found, including such unlikely species as the ferruginous hawk and California gull. The choice of such hosts is very rare and, of course, unsuccessful. But even when the mother cowbird chooses a more likely victim, the life of the young cowbird is by no means assured. If the female cowbird lays its eggs in an empty nest, the host will often desert the nest, or in some species, such as the yellow warbler, cover the cowbird egg with a new floor. Some four- or five-storied yellow warbler nests have been found, each floor covering the egg of a cowbird. This may happen even if the warbler has one or two eggs of its own. But most species, the yellow warbler included, will accept the cowbird egg if it appears after they have a full clutch of their own. Robins and catbirds, however, seem able to discriminate between their own blue eggs and the white, brown-splotched eggs of the cowbird, and will immediately throw out the foreign egg.

The female cowbird lays from four to six eggs in as many days, each usually in a different nest. A scarcity of nests within her territory may force her to frequent the same nest twice, however, and two or even three young cowbirds are sometimes found in the same nest. In some cases this may be due to visits by two different cowbirds, though normally the female cowbird stays within her own territory.

Cowbird eggs hatch more quickly than those of other species. Consequently the young cowbird often smothers or otherwise destroys the eggs of the host. Even if the fledglings of the host should hatch, they seldom survive. They are crushed, thrown from the nest, or deprived of their food by the larger, more powerful young cowbird. Receiving the entire benefit of food supply, normally consumed by three or four nestlings, the cowbird develops rapidly. It soon dwarfs its foster parents, but remains dependent on them even for two or three weeks after leaving the nest, following them about and constantly begging for food.

During the winter months, when insect food is scarce, the cowbird subsists almost entirely on seeds, especially at the northern limit of its winter range. A roving flock discovering a feeding station will often settle down to spend the winter, this time at the expense of a human host. Cowbirds are quiet, well-mannered birds around the feeder. Their usual calls are a soft, throaty *chuck* and a plaintive, high-pitched *peeeee*. They seldom exhibit aggressiveness, feeding amicably with smaller juncos and sparrows. On the other hand, a small flock can consume an enormous amount of food while offering little esthetic pleasure in return, either in appearance or voice. They are fond of the seeds of hemp, millet, and sunflower, but are quite willing to accept almost anything offered.

Description: Length, 8 in. Thick and conical bill; broad and rounded wings. "Bounces" slightly in flight; on ground, walks with head up, feeds with tail up. Male: black, glossed green, head brown. Female: plain dull gray. Immature male: blotched and patched gray, and glossy bluish black.

Incubation, 10 days; young stay ten days in nest.

Size of eggs, 0.86 x 0.65 in.; one brood per year.

TANAGERS / *Thraupidae*

WESTERN TANAGER (*Piranga ludoviciana*)

This species was originally named the Louisiana tanager because it was first discovered by the Lewis and Clark expedition of 1804 in the Louisiana Purchase, which embraced much of our present West. The bird breeds in summer all over the open pine and fir forests of the Canadian and Transition life-zones of the West, from British Columbia to Mexico and from the Black Hills to the Pacific. It nests as low as 1,500 ft. in the state of Washington, up to 10,000 ft. in Utah and New Mexico, and in the Sierra Nevadas from 3,000 ft. to the summits.

After the breeding season the birds wander. Sometimes they are seen above timber line, but more often come down into the oak-zone and scatter out among streamside willows and cottonwoods. In migration they are widely distributed in the lowlands. They winter in Central America.

The habitat of the western tanager is the leafy canopy of the pine forest, but it is also found in deciduous and mixed woods and along the edges of woods. On its arrival in its breeding grounds in spring, the males often sing at daybreak from the tops of the tallest conifers. In British Columbia these may reach a height of 300 ft. In the pine

forests of the Sierra Nevada its songs and notes are among the most
common bird sounds, but except for a distant flash of gold on green,
the birds themselves are seldom seen. They spend the day foraging
through the upper foliage with the usual tanager deliberation. The
flight of the western tanager is straight, its wingbeats rapid. It catches
insects on the wing, like a flycatcher, and from a roadside fence in
migration will dart down to pick insects from the ground.

Each species of migratory bird has a different migration route and
a different winter range. Frederick C. Lincoln, an authority on this subject, explains the unusual spring migration of the western tanager:

On the spring migration the birds enter the United States about April 20,
appearing first in western Texas and the southern parts of New Mexico and
Arizona. By April 30, the van has advanced evenly to an approximately
east-and-west line across central New Mexico, Arizona, and southern California. But by May 10, the easternmost birds have advanced only to southern
Colorado, while those in the Far West have reached northern Washington.
Ten days later the northern front of the species is a great curve, extending
northeastward from Vancouver Island to Central Alberta, and thence south-
eastward to northern Colorado. Since these tanagers do not reach northern
Colorado until May 20, it is evident that those present in Alberta on that
date, instead of having traveled northward through the Rocky Mountains,
which from the location of their summer and winter homes would seem to
be the natural route, have reached that province by a route through the
interior of California, Oregon and Washington to southern British Columbia and thence across the mountains, despite the fact that these are
still partly covered with snow at that time.

Although the eastern seaboard is far outside the normal breeding
range or migration route of this species, a few of the birds turn up
there almost every winter. Hardly a year goes by without a report of
a western tanager at a Christmas census or at a feeder in the East.

Little has been recorded on the courtship of this species, if indeed
it has any. A possible courtship rite was reported once from the Grand
Canyon when a male was seen offering food to a female who seemed
to be his intended mate. Further studies are needed, however, to discover whether this is a regular performance.

The rather frail, 5 in. wide, saucer-shaped nest of the western tanager
is made primarily of grasses, bark shreds, and twigs, though sometimes

pine needles, rootlets, and mosses are also used. It is lined with fine rootlets and hair. The structure is usually saddled on a horizontal branch of pine, spruce, or fir, 3 to 25 ft. from the trunk and 5 to 30 ft. from the ground. Sometimes, however, it may be higher, or it may be placed in an oak, sycamore, or aspen.

The three or four pale greenish blue eggs are spotted with brown, principally at the larger end. The female is a close sitter. When egg collecting was legal, collectors sometimes had to lift the bird off the nest by hand in order to secure her clutch. Only the female incubates; the male helps feed the young.

The song of the western tanager is similar to that of the robin (p. 136), but it also suggests the song of the scarlet tanager, though it is less hoarse.

Ralph Hoffmann, in his *Birds of the Pacific States,* gives a good description of its voice:

A tanager is always deliberate and often sits for a long period on one perch singing short phrases at longish intervals. The song sounds much like a robin's; it is made up of short phrases with rising and falling inflections *pir-ri pir-ri pee-wi pr-ri pee-wi.* It is hoarser than a robin's, lower in pitch and rarely continued for more than four or five phrases; it lacks the joyous ringing quality of the robin's. The tanager's call note is one of the most characteristic sounds of the mountains of California and the evergreen forests in the lowlands of Oregon and Washington. It may be written *prit-it* or *pri-titick,* followed often by a lower *chert-it.*

Dawson in California, however, and Aretas A. Saunders, the birdsong expert in Montana, both thought the song of this species closely resembled that of the scarlet tanager.

Its call is a *pit-ik, pit-ik,* or *pit-itik,* sometimes written as *pitter piterick.* It has a *cheep-churr* note something like the *KIP-purr* of the scarlet tanager; and when going about with their young, the parents utter a plaintive *tu-wheep.*

The natural food of the western tanager is insects, fruit, and berries. It gleans the insects all summer long from the leaves overhead. In migration, however, it has at times made substantial inroads on cherry orchards. On occasion it feeds on tent caterpillars and the buds of greasewood and hawthorn. A study of 46 stomachs by California's

Department of Agriculture biologists showed that from April to September insects made up 82 percent of the diet; fruit, about 18 percent. Most of the insects were wasps and ants. Its picnic table fare is more varied; there are few scraps it will not sample.

Description: Length, 7 in. Bill heavy, blunt; tail notched. Male: yellow with a red head and black back, some black also on wings and tail; two pale-yellow wing bars (or one white and one yellow); yellow rump; face in fall, largely yellow. Female and young: olive upperparts; yellow underparts; two pale-yellow or white wing bars. Female orioles have sharp-pointed bills and lighter cheeks.

Incubation, 13 days; young stay 13 to 15 days in nest.

Size of eggs, 0.95 x 0.65 in.; one brood per year.

SUMMER TANAGER (*Piranga rubra*)

The male summer tanager is our only all-red bird. It has no crest, as has the cardinal; its color is a rose-red, not a cardinal red. The female is olive-green above, brownish orange below. The species is found in summer throughout the lowlands and foothills of the southern United States from coast to coast. It breeds northward almost to the Mason and Dixon Line in the East and to the latitude of northern Arizona in the West. A few occasionally wander farther north after nesting. It winters from central Mexico to Bolivia, and a substantial portion of the total population migrates twice yearly across the Gulf of Mexico.

The favored habitats of this bird are dry, open, pine groves, mixed woodlands and hardwood groves, especially oak and hickory. It particularly likes pine woods with an understory of oaks. It is also fond of shade trees, mulberry orchards, and clumps of trees in villages and towns. In the West it is found in streamside willows and cottonwoods.

Like other tanagers this species is sluggish in its movements and somewhat solitary in habits. It forages for insects among foliage, feeding at various levels and not only in the canopy, as do the scarlet and western tanagers. It also catches insects in the air like a flycatcher.

When migrants cross the Gulf of Mexico in good weather, most of them pass over the coastal strip without stopping. But if they encounter rain, fog, a north wind, or a cold front while crossing the Gulf or on reaching land, then the birds drop down exhausted into the nearest patch of woodland. They feed and rest and wait for the weather to improve. On such occasions the parks and gardens of any city along the Gulf coast may suddenly be filled with a "rain of red birds."

Tropical disturbances occasionally carry these tanagers far out of their usual range. A great storm in the spring of 1929 brought hundreds to New England. After every violent storm from the South, bird watchers in the North keep a sharp lookout for hurricane waifs of this species.

The nest of the summer tanager is a thin, cupshaped affair made of grasses, rootlets, leaves, bark shreds, and, in the Deep South, Spanish moss. It is lined with fine grass that often bleaches yellow. The nest is usually placed near the end of a limb, 5 to 20 (sometimes up to 60) ft. above the ground in pine, dogwood, or scrub oak. The nest is shallow, often frail. The eggs sometimes can be seen from below, as with the mourning dove. The birds build in woods, groves, edges of clearings, along roadsides, and around houses and gardens. From scanty evidence it appears that the female builds the nest alone in about two weeks.

The three or four bluish green eggs are spotted with various shades of brown, often most heavily at the larger end. The female incubates alone; the male joins her in feeding the young.

The male summer tanager has a delightful, rollicking, robinlike or grosbeak-like carol, which is often delivered from a treetop. In the northern part of its range the bird seems to sing infrequently, but in Louisiana it carols with a persistence that is monotonous.

The most characteristic sound of this species is the *chicky-tucky-tuck* call note, with which it keeps its mate and the world at large posted throughout the day as to its movements and state of mind.

Dr. J. G. Cooper, after whom the western subspecies was named, first studied the bird in the neighborhood of Fort Mojave on the lower Colorado River in 1869. He said the call note, which he wrote as *ke-dik,* meant "come here" in the language of the Mojave Indians. T. W. Brewer, a famous authority of the past century, said of this western subspecies: "They sing in a loud, clear tone, and in a style much like that of the robin, but with a power of ventriloquism which makes the sound appear more distant than it really is."

This species is primarily insectivorous. It includes in its diet bees (mostly drones), wasps, flies, beetles, wood borers, weevils, cicadas, tomato worms, spiders, and dragonflies. It seems to be particularly fond of wasps and wasp larvae, and it will sometimes tear apart a wasp's nest to get at these succulent grubs. The beetles it eats may be quite large. If so, the bird ejects as a pellet a consolidated globule of the indigestible shells, legs, and feet. This tanager also eats some fruit, such as blackberries, figs, mulberries, and whortleberries.

At feeders the summer tanager likes bananas and bread crumbs.

Description: Length, 7½ in. Heavy, blunt, yellowish bill; tail notched. Adult male: rose-red with no black and no crest. Female: upperparts, olive-green washed with yellow; underparts, light brownish orange. Immature male: same as female or with patches of rosy red. Orioles have wing bars. Female scarlet tanager has yellowish (not orange) underparts and dark gray wings. Spring male is our only red bird with black wings and a black tail.

Incubation, 11 to 12 days; young stay 7 to 10 days in nest.

Size of eggs, 0.9 x 0.7 in.; one brood per year.

FINCHES, GROSBEAKS, BUNTINGS, SPARROWS

/ *Fringillidae*

CARDINAL *(Richmondena cardinalis)*

The male cardinal is our only crested red bird. A black throat and forehead point up the brilliance of the rest of its plumage. The dove-colored female has red only on crest, wings, and tail. The brilliant color is due to pigment in the feathers. Both sexes have a big bill, and a former name for the species was cardinal grosbeak.

The cardinal is resident throughout southeastern states. It ranges north to Ontario and Connecticut, northwest to South Dakota, west to southern California and south through Mexico to British Honduras. It has been introduced into Bermuda and Hawaii. The subfamily to which it belongs is thought to have originated in South America. The cardinal has increased its continental range since Colonial days, and is still spreading slowly northward.

This grosbeak is a bird of thicket and tangle, where it forages, nests, and roosts; but it sings from an elevated perch. Other favorite habitats

199

include gardens, shrubbery, hedgerows, roadsides, orchards, parks, swamps, and the edges of woods and watercourses. In Maryland, Stewart and Robbins describe favored habitats as "brushy, cut-over floodplain and swamp forests, and rich, brush, moist forests on the upland." In the South it is a bird found both in suburban dooryard and gum and cypress swamp.

Around dwellings, the cardinal is tame. A New Jersey survey showed it to be the first species to come to the feeder on a winter morning. It usually is found in pairs; sometimes in winter two or three pairs may occur together. The average flock is 4.3 birds. It does not migrate.

The male cardinal establishes a breeding territory and uses song to mark its borders and to warn off rivals. A male may engage in reflection fighting with its own image in a hubcap, mirror, or window. The male also fights an intruding male. It does not seem to enjoy bathing.

The cardinal is monogamous. The male's courtship is a somewhat rough and tumble affair. Verna R. Johnston describes an instance she observed along the Sangamon River, 40 miles west of Champaign, Illinois:

On March 2, 1940, two male Cardinals chased one female up and down and around trees for twenty minutes, the female always in the lead. The two males flew at each other several times, pecking and ruffling their feathers and uttering an angry buzzing note when in combat. Several times the males dashed headlong from the top branches of a tree toward the ground, only to swoop up again when within six feet of it. When the female stopped and perched in a tree, usually high up, the two males perched close by and took turns singing, flying at each other and diving toward the ground while the female watched them.

The female cardinal chooses a nesting site in a bush, thicket, grape tangle, briar patch, brush heap, or low tree, either evergreen or deciduous; sometimes the bird selects a vine-covered porch, fence, or stump. The site often is near a dwelling.

The nest is not well concealed. It is loosely constructed of twigs, leaves, weed stalks, bark shreds, rootlets, and grasses. The deep cup is lined with hair, grass, or rootlets. It is usually within 8 ft. of the ground, but nests 30 ft. up have been recorded. The female alone builds it, but the male helps by bringing material. The three or four eggs are white or greenish white, generously marked and spotted with lilac and various shades of brown. The markings of individual eggs vary considerably. The species has a long nesting season. In some parts of the United States, eggs may be found as early as February, nestlings as late as October. In Georgia the customary three nestings take place in March, May, and July.

The female alone incubates the eggs, as is often the case in species with brightly colored males. Sometimes she sings on the nest, where the male brings her food. Both parents feed the young. Amelia R. Lasker, who studied the species in Tennessee, noted that the parents kept the nest sanitary by eating the pellet-like excreta of the young for the first four or five days, after that carrying the pellets away. The parents show marked anxiety if the nest is disturbed.

After the young leave the nest the male may take complete and highly solicitous charge of the fledglings for another three weeks or longer while the female nests again. In one nesting, Hervey Brackbill of Baltimore reported partial independence of the young at 44 days after hatching, complete independence at 50 days, and total severance of family ties at 70 days.

Cardinal nests are easy to observe, and some have proved unusually interesting. Occasionally two females share the same nest to try to incubate two sets of eggs, usually with indifferent success. One joint nesting with a song sparrow has been reported, in which the cardinals brought off their brood first; subsequently the song sparrows brought off theirs. On one occasion a male cardinal that had lost his own brood, helped feed young robins that happened to hatch nearby at the time of his bereavement.

The voice of the cardinal is a varied series of loud, clear whistles, frequently written as *wheat wheat wheat what-cheer what-cheer what-cheer,* or *wet year wet year wet year weet weet weet,* or *birdy birdy birdy,* or *boys, boys get up.*

Chamberlain noted 16 variations of the song in South Carolina. Amelia Lasker, in a study of the bird in Tennessee, distinguished 28 different variations, as did A. A. Saunders in Delaware. Saunders points out that the cardinal's song is often confused with the Carolina wren, but the cardinal is more inclined to slur and repeats its slur or phrase many more times than the wren. The call of the cardinal is a sharp heavy *tik*.

The cardinal is one of the first—often the very first—species to sing at dawn. Sometimes it is also heard at night. Unlike most species in many parts of the country, it sings throughout the year, perhaps with greatest vigor in spring. Unlike most other species, the female also sings. Her offering is somewhat softer than the male's, but is of equal beauty. In courtship she sings as an invitation to mating. Later she often gives voice from the nest. One of her common songs has been rendered as *we-oo, we-oo, we-oo, we-oo, we-oo*. But her season of song is shorter than the male's and she chooses a less exposed perch.

Its powerful bill identifies the cardinal as a seed eater, and vegetable matter accounts for 71 percent of its diet. Half of this is seeds, a third wild fruit, the balance largely corn, rice, and millet. Its principal insects are such pests as the Rocky Mountain locust, 17-year cicada, Colorado potato beetle, cotton worm, boll weevil, cotton cutworm, codling moth, rose beetle, cucumber beetle, leaf hopper, fig eater, zebra caterpillar, and plum scale.

At the feeder the cardinal prefers sunflower seeds, but also likes seeds of melon, squash, pumpkin, and cantaloupe. It takes small grains and attacks with relish suet and nut meats, notably pecans and peanuts. Cardinals eat the fruit of mulberry, hackberry, pokeberry, raspberry, blackberry, blueberry, elderberry, greenbrier, grape, cherry, dogwood, sumac, and Russian olive.

Description: Length, 8 in. Female smaller than male. Red, strong, short, and conical bill; crest conspicuous; tail rather long; short and rounded wings. Male: all red except for black face and throat. Female: bill paler than in male; red confined to crest, wings, and tail; face black; brownish gray upperparts; buffy underparts. The young resemble the female but are darker and have little or no red. (The male summer tanager, our only other all red bird, has no crest. The female pyrrhuloxia has a gray back and yellow bill.)

Incubation, 12 to 13 days; young stay 9 to 10 days in nest.

Size of eggs, 1.1 x 0.8 in.; two broods per year; three in South.

ROSE-BREASTED GROSBEAK (*Pheuticus ludovicianus*)

The rose-breasted grosbeak breeds in Canada and the northern United States, from the Plains to the Atlantic, and south in the Appalachians and Georgia. It winters from southern Mexico to Colombia, Venezuela, and Ecuador, and casually to the Greater Antilles.

The rose-breast is a bird of open deciduous or mixed woodlands, wood, stream, and road edges, shade trees, orchards, second growth, swamps, and thickets. Its preferred breeding location, according to Richard H. Pough, the conservationist, is the borderline area where a stand of fairly large trees adjoins a shrubby area. Under natural conditions such a situation usually occurs along a stream or around a pond or swamp. The bird has adjusted, however, to the so-called disturbance communities of suburbs and farms. There it seems to find shade trees and garden shrubbery quite acceptable. In Georgia, where it breeds in the mountains above 3,000 ft., it is particularly attached to rhododendron thickets.

The rose-breasted grosbeak is deliberate in its movements. Once located in the binoculars, it is easily kept in view, unless it retreats behind the wealth of encompassing greenery. The bird is found at every level of woodland branches. It feeds from the treetops almost down to the ground, but usually sings from an elevated perch. In flight it flashes large patches of white on its wings and rump.

At the extreme limits of its summer breeding range, the rose-breasted grosbeak occupies a territory 2,500 miles wide. As they migrate south in fall the birds gradually funnel into a narrower region, which, by the time they reach the Gulf coast, is about 700 miles wide and stretches from eastern Texas to Apalachicola Bay, Florida. From this section of the Gulf coast the grosbeaks migrate across the Gulf of Mexico to the Isthmus of Tehuantepec and Yucatan, and from there on south, some of them as far as northern South America.

In the spring, from mid-April to mid-May, the birds come north through Louisiana. Males usually precede the females. The vanguard of the flight arrives in New York and New England early in May. The southward movement departs from Massachusetts in September, although a few birds occasionally linger at feeders into December. The last individuals leave Georgia in late October. The main flight goes through Louisiana and the adjacent Gulf coast from the end of September to early November. Rarely, an individual, perhaps sick or injured, may winter in Louisiana or occasionally elsewhere, usually at a feeder.

Edward Howe Forbush, author of *Birds of Massachusetts,* writes of its courtship in spring:

The males usually come first, and when the modestly attired females arrive they are pursued with fierce rivalry. Sometimes from four to six males may be seen paying attentions to one female. They dart from twig to twig, pouring forth their sweetest songs, or hover about her in the air, both singing and fighting at the same time. Their battles sometimes are sanguinary as the beak of the bird is a powerful weapon. I have seen such a fracas but once, but it is well worth seeing. When the battle is won the female, though apparently indifferent during it all, accompanies her conquering hero as he leaves the scene. Having won her he seldom leaves her for long until the young are able to care for themselves.

The rose-breasted grosbeak builds a rather loose, saucer-shaped nest of twigs, weed stalks, and grasses, and lightly lined with somewhat finer material. The nest site is usually from 5 to 20 ft. up (rarely higher) in a fork of a shrub or sapling in a thicket or along a woodland border. In Georgia the birds often build at the outer ends of rhododendron limbs.

The three to five bluish green or grayish eggs are spotted and blotched with various shades of lilac and brown. In species where the males are brightly colored, they do not usually help incubate (possibly because their colors might attract attention). The rose-breasted grosbeak is an exception to this rule. The male rose-breast shares part of the duties of incubation with the female, and when on the nest often sings, sometimes in a low or even a ventriloquial voice. When the female is sitting, the male often feeds her.

The song of the rose-breasted grosbeak is a long, smooth, somewhat hurried, liquid carol. It is heard from the time of the birds' arrival in spring until the second week in July. It somewhat suggests the song of a robin, a robin that has had singing lessons, as someone once said.

The song differs from the robin's in that the grosbeak's song has a rising inflection at the end, and its pauses are the briefest possible, whereas in the robin's song, each pause is about as long as the phrase that preceded it. F. S. Mathews, author of the *Field Guide of Wild Birds and Their Music,* states that from a musician's standpoint the

female

male

BLACK-HEADED GROSBEAK

songs of the grosbeak and the robin are absolutely dissimilar. Unlike most other species of birds, the female rose-breasted grosbeak has a good voice and also sings. The grosbeak's call note is a highly distinctive *ik* or *eek,* which is frequently heard, even when the bird cannot be seen.

According to the researches of Department of Agriculture biologists, 52 percent of the diet of the rose-breasted grosbeak is of animal origin, and 48 percent of vegetable matter. The bird is one of the few that seems to relish Colorado potato bugs. Its diet also includes such other insects as cucumber, click, and leaf beetles; tent caterpillars, wood borers, curculios, scale insects, plant lice, stink bugs; and the caterpillars of army worms and of tussock, browntail, and gypsy moths.

The grosbeak's vegetable diet includes weed seeds, tree seeds, wild fruits, and berries (notably those of the sour gum), the buds and blossoms of forest trees, and at times young vegetables such as squash and peas.

Description: Length, to 8 in. Female slightly smaller than male. Large, ivory white bill; very slightly notched tail. Male in spring: breast with notable rose triangle pointing down; black head and upperparts; white on rump and wings is conspicuous in flight. Male in fall: black wings and tail, but rest of black upperparts replaced by streaked brown; white and rose of underparts spotted with dark markings; individuals show considerable variation in plumage. Immature male: resembles female but is buffier, more profusely streaked below, and often has some rose on its breast; molts into adult plumage in second August when 14 months old. Female: resembles a big, brown sparrow or an oversized female purple finch; light line through crown; two white wing bars and white line over eye; underparts streaked throughout (underparts of black-headed grosbeak are browner and it is streaked only on sides); saffron-yellow underwing (not canary-yellow as in black-headed grosbeak).

Incubation, 14 days; young stay 14 to 16 days in nest.

Size of eggs, 1.0 x 0.7 in.; one brood per year.

INDIGO BUNTING (*Passerina cyanea*)

The male indigo bunting is blue all over appearing very dark at times. The female is rusty brown, darker above than below, with faint streaks on the sides. Young males are mottled blue and brown. They do not assume full blue adult plumage until their second year.

The blue of this bird's plumage is caused by the refraction of light back through the outer feather cells from the basal pigment cells which absorb all but blue light. Owing to this kind of feather structure the color itself changes with the angle of refraction. Thus, from an acute angle the feathers look green; from an obtuse angle, blue; and at a distance they look black. Intermediate angles give other colors, which have been called cerulean, azure, deep ultramarine, Prussian blue, olive-blue, and grayish blue.

The indigo bunting breeds over the United States and southern Canada from the Plains and the Black Hills east, except in southern Florida and southern Texas. It winters from central Mexico south to Panama and in Cuba, Jamaica, and the Bahamas.

Due to recent climatic changes and the effect of civilization, the range of the indigo bunting now joins, over a wide area, the range of the somewhat similar lazuli bunting of the West. Before the settlement of the continent by Europeans the points of range infringement were slight, if indeed there were any at all. Today, in this wide and increasing zone of contact, extensive hybridization between the two species is taking place, apparently resulting in fertile offspring. An investigation of this situation leads some students to believe that both the lazuli bunting and the indigo bunting should be treated together as one species. Other students, from the same data, find confirmation for considering them two separate species, as does the official *A.O.U. Checklist of North American Birds,* and as we do here.

The indigo bunting in the breeding season is a bird of roadsides, dry hillsides, brush and thicket, young second growth, clearings, the edges of shrubby fields and pastures, open woods, orchards, burnedover and cutover land, and the edges of swamps and river valleys. Because such habitats today are much more common than in the days of the Pilgrims, this species is undoubtedly more abundant now than it was then.

The maximum breeding population density in recent years in Maryland (in Allegany County in 1948) was 52 pairs per 100 acres in "unsprayed apple orchard with unmowed ground cover." It might be reasonable to expect similar population densities in the breeding season in similar habitats elsewhere within its range.

Population densities, however, change over the years. Ludlow Griscom, an expert in avian population trends, supplies us with the following picture of the situation around Concord, Massachusetts, over the past 130 years. Were other areas studied as intensively as Concord has been, they might yield similar histories.

In his *Birds of Concord,* under the heading, "Complex Cases, Unknown Causes," Griscom states:

A further illustration of the complexities involved (in analyzing population trends) is afforded by the local history of the indigo bunting. It ranges widely throughout the eastern United States, and is one of the strikingly numerous birds, wintering in Central America. Its preferred haunts are woodland edges and clearings grown up to slash, so that favorable territory has been increasing for decades.

1830–1879. Very common summer resident north to central Maine, where ten males can be found in a day.

1880–1890. Some decrease noted.

1890–1905. Slow but steady decline, virtually disappearing from Maine and New Hampshire.

1905–1930. Continued decline; now so rare and local in Essex County that numerous active observers have to work hard to find two to three pairs in the whole county [in] a season. A rare summer resident generally.

1935–1948. Slow but steady increase. At the moment an uncommon summer resident generally, most numerous in Sudbury Valley, where ten males were noted in one day in July 1948, the best count in over half a century.

Lawrence E. Hicks made a study in northeast Ohio of the succession of plants and birds that follow lumbering of a beech-maple forest. He found that in the first stage, when sprouts and seedlings were from 1 to 10 ft. high and there were large open spaces between the crowns, the indigo bunting was one of five bird species that dominated this microcosm. [The others were the blue-winged warbler, chestnut-sided warbler, field sparrow (p. 269), and rufous-sided towhee.]

In migration the indigo bunting is seen in its favorite breeding season habitats but also in other less familiar places. In Louisiana, as in Texas, great swarms of buntings pass through in migration. And all over the country the characteristic *chit* call note of night migrants can be heard overhead.

In spring the males arrive before the females. The male sings persistently from a bare twig, roof, chimney top, lightning rod, telephone wire, TV antenna, or other exposed perch. One study in Wisconsin showed that the minimum acceptable elevation for a perch was 13 ft. with a ground cover of 5 ft. Sometimes the bird starts singing from a branch near the foot of a tree and jumps up from branch to branch, singing as he goes, until he has reached the topmost spire. If disturbed, he dives into the thicket below.

Unlike most other birds the indigo is not deterred by the heat of noontime, and his pleasant song can be heard regularly all through the long hot day. He is one of the few birds in North America that sings more as the season progresses. Indeed, we hear the male's persistent song into the middle of August, right up to the time of the molt.

The female, at least when nesting, is suspicious, shyer than the male, and is seldom seen. If disturbed on or near her nest, she flits about, nervously twitching her tail and uttering a *chit* of alarm that soon brings the male down to join her in anxious agitation.

In Virginia and North Carolina along the Blue Ridge Parkway, which traces the crest of the eastern range of the Appalachians for hundreds of miles, the indigo bunting is one of the commonest birds. Dead trees alongside the Parkway supply excellent perches, and the motorist whose ears are attuned to bird voices can hear the song (and sometimes see the singer, a little black dot on a big black branch) for mile after curving mile.

The many hazards of a bird's life make us wonder what happens when one of a mated pair is killed during the nesting season. Researches have shown that for various reasons (lack of available nesting territory, etc.) there are numbers of unmated birds at large during the breeding season. If one member of a pair is killed, his or her place is soon taken by one of these unmated standbys, usually within 24 hours.

In a scientific experiment, an investigator once shot the male of a mated pair of indigo buntings. Overnight the female acquired a new mate. This one, too, was shot. By the next morning another male had replaced him. The same fate met this third husband, and a fourth, and a fifth, and so on, until nine skins hung on the collector's belt, if not on his conscience. This investigation, however, showed that there was no shortage, in that region at least, of available males. The tenth suitor was allowed to enjoy his conjugal rights and duties undisturbed.

In an open, bushy location the smallish cupshaped nest is cleverly hidden in underbrush or a thicket (in the South sometimes in a cane thicket). It is built in a crotch of a bush, usually within 4 ft. (maximum 12) of the ground, and is made of twigs, grasses, weed stalks, and a few leaves (cane leaves, if amid canes). It is lined with fine grass, hair, or feathers. A pair or its successors may occupy the same nest for five summers or more, repairing it each year.

It is obvious that over the centuries the breeding preferences of each species of bird have gradually evolved from those of its ancestors. We are seldom privileged to witness significant changes in these preferences in a short time. Such, however, took place among the indigos on the Sherwood Plantation in Georgia when the cultivation of tung trees was started. H. L. Stoddard, the great authority on that area around Thomasville, says:

This species has during recent years "taken over" the tung groves on Sherwood for breeding (although the "natural" location is shrubby growth on field edges and in the open piney woods). When the leaves drop in the fall, we find two or three to a half dozen of the characteristic nests in each grove. This, coupled with the observation of the singing males, is the basis of our estimate of a maximum nesting population of one breeding pair to each two or three acres of grove. As there are thirteen of the groves totaling some 125 acres, a considerable breeding population is indicated. Very few pairs, however, continue to nest in the open piney woods of the place, to which they were largely confined as breeders before the tung groves were planted. On July 20, 1940, a nest with three eggs was noted near the end of a tung branch not over eighteen inches above ground. The more usual situation in tung trees is from five to fifteen feet up.

The female lays three or four pale blue eggs, which in different lights may look whitish or pale greenish. Very rarely they may have a few dots. She does almost all the incubating. The species is often victimized by the brown-headed cowbird.

Studies in the winter range of this bird in Guatemala suggest that the same group of individuals that associates together one winter tends to do so the next winter, and that the birds also tend to winter in the same place; for example, a particular jungle clearing, as in the previous winter.

The indigo bunting has a short, pleasant song, sometimes described as canarylike. The notes usually come in pairs—usually three to five pairs—and to me at least the song seems to "change gears" in the middle. Saunders, the great authority on bird voice, describes it as "a high strident whistle, *sweea sweea sit sit seet seet sayo*." He lists from 6 to 20 notes and points out that the summer songs are longer than those of spring.

Ralph Hoffman, who had an apt way of rendering bird songs so others could recognize them, wrote it as *swee-swee-swee, swee-swee* (slightly lower) *sweet-sweet-sweet, swee-swee* (slightly lower), *swee, swee, swee,* and said "the song finishes diminuendo."

F. S. Mathews, in his *Field Guide of Wild Birds and Their Music,* stated that no two buntings sing exactly alike, but that there is a resemblance between the songs of individual families. He traced one family through three generations, grandfather, son, and grandson, noting that the songs all had a family resemblance and that the song of each individual developed and perfected itself, so to speak, through the season. He counted five songs a minute, for an hour at a time, and estimated 2,000 songs a day. The similar raw data of T. S. Roberts, who did much of his work in Minnesota, might lead one to estimate a season's total of over 250,000 songs.

The food of the indigo bunting is largely insects in summer and seeds in winter. Among insects taken are caterpillars (including cankerworms and those of the brown-tailed moth), beetles, curculios, grasshoppers, and measuring worms. Seeds include weed and grass seeds.

Description: Length, 4¾ to 5¾ in. Short, strong, conical bill. Spring male: bill, dark above and pale blue beneath; bird blue all over, looks black at a distance. Fall male: brown but shows blue on wings and tail, some whitish below. Female and immature: bill horn-colored; rusty brown upperparts; paler underparts, and faintly streaked. Female is our only brown finch that lacks wing bars, prominent streaks below, or any other distinctive marks; male does not assume full plumage till second year. Immature males, molting males, and old females present a mottled appearance of brown or blue. This bird suggests a miniature blue grosbeak, but has a much smaller bill and no wing bars.

Incubation, 12 to 13 days; young stay 10 to 13 days in nest.

Size of eggs, 0.8 x 0.6 in.; often two broods per year.

PAINTED BUNTING (*Passerina ciris*)

The male painted bunting is one of the most gaudily colorful birds in North America. Scarlet, green, and violet-blue, all the brightest colors of the rainbow, shimmer over his small frame. His only rivals are the hummingbirds.

One spring at the Welder Wildlife Refuge at Sinton, Texas, I observed a number of these birds. Despite their bright hues, when one of these buntings is perched on top of a mesquite and silhouetted against the sun, it looks like a dark blob. All its colors vanish against the brilliant blue of the Texas sky.

In the wide-open spaces the song seems to have an indefinable quality of mellow farawayness. It is finchlike, a little hard to separate into its component phrases, but not too difficult to learn. As I heard it again and again, it seemed to become an integral part of the dryness and heat, the arid canyons, and oak mottes (groves) of the endless south Texas plains.

The painted bunting breeds from Kansas and North Carolina to the Gulf coast and southern New Mexico. It winters from the Gulf coast and southern Florida south through Mexico to western Panama. Its favorite habitats include gardens, hedgerows, roadsides, dry scrub, old pastures, isolated trees in open fields, the edges of woods and pastures, and brushy streamsides. It is especially partial to rice plantations, bushes along drainage ditches, and myrtle thickets by live-oak groves. It is also found in towns and even cities. The pioneer ornithologist, Alexander Wilson, wrote, "They frequent gardens, building within a few paces of the house; are particularly attached to orangeries; and chant occasionally during the whole summer."

Like many other members of the sparrow family, to which it belongs, this species sings from an elevated perch, such as a bare treetop twig, roof top, telephone pole, telegraph or power wire. When disturbed, however, it plunges into the nearest thicket.

Alexander Sprunt, Jr., writing in his *Florida Bird Life,* says:

The males fight viciously for territory. Often the battles terminate only when one or the other is blinded, or wounded. Sometimes a fighting pair can be picked up in one's hands, so utterly oblivious are they to anything but combat. The writer has seen birds whose heads were almost denuded of feathers and bleeding profusely. This tendency made it easy to trap the bird when they were caged and sold. A dummy, or a mounted bird in a trap was a lure which never failed.

In migration great numbers of this species come up from Mexico along the Gulf coast and swarm through Texas and Louisiana, particularly along rural roads, just as its more common relative, the indigo bunting, does. The males precede the females by about a week.

T. Gilbert Pearson, in his *Birds of America*, writes, "The male struts before his modest colored mate in the mating season. With spread wings and tail he makes a very interesting picture parading up and down on the ground." Writing of this species in South Carolina, Sprunt says:

Mating starts as soon as the females arrive and the period of mating is tempestuous. The males have violent tempers and are as pugnacious as any bird could be. There is little of the bluff which characterizes many small birds in their conflicts. The battles are fought to an unquestioned conclusion and often terminate fatally.

If we are lucky, we shall find the nest of this bunting amid thick foliage in a briar patch or in a crotch of a bush or branch from 3 to 6 (sometimes 20) ft. above the ground, often in a river flood plain or dry canyon. In live-oak country the nest is often placed in, and completely hidden by, a clump of Spanish moss. The cupshaped structure of twigs, leaves, rootlets, bark strips, weed stalks, and grass, sometimes bound together with caterpillar silk, is lined with fine grasses and rootlets, and perhaps horsehair. The nest is similar to, but neater than, that of the indigo bunting.

The three or four creamy to bluish white eggs have red-brown markings. In the days of egg collecting, happily now long past, the female was known as a "close sitter" and sometimes allowed herself to be lifted off the nest by hand.

Opinions on the song of this species vary. Most authorities find it bears resemblance to that of the indigo bunting. Some think it is more musical, some less. Roger Tory Peterson, author of the *Field Guide to Bird Songs*, says it resembles the song of a warbling vireo but is more wiry.

A. A. Saunders, whose statements on bird songs bear the stamp of a lifetime of listening, says it is "a high-pitched, sweet, but tinkly song. It is more musical in quality than that of its relative, the indigo bunting, but it is not as loud, and does not carry far . . . abrupt two-note phrases are common."

The males sing from April to July, but with some falling off in intensity in June and a resumption of vigor in July. Although the males of most species do not give a complete song until they are in adult plumage, this is not true of the painted bunting. Immature males will often sing a song indistinguishable from that of the full-plumaged adult.

The alarm note is a sharp *chip*, sometimes *chip-chip*, or *chip-chip-chip*.

Food of vegetable origin constitutes about three-quarters of the diet of this species. Notable ingredients are weed and grass seeds, especially the seeds of foxtail grass, pine seeds, sunflower seeds, and rice. Insects include beetles, flies, wasps, crickets, and, of special interest, cotton worms and boll weevils. These latter make up one-quarter of its animal food diet.

Favorite feeder foods include mixed seeds and peanut hearts.

Description: Length, 5¼ in. Short, conical bill; no wing bars. Male: violet-blue head and nape; yellow-green back; dragon's blood red rump; scarlet eye ring and underparts; colors sharply demarcated; all colors darker after the fall molt; full plumage not attained until the fourth or fifth year. Female: bright apple-green above, lemon-green below, shading into yellow on belly. Females and immatures are our only green finches. Fall immature resembles female. Immature male in spring resembles female but has some blue on the head.

Incubation, 10 to 12 days; young stay 12 to 14 days in nest.

Size of eggs, 0.75 x 0.55 in.; two to four broods per year.

DICKCISSEL (*Spiza americana*)

Usually, when a species of bird becomes established in a new area or disappears from an old area where it was common, at least some of the reasons are readily discernible. It may be attributable to human activity; man may destroy an old habitat or create a new one, or hunt one species to extinction while vigorously protecting another. Or the reasons can be completely natural ones, such as the spread northward of many southern species because of a gradual amelioration of climate. In all events, by considering these factors, singly or in combination, it is usually possible to arrive at a plausible theory accounting for the change.

But occasionally a mysterious change occurs that cannot be accounted for, that fits no known pattern and for which no acceptable theory can be formulated.

Until about 1870, the dickcissel was a common breeding bird on the Atlantic seaboard from Massachusetts to South Carolina. Then suddenly, within the space of a few years, this eastern population completely disappeared. Conceivably this may have been due to some great natural catastrophe, either a disease or migration disaster that reduced the population below the self-sustaining level. But the cause seems more likely linked to an intrinsic behavior trait of the species, a trait that has been observed but is not yet fully understood.

Even in the middle west, where the species is abundant, dickcissels may be absent from an area for a year or more, then suddenly reappear in numbers. Thomas Roberts, in *Birds of Minnesota*, comments:

There is always a pleasant excitement as to whether or not Dickcissel can be found and where. When it leaves in the fall, after perhaps a season of abundance and intimate acquaintance, it may be lost almost entirely from that locality for no one knows how long. Each year about the time it should return, in late May or early June, it is in order to search the clover-and-alfalfa-fields, pastures, and upland hay-fields, in the hope of finding it once more in its favorite haunts. Now and then a few scattered arrivals may be found or perhaps none at all, and then after a lapse of several years there comes, most unaccountably, a veritable "Dickcissel year" when every place is full of them.

Whether this trait accounts for its wholesale disappearance from such an extensive area as the eastern coastal plain for so long a period of time is open to question.

But again, "a long period" is so relative a term as to be rather meaningless. One hundred years is indeed a long time in relation to the time North American birds have been studied and observed, but perhaps not in relation to the idiosyncrasies of the dickcissel. For all we know, this cycle of appearance and disappearance may have been going on for eons. The disappearances are longer and more complete in the isolated eastern extremity of its range than those noted by Roberts and others at the center of the species' abundance.

Whatever the case, it is of some interest that in recent years the dickcissel has again appeared as a breeding bird just east of the Alleghenies in Maryland and has become increasingly common along the Atlantic coast during the fall migration. It is quite possible that someday the dickcissel will repopulate the Atlantic coastal plain.

At present, except for the Maryland birds noted above, the breeding range of the dickcissel is confined entirely to the area between the west slope of the Appalachians and the eastern edge of western short-grass plains, from eastern Montana and Ontario south to east-central Texas, Louisiana, and central Alabama. Dickcissels winter entirely south of the United States, the majority in northern South America, but a few as far north as southern Mexico.

The dickcissel is a sparrowlike bird with a thick conical bill and streaky brown upperparts. The male in spring has a bright-yellow breast crossed by a black V, and a yellow eye line and rusty shoulders. The pattern of the underparts is remarkably similar to the meadowlark, but the male dickcissel is hardly likely to be confused with that or any other species. Winter and immature males are much duller, but show enough of the distinctive spring pattern to be recognizable.

Adult and immature females are quite variable and more or less resemble the winter male, but have no black on the breast. Most show at least a trace of yellow below and a touch of rust on the shoulders, and all have conspicuous white or pale yellow eye lines. Some individuals are quite like female house sparrows, but even the most dingily colored can usually be distinguished by their pale bluish bill. The house sparrow's bill is a yellowish horn-color.

The dickcissel is pre-eminently a bird of open grasslands. It adjusted easily to the disappearance of the original tall grass prairie, and quickly became established in agricultural areas that offered similar nesting cover. Though dickcissels can be found in almost any kind of field, pasture, or meadow, they seem to have a definite scale of preference.

Roberts comments: "To find the Dickcissel one should search first the clover fields, then the alfalfa fields, upland grasslands, grain-fields, weed-grown pastures, and, lastly, open brushlands with scattered small trees."

The spring migrants reach the southern states in May and by the end of the month most of the population is presently throughout the breeding grounds.

All the sparrows and finches dwelling in the open grasslands of North America have two vocal traits in common. Their songs are invariably monotonous insectlike buzzes or rasps delivered with a monotonous insectlike regularity hour after hour throughout the breeding season. The dickcissel is no exception to this. Perched on a grass stem, fence post, or power line, all day long, from May to August he utters his unvarying *Dick dick cissel, cissel, cissel,* the *dick* notes quick and sharp, the *cissels* blending into a buzzy trill.

Needless to say, with the male so busily occupied, nest building is done almost entirely by the female. The nest is rather large and bulky and made of weed stalks and grasses and lined with softer material. It is usually located on or very close to the ground, but may occasionally be as high as 15 ft. in a bush or small tree. The eggs are an unmarked pale bluish, four or five to a clutch, and hatch in about 10 to 12 days. The young remain in the nest about the same length of time. There are usually two broods a year.

Dickcissels are accounted highly beneficial birds, during the breeding season at least. They eat a much greater amount of insect food than most small finches, mostly grasshoppers, locusts, and crickets, and a few ants, beetles, and other forms captured on the ground. The remainder of the summer diet is weed seeds and a very small amount of waste grain. Fruit and other crops are not touched.

When the nesting season is over in late August, dickcissels gather into flocks and begin to move southward almost immediately. Most are gone from the northern states by the end of the month. As they move southward they are joined by more southerly nesting birds, and by early September countless flocks of as many as 200 or 300 individuals each are pouring through southern Texas bound for their South American winter grounds.

By the first days of October, the dickcissel is gone almost entirely from inland areas, including its major breeding grounds, but the light but steady flight down the Atlantic coastline may continue into November. This appearance of dickcissels on the Atlantic coast in late autumn is paralleled by several other western species and is generally assumed to be composed of individuals that for one reason or another have become disoriented, drift eastward with the prevailing west winds, and do not turn southward until faced by the impassable barrier of the Atlantic. There are a few winter records, mostly from the Atlantic coast, but the majority of dickcissels spend the winter roaming the savannas and llanos of the tropics until the beginning of the spring migration in March.

The behavior of the dickcissel on its northward flight offers a good example of how a slight variation in the habits of a bird can bring about very different opinions as to its "beneficial" or "harmful" nature.

Dr. Alfred Gross, *Auk*, Vol. 38, 1921, estimating the total number of dickcissels in the state of Illinois at 1 million and making a series of calculations involving the destruction done by a single grasshopper, the number of grasshoppers eaten by dickcissels, and so on, came up with the result that dickcissels save the farmers a total of $4,680 a day during the nesting season. Even if these calculations were only 50 percent accurate, projecting the totals for the entire Midwest would result in at least a few million dickcissels and a considerable amount of cash. However, the majority of these birds winter in South America and must funnel through the narrow strip of Panama during migration. In spring this movement corresponds exactly with the ripening of the rice crop. The amount of crop destruction reported there is almost unbelievable. The dickcissel, its annual southern fling over, returns to its northern home, dutifully eats grasshoppers and is praised by one and all as a model citizen.

Most of the late fall and winter records of dickcissels are from feeding stations, for like other half-hearty birds that occasionally winter in the north, they will quickly seek out a feeder if one is available. They apparently have no special or unusual dietary requirements, but seem to do well enough on the usual fare offered other finches, i.e., sunflower seeds, hemp, millet, and chickweed. They are also reported to be fond of peanuts, doughnut crumbs, and occasional bits of suet.

Description: Length, 6¼ in. Sparrowlike, with streaked brown back; conical bill. Male easily recognized by yellow breast, black bib, rusty shoulders; females and immatures by bluish bill and pale eye stripe; also by usually having tinge of yellow on breast and eye line, and tinge of rust on shoulders, or some combination of these markings. Flight swift, slightly erratic or undulating.

Incubation, 10 to 12 days; young stay 10 to 12 days in nest.

Size of eggs, 0.80 x 0.66 in.; two broods per year.

EVENING GROSBEAK (*Hesperiphona vespertina*)

Until recently the evening grosbeak was one of the least known of North American birds. To the great majority of ornithologists, both professional and amateur, it was a mystery bird of far-off places, known from books and museum specimens, but very seldom observed in life. It was known to breed in the boreal forests of the northwest, from extreme northern Michigan to central British Columbia, thence south through the high Rockies to Mexico, but otherwise was recorded only as the rarest of winter visitors. It was undoubtedly a fairly regular visitor in winter to the lowlands of the Pacific northwest and the plains adjacent to the Rockies (as it is today in both areas), but both regions were sparsely populated until late in the nineteenth century, and humans—let alone bird watchers—were few and far between.

In the last years of the nineteenth century, winter reports of the grosbeak from the north-central states began to increase. Like many other finches of the northern forests, the evening grosbeak is a highly gregarious species, wandering erratically during the winter months and overflowing its normal wintering grounds at irregular intervals in years of poor food supply or high population levels. (See pine siskin, p. 239.) Since the grosbeak had always occurred sporadically in the north-central states in winter, in all probability the increase of records from this area was due at least in part to an increase in the number of interested observers. But there also seems little doubt that there was an actual increase in the numbers of the bird.

In New England, bird life had been intensively studied since early in the nineteenth century, yet Stearn's *New England Bird Life,* published in 1881, does not list the evening grosbeak among the birds recorded even once in the New England states. Then in the winter of 1889 to 1890 a great invasion of evening grosbeaks reached New England. During the succeeding winters there was a scattering of records, followed by another invasion in the winter of 1910 to 1911, which marked the first recorded occurrence of the bird in New York City. Since that date the evening grosbeak has been a regular winter visitor to the New England states and has been steadily increasing its winter range southward. Writing in 1929, Forbush commented:

It is a typical seed-eater with a large powerful fringilline bill, and was regarded until within the past fifty years as typically a bird of the far northwest. Its generic name is derived from the Greek, referring to the Hesperides, "Daughters of the Night," who dwelt in the western verge of the world where the sun goes down. It was discovered in 1823 by Henry R. Schoolcraft and named in 1825 by W. Cooper from a specimen taken at Sault Ste. Marie, Michigan. It was called the Evening Grosbeak as it was observed to sing only at evening. Whatever may have been its distribution and habits then, it is no longer a distinctively western bird nor does it sing only at night.

Though by that time a regular visitor in New England, the evening grosbeak was still by no means a familiar bird through the rest of the northeast. As late as 1940 Cruickshank considered the new portion of its wintering range to be located just north of the New York City region (New York City and its environs, including northern New Jersey and Rockland and Westchester counties in southern New York) and commented that: "I must emphasize that the recording of this species in the New York City Region is still a red-letter occasion and I know many an active observer who has yet to see the species locally."

It has only been in the approximately 25 years since Cruickshank's writing that the grosbeak has extended its winter range southward to become a regular winter visitant to the New York City region. Today, though much rarer in some years than in others, it is always to be expected somewhere in that region in at least small numbers every season. Its presence, though still generating some excitement in those who remember its relative scarcity not so long ago, is accepted rather matter-of-factly by the younger generation of bird watchers, and one would be hard-put to find an active observer who has not seen the species locally, or indeed, does not record it every season. It is now the Baltimore-Washington area that lies at the southern edge of the species' winter range, and the bird's frequency of occurrence there is about the same as it was around New York 25 years ago.

Coincident with this expansion of its winter range has been the even more interesting phenomenon of a slow but steady expansion of the breeding range of the species eastward and southward. About ten years ago it began nesting in the Adirondacks of northeastern New York and recently (1962) has been found nesting in the highlands of northern New Jersey.

The most generally proposed explanation for this spread of the evening grosbeak is especially interesting to amateur bird watchers, most particularly those who maintain feeding stations. In all such cases of species expansion a complex of factors is involved, based mainly on changes in the natural environment brought about by the civilization of the North American continent. Almost every species of North American bird has been affected by these changes: suitable breeding places have been destroyed or increased; food supplies depleted or enriched; enemies and competitors removed or introduced; and each individual species has flourished or declined according to whether the changes in its environment were or were not advantageous to it.

In the case of the evening grosbeak there has been little or no change in the environmental conditions of its main breeding grounds; i.e., no alteration of the forest nor any significant reduction of predators or possibly competitive species. The only significant environmental change presented to the grosbeak has been a marked increase in winter food supply.

In the late nineteenth and early twentieth centuries extensive plantings of trees attractive to the grosbeak seem to have provided the first stimulus to the extension of its wintering range. Forbush commented:

It was first suggested by Dr. Walter Faxon, I believe, that the movement of these birds east in the winter was facilitated by the planting of the ash-leaved maple or box-elder (*Negundo aceroides*) in tree chains across the western plains as well as in the East. The buds and seeds of this tree seem to be preferred by these Grosbeaks to those of all other trees.

In more recent years there seems little doubt that the tremendous increase in the number of feeding stations in the northeast has had the most significant influence on the grosbeak. This becomes especially evident when it is noted that many persons who maintain feeders cater especially to the grosbeaks, providing them with large amounts of their favorite foods and discouraging by one means or another less "desirable" species that may compete for this food. To such people the romance of playing host to these wanderers from the far north has an undeniable appeal, heightened in the case of more knowledgeable individuals by the exciting possibility that, by so doing, they may actually be participating in a course of events significantly affecting the distribution of this species.

Then, too, there remains the simple fact that the evening grosbeak is a strikingly handsome bird, especially amid the bare branches and snowy backgrounds of winter, an inducement enough to attract it to one's home for this reason alone. It is a stocky, medium-sized bird with an enormous, conical, pale-yellow bill. The boldly patterned black, white, yellow, and brown-olive male is absolutely unmistakable; note especially the conspicuous yellow band across the forehead and the bold white patches in the black wings. Females and immatures are much less conspicuously colored. They are mostly gray-olive with a faint wash of yellow on the underparts, but show the boldly patterned black and white wings of the male and in addition have the same white spotting in the tail. The wings and tail markings, together with the enormous pale bill, will identify them easily.

As a result of all this attention, the pattern of nomadic wandering characteristic of the evening grosbeak in winter has to some extent been altered; there is now more of a tendency for a flock to remain in one place for the entire winter, to leave for the north much later in the spring, and if the environment is at all suitable, occasionally to nest in small numbers. Thus breeding colonies are established far south of the normal nesting grounds.

This raises the question of why certain species such as the grosbeak respond so well when a chance of expansion presents itself, while others do not. Many other species have been fed regularly in the winter for many years without any significant extension of their wintering ranges, let alone a southward expansion of their breeding ranges. The answer seems to be that the introduction of favorable factors in one direction does not necessarily offset the lack of favorable factors in another. In other words, if a species needs, for instance, certain precise environmental conditions in which to nest, and these requirements are not available in the wintering grounds, no food supply, no matter how bountiful, will entice normally developed, sexually potent individuals of that species to remain in an area where nesting is impossible for them. The grosbeak, however, has a wide enough latitude in its nesting requirements to allow it, within certain limits, to nest in any area that approximates its original home.

The northward migration usually takes place in late March, but varies considerably from season to season. In years of heavy flights, flocks often linger to late April or early May, especially when food is abundant. Among most species of birds, each spring as the reproductive cycle begins anew, the mature individuals undergo a series of complex physiological changes, one of which is the stimulus producing song. The late lingering flocks offer the only opportunity for most observers to hear the song of the male evening grosbeak, for among them there are usually a few individuals in which the reproductive cycle is far enough advanced to trigger the internal mechanism of song.

This song is a series of short, loud warbles terminating in a characteristic sharp whistling note. It is ridiculous, of course, to attribute to the purely mechanical response that is the song of a bird any suggestion of conscious commentary, but it is difficult nevertheless to avoid reading into the ringing notes of the evening grosbeak a touch of an expression of wildness and a hint of the awareness of the limitless forests of the north. More prosaically, it may be described as slower, rougher, and more ringing than the song of the rose-breasted grosbeak (p. 205), and is generally shorter and less complex. Other call notes of the evening grosbeak, heard throughout the year, include a rattling whistle and a loud ringing *chirp*. The latter note is very similar to the *chirp* of the house sparrow, but is much louder and with more of a metallic ring.

Nesting begins in late May or early June, and even at this season the gregarious nature of the grosbeak is evident. Several pairs are often found nesting together in close proximity, though they do display some inclination toward territoriality, since normally there is never more than one nest in any one tree.

Conifers are generally preferred for nesting sites, though the birds will frequent a variety of trees including willows, maples, and ashes. The nest is usually located in a leaf cluster at the end of a branch, 15 to 60 ft. from the ground. It is a loosely constructed, saucer-shaped affair, built mostly of twigs and lined with fine grass or rootlets. The eggs are blue-green, blotched with brown or olive, three or four to a clutch.

During the summer months the grosbeaks take some insects, principally beetles and caterpillars; the nestlings especially receive considerable amounts of this food. But the grosbeak is primarily herbivorous, and finds in each stage of the vegetative cycle some sort of plant food attractive to it.

Early in the year they feed on the buds of a variety of deciduous trees, including elm, maple, and apple, and to a limited extent also browse on the buds of conifers. As the leaves begin to sprout, grosbeaks feed on the more tender varieties, but it is not until cones and seed pods begin to ripen that the grosbeak really begins to concentrate on plant food. They eagerly devour the offerings of a great variety of trees and shrubs, both coniferous and deciduous, for few seeds are secure against the power of the grosbeak's enormous bill. It is the kernel itself that is most attractive to the grosbeak; usually the soft, pulpy portion of fruits such as wild cherries or chokeberries is disregarded and the pits are cracked for the inner seed.

The grosbeak is normally arboreal, foraging through the tree tops in a leisurely, almost stolid, manner. The usual method of feeding is to gather by much twisting and craning of the neck all the food that can be reached from one spot, then to hop solemnly a little farther along the branch and repeat the procedure. Occasionally, when hard put for food, they will forage closer to the ground, feeding among the tall stalks of ragweed, sunflowers, and similar plants, and even picking fallen seeds off the ground.

Gradually these groups of foraging grosbeaks wander farther and farther from their nesting grounds, drifting southward with their characteristic undulating flight along the mountain ridges and river valleys. In the latitude of New York observers watching the hawk migration along the mountain ridges in October are often the first to report these birds in the fall as flocks of evening grosbeaks swing by on their southbound migration. By November or early December the winter's population, whatever it might be that particular year, is fairly well established, though occasionally there are marked incursions later in the winter.

At feeder stations grosbeaks will eat almost any sort of seeds offered, but sunflower seeds seem far and away their favorite. The amount of this food even a relatively small flock can devour during the course of a winter is truly prodigious, and since sunflower seed usually costs about twice as much as the normal wild-bird mix available on the market, maintaining a flock of evening grosbeaks through the winter can cost more than a few dollars. To the true grosbeak enthusiast, however, this means nothing. In fact they take a good deal of delight in reporting how much their grosbeaks ate.

Description: Length, 8 in. Heavy-bodied; tail short, forked; bill huge, very thick. Male body pattern yellow, golden brown, black and white; unmistakable. Female much duller, but has easily recognized note; pale bill, white spotted wings and tail. In most places, an erratic winter visitor, usually in flocks. Flight strongly undulating.

Incubation, 12 to 14 days; young stay 14 to 16 days in nest.

Size of eggs, 0.90 x 0.65 in.; one brood per year.

PURPLE FINCH (*Carpodacus purpureus*)

Closely related species of similar habits seldom occur together as nesting species. (See myrtle warbler, p. 157.) Instead, they avoid the undue competition sure to arise under such circumstances, and each occupies a different habitat or geographic range. Thus the three American species of Carpodacus occupy breeding territories that for the most part are mutually exclusive: the house finch (p. 231), the arid open country of the west; Cassin's finch, the coniferous forests high in the western mountains; and the purple finch, mostly in the coniferous forests and mixed woodlands of the east and far north.

The breeding range of the purple finch is from northern New Jersey, northern Maryland (mountains), northern Illinois, and eastern North Dakota north to Newfoundland and northern Ontario, thence west through the forests of northern Canada to British Columbia. It also occurs on the west slopes of the Cascades and Coast ranges from British Columbia to northern Baja California, breeding in a belt of mixed coniferous and deciduous woodland that is for the most part intermediate in altitude between the ranges of the house and Cassin's finches. It does not breed in the Rocky Mountain chain.

It winters from southern Canada and central Minnesota south to Florida, the Gulf coast, and the southwestern border states. The number of birds remaining in the north depends to a great extent on weather and food supply, and varies considerably from year to year. For the most part, the purple finch is rather uncommon in winter north of Virginia and the Ohio Valley. Birds of the western mountains often simply move down to lower elevations rather than migrate southward.

During the breeding season the purple finch prefers a location that provides both a scattering of tall evergreens for nesting and a variety of berry- or catkin-bearing deciduous trees and shrubs for food. Its native home is around the edge of a bog, natural meadow, or other small clearing in northern or mountain forests where the evergreens tend to be somewhat spaced and there are likely to be patches of alder, birch, or similar deciduous growth.

In settled areas they have learned to accept quiet, well-watered parks, cemeteries, or estates that provide essentially similar conditions, but the purple finch has never achieved the close relationship with humans established by its relative the house finch, and for the most part it remains a bird of the forests and woodland.

The male purple finch is mostly bright rose red with white lower underparts, a brownish cast to the wings and tail, and some brown streakings on the back. Why it was named "purple" finch is rather puzzling; Forbush, in *Birds of Massachusetts,* offers this explanation:

According to our color standards of the present day, the name "Purple Finch" is a misnomer. Doubtless the term was first applied by someone collecting for the first time a highly plumaged adult male. In full breeding plumage it displays some tints approaching the "royal purple" of the olden time, and to that color very likely was due the origin of its name.

Around New York City the male might be confused with the house finch, and west of the Cascades and Coast ranges with either the house or Cassin's finch (see house finch, p. 231), but through most of its range it is not likely to be mistaken for any other species.

Females and immatures are sparrowlike birds with white, heavily streaked underparts and conspicuous white eye lines. They are distinguished from similar sparrows by their eye lines and more arboreal habits, and from female Cassin's finch by their dingier, less sharply streaked underparts and different call notes. (See also female house finch, p. 236.)

Full-plumaged males are scarce in proportion to the total number of purple finches. Although a few young males molt into a duller version of full-adult plumage during their first winter, the majority retain female-like coloration much longer, only gradually becoming more and more rose-colored with each succeeding molt. In either case it may take several years before the final adult male coloration is attained. A few individuals apparently never change at all, retaining a "hen-feathered" plumage for life. Birds in any of these intermediate stages are fully mature otherwise, and regularly mate and raise broods.

Purple finches may begin singing as early as late March, though mid-April is a more normal time, and actual courtship does not usually begin until May.

The song is a rapid, jumbled caroling similar to the house finch, but fuller and richer and without the distinctive, slurred, ending note. It is usually delivered from a partially concealed perch at the very top of a tree, and even a highly colored male is often surprisingly difficult to pick out, especially if he is among bright red buds or blossoms. When actually courting, the male raises the short feathers of his crown, tilts back his head, and with rapidly vibrating wings dances about before the female. At the height of this performance he may occasionally make a short, fluttering song-flight.

In the east the purple finch song might be confused with the song of the warbling vireo, but it is deeper and richer, with considerable more internal variation. As F. S. Mathews commented in *Field Guide* of *Wild Birds and Their Music,* "The Vireo's warble is stereotyped, that of the Finch is untrammelled and characteristically variable."

The call note of the purple finch is a sharp metallic *pink.* Easily learned and immediately recognizable, it is a valuable aid to identification.

The nest is a deep cup made of twigs, weeds, and grass, lined with softer material. It is usually hidden among the branches of a dense evergreen, anywhere from 5 to 60 ft. from the ground. Occasionally the purple finch will nest in a deciduous tree, but only if the foliage is thick enough to conceal the nest well. The female does most of the actual construction, though the male will help occasionally, at least to the extent of gathering a few bits of material.

The eggs are greenish blue, blotched or lined at the larger end with brown or black. The normal clutch of four or five hatch in about 13 days. While the female is incubating, the male feeds her, and when the young hatch out, he shares equally in the task of feeding them. There is one brood a year.

The purple finch is primarily a seed-eating species, supplementing its diet with buds and young leaves in spring and fruit and berries in summer. During the warmer months a considerable amount of animal food is also taken, especially for the nestlings, which are fed quantities of plant lice, caterpillars, cutworms, and similar insects.

As might be expected from its food habits, the purple finch occasionally does some slight damage to crops, mostly to buds and leaves in early spring. Immediately after nesting, purple finches gather in flocks that occasionally visit orchards, but they are never found in the great concentrations that make the house finch a serious pest. For the most part these flocks of purple finches remain in the woodlands, not becoming common about agricultural and residential areas until the southward migration in late September and October.

Of the winter diet of the purple finch, 75 percent consists of weed seeds; ragweed and smartweed are special favorites. The remaining 25 percent includes seeds of maple, ash, and pine, and the offerings of alders, junipers, hawthorns, and other plants that retain their fruit through the winter.

In the winter season purple finches are frequently found in company with other finches of similar habits, notably goldfinches and siskins. Less active than either of these two nervous, constantly flittering species, the purple finch forages in a methodical manner, more like the larger grosbeaks. They can be found wherever food is available, high in the tops of elms or maples, or almost on the ground among the stalks of ragweed, goldenrod, and sunflowers.

Purple finches regularly visit feeders: in the northeast mostly during migration in October, early November, and again in March, but farther south and in the far West they can be expected throughout the winter. Sunflower seeds seem to be their favorite choice, but they are also fond of millet, hemp, and of bread, doughnuts, and cheese, but only for occasional variety; a good supply of the favored seeds is necessary to keep them permanently attached to the feeder.

Description: Length, 6¼ in. Tail forked, rather short; bill thick and conical. Male mostly bright rose red with brownish cast to wings and tail. Distinguished from house finch by greater extent of rose coloration and clear (unstreaked) white abdomen; from Cassin's finch by deeper coloration and more uniformly rose-colored head. Cassin's has a distinct contrast between bright cap and dull nape. Female and immatures are brownish above, white below, streaked dark. Distinguished from house finch and similar sparrows by conspicuous white eye line and by voice; and from Cassin's by less sharply streaked underparts.

Incubation: 13 days; young stay 12 to 14 days in nest.

Size of eggs: 0.79 x 0.56 in.; one brood per year.

HOUSE FINCH (*Carpodacus mexicanus*)

Most Americans are quite aware that there are numerous differences between eastern and western United States. But the question of where one begins and the other ends is likely to be decided entirely by the individual's point of view. Everyone is familiar with the tired old story of the ultra-sophisticated Manhattanite who considers anywhere west of the Hudson as Indian territory. But a Californian would certainly view things quite differently, and for years small boys have known

for a certainty that, no matter what else, the dividing line is indis-
putably east of Texas.

The zoologist has his point of view, too, but it is based on ecological
factors rather than concepts of urbanity or romantic legendry. It is a
north-south line, roughly approximating the 100th meridian, that
bisects the Dakotas and Nebraska, crosses the western third of Kansas
and the Oklahoma panhandle, and divides Texas from the vicinity of
Perryton on the Oklahoma border to Del Rio on the Rio Grande.
East of this line most of the land is well watered, the natural vegetation
is forest or rich tall-grass prairie; west of it begins the high, dry, short-
grass plains that extend to the base of the Rockies.

This division is not absolutely abrupt; a belt populated by a mixture of eastern and western forms extends for some miles on either side
of the dividing line. But the transition is nevertheless rapid, and an
observer traveling westward from the 100th meridian would in a short
time find himself in country dominated by western forms of animal
and plant life. Among the first of these encountered would be the most
typical of western birds, the house finch.

It is a sparrow-sized bird with the typical thick, conical bill of a
seed eater. The male is easily recognized by the bright coloration of
the crown, throat, and rump. The exact shade varies, according to
geographical race, from orange-red to dusky red; in most races it is
bright rose-red. The remainder of the upperparts are gray-brown; the
underparts are whitish, streaked dusky. Females lack any trace of bright
coloration; they are gray-brown above and whitish below, streaked
darker brown.

The house finch is a permanent resident almost everywhere in the
west from southern British Columbia east to the 100th meridian and
south through the drier parts of western and central Mexico to the
south edge of the Mexican Plateau. Its requirements are few and
flexible: water, which may be located a considerable distance away;
fleshy fruits or berries, important for nestling food and to substitute
for water in dry spells; open ground with a covering of seed-producing
plants; a place to roost above ground level. Only areas of dense mountain forest and the alpine meadows above the timber line fail to fill
these requirements completely, and here the house finch is absent. But

everywhere else, deserts, scrub lands, open woods—any place in fact with a clump of trees or a patch of brushy growth at low to moderate elevation—is sure to be populated by this species.

Two other closely related and very similar birds also occur in parts of the West, but for the most part their ranges are separated from the range of the house finch by a combination of geography, altitude, and habitat. The Cassin's finch inhabits the high mountain forests of the Rockies and Sierras, invading the house finch's range only in winter when, following the pattern of many high mountain species, it drifts downslope to the relatively warmer foothills and adjacent lowlands where food is more easily obtained.

The second species, the purple finch (p. 225), occurs west of the Cascades and Coast ranges, from northern British Columbia to lower California. It is primarily a bird of conifer and oak forests, but in the winter months wanders into more open country inhabited by the house finch.

The best way of distinguishing the male house finch from males of these two species is by the pattern on the lower underparts. The whitish belly of the house finch is distinctly streaked; the other two species have clear whitish bellies. Females are more difficult to separate, but the female house finch usually lacks the distinct whitish superciliary, or eyebrow, of the female Cassin's and purple. In addition, the call notes of the house finch, a wheezy, English sparrow-like *cheep* and musical twitterings are quite different from the sharp metallic *pink* of the purple finch and the clear *tree-lip* of the Cassin's.

All in all, the area inhabited by Cassin's and purple finches is rather insignificant compared to the range of the house finch. The habitat requirements of the house finch have given it undisputed possession of the majority of the land area of the western United States where, unhampered by the presence of similar competitive species, it has had opportunity for almost unlimited expansion.

The house finch has taken full advantage of this opportunity. Not only has it made itself at home in a wide variety of natural habitats, but, hardy and adaptive, it has also been able to weather and even capitalize on the profound effects of civilization upon its natural range. As its name implies, it is particularly abundant in the vicinity of human habitations, attracted by the increased food and shelter offered by gardens, orchards, irrigated farmlands, shade trees, and other artificial plantings.

Further proof of its adaptability is its success in areas where it has been artificially introduced. The house finch was liberated in the Hawaiian Islands in the early part of the twentieth century, and the species is now well established on all the main islands where it competes successfully not only with the native species but also with a hodge-podge mixture of other introduced species from all parts of the world.

The males of the various Hawaiian Island populations, by the way, vary in coloration from yellow to reddish-orange; very few are the bright rose-red of the mainland birds. These color variations are not genetically controlled; i.e., they are not transmitted from generation to generation, but are due entirely to an environmental effect on each bird individually. Experiments with captive specimens have shown that the chemical compound forming the red pigment of the house finch is highly susceptible to variations in temperature and humidity; individuals transported to a different climate soon became the same color as the native house finch of that area.

House finches have also been established in the vicinity of New York City since the early 1940s. Though the reasons behind their appearance have not been absolutely established, the evidence seems to indicate that they are the descendants of birds released just beyond the reach of the law.

Early in 1940 Dr. Edward Fleisher, of the Linnaean Society of New York, discovered house finches for sale in a local pet shop. Since part of the federal law protecting native songbirds prohibits their possession or transportation for commercial purposes, Dr. Fleisher immediately notified the federal authorities. Subsequent investigations revealed that, for several years, house finches (under such names as Hollywood finches and red-headed linnets) had been and were being sold in pet shops all over New York. Thanks to vigorous enforcement of the law by federal wardens, these sales in New York and the rest of the country were effectively stopped.

A year or two later house finches appeared in several localities in western Long Island, and in 1942 the first nesting pair was found. According to Elliot and Arbib, *Auk,* Vol. 70, No. 1, from whom the preceding information was obtained: "The origin of the House Finch in the East appears to be in the release of caged birds by bird dealers following a ban on their sale commercially, enforced early in 1940. These caged birds had been trapped in California and shipped east in quantities during the preceding ten years."

Today the house finch is firmly established in its eastern enclave. It has spread over most of Long Island, along the south shore of western Connecticut, often appears and occasionally nests in northeastern New Jersey, and has been recorded as far south as Philadelphia.

These eastern birds also appear a bit off-color; they are distinctly duskier than any of the birds from the places in California from which they supposedly came. According to Elliot and Arbib:

The possibility that the Long Island birds might be "sooted" was considered improbable, since the areas frequented by the House Finch on Long Island are suburban, close to the sea, non-industrial and relatively clean. . . . Subsequent examinations of freshly collected specimens from Long Island, however, prove conclusively that these birds are heavily sooted. In New York, Dean Amadon compared newly-collected, washed House Finches with earlier unwashed specimens from Long Island and found that the darker color of Long Island birds was attributed to dirt-stained plumage.

Long Islanders may take consolation in the fact that both factors are probably at work here. They can always conclude that their house finches are climate-affected, whereas the ones in the next town are dirty.

In early spring, house finches, which have congregated in flocks since the end of the previous breeding season, begin to pair off, and the breeding season begins. Pausing only for brief intervals of feeding, the male spends the entire day absorbed in the ritual of courtship. His song, heard constantly throughout the daylight hours, is one of the commonest sounds of the western spring; a rapid jumble of disjointed warbling notes lacking form or pattern, but cheerful and spritely. It is very similar to the songs of purple and Cassin's finches, but is less full and rich and usually ends in a distinctively strident *wheer* or *which ear* note, which the other two lack.

The male now becomes highly excited in the presence of a female.

Circling her with short strutting hops, he displays his bright coloration by drooping his wings and raising the short feathers of his crown and breast, accompanying this performance all the while with chirping notes and brief snatches of song. The intrusion of another male at this point is sure to provoke a fury of aggressiveness, climaxed by a swirling battle that to all appearances seems a violent life-or-death affair, but in reality is a part of a stylized ritual in which the defender invariably triumphs and the intruder invariably retreats, with very little physical damage on either side.

The pair now settle down to the business of selecting a site and building a nest, demonstrating in this process the amazingly adaptive and versatile nature of the species. In settled areas, eaves, rafters, shade trees, vines, and arbors are the most usual locations, but house finch nests have been found in almost every conceivable location including hayricks, empty boxes, and even old tin cans. In wilder areas, any sort of tree or bush, from a cactus to a pine, is entirely satisfactory.

The nest itself is a large bulky affair composed of any of a variety of materials; grass, bits of string, rag or newspaper, strips of bark, wool, or hair from domestic animals; in fact, any fairly soft material the bird can manage to carry is likely to wind up tucked into the nest.

The eggs, pale greenish blue and sparsely speckled brown or black, are four to six to a clutch. Incubation lasts 12 to 14 days, and the young remain in the nest about the same length of time. Usually only the female incubates, but the male assists in feeding the young. There may be two or even three broods a year.

House finches are almost entirely vegetarian, but occasionally vary their diet with plant lice or other animal matter and are quick to take advantage of any unusual food supply. Describing his observations of the house finch of San Clemente Island, W. L. Finley commented: "Whenever a sheep was killed and the Mexicans hung the fresh meat out in the open, the Linnets took their share. I saw where all the meat had been picked from several bones that were hanging up."

The fledglings also are fed some insects, but the bulk of their diet is soft pulpy fruits and berries with a high water content. The kinds of fruit eaten by nestlings and adults is simply whatever is readily available, and consequently varies considerably with habitat and season.

Desert-dwelling house finches get by with only the fruit of various cacti; on the other hand, in agricultural areas their diet is sure to include some cultivated crops. For this reason, despite its attractive appearance, cheerful song, and confiding habits, the house finch is not particularly popular with agriculturalists, especially fruit growers.

Immediately after the nesting season, house finches band together in large flocks, which remain intact until the following spring. It is in late summer and fall, when these post-breeding-season flocks first begin roaming the countryside, that most crop damage occurs.

Though the total percentage of cultivated crops in the diet of any one house finch is not very great, perhaps no more than 10 percent, it is a very abundant species, and the aggregate total of crops destroyed or damaged may exceed a tolerable level in certain localities.

Yet, even during this season when fruit is abundant, 60 to 70 percent of the house finch's diet consists of weed seeds; during the winter the percentage is much higher. All in all, the house finch doubtless does more good than harm, but nevertheless it is unprotected by law in California and a few other western states, for its economically undesirable habits are easily observed and immediately obvious. Its beneficial traits, which are revealed only by careful observation and analysis, go unnoticed.

As the season advances, the house finch relies more and more on its basic diet of weed seeds, abandoning orchards and groves for over-grown fields and the weedy growth along roadsides. Though not migratory, it roams about a good deal during its winter searching for food, and at any given time may be common in one place and virtually absent from another. This is especially true in the northern portion of its range, where suitable feeding areas are likely to be widely scattered.

House finches take readily to feeders, the frequency and length of their visits varying with climate and the amount of natural food available elsewhere; in colder areas a flock is likely to remain more or less permanently in the vicinity of a well-stocked feeding station. Aggressive and pugnacious, the house finch is one of the few small birds able to outbully the house sparrow, and is always sure of obtaining a substantial share of food at the feeding tray in the face of all competitors.

As might be expected of a species as adaptive and versatile as the house finch, they are willing to take just about any seeds set out, though if a variety is offered, they do show definite preference. Commenting on their feeding-station habits in the East, Elliot and Arbib wrote: "At the feeding stations the preference is for sunflower seeds (the bait which the California trappers cited as most successful); but in the absence of this seed, hemp, millet, grape and cracked corn are readily consumed." Other types of food such as peanuts, raisins, suet, and crumbs are also taken, but these seem to be merely supplemental and are not likely to be accepted as a substitute for seeds.

Description: Length, 5 to 6 in. Thick and conical bill; moderately long, forked tail. Male: crown, throat, upper breast, and rump, some shade of red, usually bright rose. Otherwise, brown-gray above, whitish below, streaked darker. Female: like male but lacks red. Distinguished from Cassin's and purple finches by streaked belly (male), lack of distinct face pattern (female), call notes. Occurs in flocks throughout most of the year. Flight slightly undulating and erratic.

Incubation, 12 to 14 days; young stay 12 to 14 days in nest.

Size of eggs, 0.73 x 0.54 in.; one to two broods per year.

COMMON REDPOLL (*Acanthis flammea*)

Why are some years, at irregular intervals, good redpoll years? We assume it has something to do with the food supply, or the weather, or both, in their normal wintering grounds farther north. If there is a relative failure of the seed crop of birch and alder, if the weather becomes too severe even for a northern finch, or if both bad weather and food shortage combine, then we may expect a southward invasion of these hardy birds.

There may also be other, more obscure, causes relating perhaps to cyclic increases in numbers, unusual wandering propensities in certain populations or generations, heavy predation by natural enemies in some regions, and so on.

The common redpoll nests around the globe in Arctic and sub-Arctic regions, breeding south to southern Alaska, northern Canada, and Greenland. It winters from central Alaska and central Canada south over the northern half of the United States, commonly over the northern part of its range, sparingly in the southern.

The redpoll breeds amid dwarf birch, willows, and alders on the tundra, along stream banks, and in openings in the northern forest. In Alaska it frequents villages, towns, and roadsides, much as the house sparrow does farther south. During the cold months, wandering flocks roam through the northern forests. In migration and during the winter farther south the redpoll frequents weedy fields and pastures, pine groves, hedgerows, orchards, gardens, and swamps, particularly those with birches and alders.

In the United States the winter visits of the redpoll are associated with cold and snow. It is a winter finch par excellence. The sight of it afield or at the feeder suggests snowstorms and blizzards, bitter cold up north, more hard weather to come.

This finch has a habit of clinging partway down on a stalk of grass, and often hangs head downward while feeding. A flock will settle in an unmowed field and largely disappear among the weeds as they start to feed on the ground and on the stalks. If approached, the birds run through the grass or, a few at a time, will take to the air and leap-frog over the others to settle down again farther on, all the while keeping up a pleasant twittering. If startled, they all fly up at once; the flock may seem surprisingly large.

This species is gregarious and usually travels in compact flocks. A favorite singing perch is a treetop, branch, telephone wire, or building. A male may also sing in the air "during a display flight as the bird loops and circles with hesitant wing beats" (Pough). The flight is undulating, somewhat like that of a goldfinch, but with the ups and downs less pronounced. Flocks rise and wheel in unison, but after a few aerial evolutions often return to the same place. At night the birds sleep in dense cover, such as a thicket of conifers. This species often flocks with goldfinches (p. 246) and pine siskins (p. 240).

Redpolls are tame and unsuspicious and will allow a close approach.

The redpoll migrates by day. In the southward migration the young often precede the adults. Ornithologists describe this species, over much of the southern part of its winter range, as an "irregular winter visitant." Unusually heavy winter incursions of redpolls far south of their usual winter range have been noted since the early 1800s. Some of the most conspicuous recent flight years in Massachusetts were 1937–1938, 1945–1946, early 1949, and 1952–1953 (when flocks of up to 2,500 individuals were noted). In New York, 1916–1917 and 1941–1942 were exceptional redpoll years.

In New Jersey, 1836–1837, 1878–1879, March 1888, 1899–1900, 1906–1907, 1908–1909, and February 1936, stand out, although there were redpoll incursions in other years also. Usually the birds do not become common in an invasion year until after late December.

The nest of the redpoll, a deep compact cup, is placed in a crotch of a bush or low tree, usually a willow. Sometimes it may be hidden in a tussock on the ground. Grasses and plant down are the main ingredients, but twigs, feathers, rootlets, moss, and catkins are used, if available. The dense lining is largely of ptarmigan feathers or plant down. Sometimes several pairs nest together in a loose colony.

The female deposits five or six light blue eggs, sparingly spotted with lilac and brown. The species has bred successfully in captivity. In the wild it hybridizes with the more northern hoary redpoll where the ranges of the two overlap.

The song, calls, and alarm note are somewhat goldfinchlike. Townsend and Allen describe the song as "a string of *chugs* interspersed with *deé-ars* and *chee-chee-chees,* and now and then a fine rattling trill." The call that we usually hear from a winter flock in flight is a rattling *tshu, tshu, tshu.* J. Ellis Burdick, writing in Pearson's *Birds of America* analyzes its call notes as follows:

He also has at least four distinct call-notes; a loud twittering call, used when on the wing; a long buzz, not unlike one note of the pine siskin but thinner and longer; a conversational twitter, used when several birds are feeding together; and a *ker-weet,* very much like the long plaintive call of the goldfinch but different in tone.

Food of vegetable origin constitutes 75 percent of the redpoll's diet in summer and almost all of it in winter. Of this vegetable food, seeds make up 90 percent, with those of birch and alder predominating. Supplementary items include the seeds of pines, elms, and lindens, viburnum berries, and larch and lilac buds. Among weed seeds eaten are those of ragweed, pigweed, and lamb's-quarters. Animal food—largely spiders, ants, flies, and other insects—accounts for one-quarter of the bird's bill-of-fare in summer.

The redpoll in winter is a common bird at feeders, where its favorite foods include rolled oats, sunflower seeds, and the conventional wild-bird seed mixture of millet, rape, and hemp. It also likes peanut hearts and a mixture of melted suet, peanut butter, and corn meal.

Description: Length, 5⅛ to 6 in. Female slightly shorter than male. Short, strong, conical bill; notched tail. Red forehead; streaked rump. Winter: male, upperparts streaked gray-brown, paler on rump; two white wing bars; whitish underparts, blackish chin, pink breast and rump. Female and immature: similar, but with little or no pink; immature grayer and more heavily streaked than adult; young males take two years to assume full adult plumage. Summer: dull brown upperparts, pale underparts, streaked sides.

The male purple finch has the entire head raspberry red. The pine siskin is much more heavily streaked and has yellowish wing bars, not white as in immature redpolls. The common redpoll is darker in appearance than the more northern hoary redpoll, but coloration and streaking are variable enough to make positive sight identification impossible. The same is true for the rarer Greenland redpoll (*rostrata*) which is a larger, darker race, with a bulging bill, more upright posture, and louder and harsher call notes.

Incubation, 14 to 15 days; young stay 12 to 14 days in nest.

Size of eggs, 0.70 x 0.55 in.; one or two broods per year.

PINE SISKIN (*Spinus pinus*)

The pine siskin is the most common of winter finches, and during winter months is likely to occur anywhere, from the tops of trees in inland forests to the scraggly growth of goldenrod along the outer beach dunes. It is a small, plump bird, similar to the goldfinch (p. 246) in size, proportion, voice, flight, and actions. But it is easily recognized by its heavy streaking and the yellow patches in wings and tail base. There is no seasonal variation in plumage, and both sexes look alike.

During the winter the pine siskin is frequently found in association with goldfinches and redpolls, the three forming a group known collectively as "small winter finches," though a purist might deny that the goldfinch is truly a winter finch. At any rate, the three species are remarkably similar in general appearance and voice; but the siskin can be distinguished from the goldfinch by its heavy streaking, from the redpoll by the lack of any pink or rose in the plumage, and from either by the yellow patches in wings and tail. The siskin can also be recognized by voice. Its flight call is a harsh, burry *churr-it* or *chip-churf*, very different from the clear, mellow note of the goldfinch and usually distinguishable from the clipped, metallic notes of the redpoll. A second note of the siskin, a rasping screech with a rising inflection, is given while feeding or at rest, and is entirely different from the call of any other bird.

Though often a few individuals of one species may become mixed in a flock of another, the flocks usually remain discrete, shifting feeding areas independently of one another and following no fixed pattern of movement.

The flight of the siskin, like that of the goldfinch and redpoll, is extremely undulating. Unlike starlings, shorebirds, and other precision fliers, the individuals in a flock of winter finches do not move in synchronization. Each individual "roller-coasters" slightly out of phase with his companions, giving the moving flock the peculiar erratic internal motion that marks a flock of winter finches at any distance.

Siskins are frequent visitors to feeding stations, especially in flight years, and often become remarkably tame.

At the feeder, siskins take the same sort of foods as goldfinches—seeds of sunflower, melon, squash, hemp, and millet, and crumbs of bread, doughnuts, and cheese. They are flighty, restless birds, seldom content to remain in one spot for more than a short time, but are constantly milling and swirling about from ground to treetop to feeding shelf.

With the coming of spring, siskins drift northward toward their breeding grounds. No definite dates can be established for their migration, though it generally occurs in March; individual flocks may linger longer in a favorite feeding area.

In flight years especially, when the birds have penetrated much farther south than usual, flocks of siskins may be observed into May. Occasionally small flocks will spend the summer, and on rare occasions even nest far south of their usual breeding grounds.

The normal breeding range of the pine siskin is throughout the forests of Alaska and Canada, south to northern Michigan and Nova Scotia, thence south in the mountains to North Carolina in the East, and the state of Chiapas in southern Mexico in the West.

The siskin is as erratic in its breeding habits as it is in its other activities, varying apparently at random the time and place of nesting. April and May are usual breeding months, but in some seasons nesting may begin early in March and be over by early summer; in other years it may last through August. Furthermore, during the same year siskins may breed early in one locality and late in another. They also frequently shift breeding sites, nesting commonly in one locality for a year or more and then suddenly disappearing for a while to nest at another point perhaps miles distant.

The courtship and breeding behavior of the siskin is similar to that of the goldfinch, several pairs usually nesting in close proximity and using the same feeding areas.

The song of the male siskin is similar to that of the goldfinch, but less musical and admixed with harsh chattering and buzzy notes. It is often given in flight as the male bird, flying a few feet from the ground, slowly circles an open patch or small meadow. The song of the siskin is not often heard away from the breeding grounds, but occasionally on warm sunny days in late winter or early spring the males can be heard tuning up in anticipation of the coming nesting season.

The shallow, saucer-shaped nest is carefully concealed in a fork at the end of a branch of evergreen, 8 to 30 ft. from the ground. It is made of twigs, strips of bark and moss, densely lined with fur, hair, plant down, or moss. The eggs are three to six in number, pale bluish green spotted, and speckled at the larger end with purplish or black. Incubation is from 12 to 14 days and is chiefly by the female. There is usually one brood, sometimes two, per year.

During late spring and early summer, when ripe seeds are not yet plentiful, the siskin supplements its diet with buds and tender young leaves of deciduous trees and shrubs. It also takes some insects, mostly caterpillars, aphids, and various insect larvae gleaned from leaves and needles of forest trees. Its manner of feeding is the same as in winter. Working among tips of outer branches and tops of weed stalks with much fluttering activity, often hanging upside down from the tip of a branch to secure some otherwise inaccessible morsel, siskins flit nervously from tree to ground and back to tree. As dandelions, thistles, and similar plants begin to bear seed, the siskin turns immediately to them, subsisting mainly on such food until the cones of evergreens ripen.

In late summer, flocks gather and the siskins begin their annual wanderings, roaming through the forest in groups of a few dozen to several hundred. At this season they sometimes visit nearby settled areas where they occasionally do some damage to crops and garden flowers. Usually, however, the siskin confines foraging to the seeds of elms, maples, and similar deciduous trees.

By the time of first heavy frost the flocks have settled into the winter routine, which may see them either spending the entire season in northern wilderness or pouring south in a mass invasion.

Description: Length, 5 in. Small, plump; tail forked; stubby and conical bill. Dull grayish or liver-brown; heavily streaked blackish above and below; a yellow band through the wing, usually visible only in flight, and a yellow patch at the base of the tail. Distinguished from winter goldfinch by streaking, from redpoll by greater profusion of streaking, yellow patches, and lack of red crown patch or rosy breast.

Incubation, 12 to 14 days; young stay 12 to 14 days in nest.

Size of eggs, 0.62–0.72 x 0.44–0.52 in.; one brood per year.

AMERICAN GOLDFINCH (*Spinus tristis*)

The goldfinch is a small, plump bird with a short, conical bill and short, forked tail. In spring the male is bright canary-yellow with jet-black wings, cap, and tail. The wings and tail are spotted white. The female is plain, unstreaked buffy-olive above and plain whitish or yellowish buff below. She has white wing bars and a pale whitish bill.

Males in winter resemble females, but retain the black-and-white wings of spring plumage. The flight is undulating, a characteristic shared with some closely related species. In West, see dark-backed goldfinch.

The goldfinch, known to many as "wild canary," is found throughout North America from central British Columbia and central Quebec

BLACK-BACKED
PHASE

male

female

DARK-BACKED GOLDFINCH

to northern Baja California and the Gulf Coast. It is a permanent resident, and though in winter there is a decided southward population shift, at least some individuals can be found in any part of the species' breeding range at any time of the year.

Despite the fact that the goldfinch occupies its breeding grounds the year round, it does not begin nesting activities until July or August when the wild thistles begin to bloom. For not only does the goldfinch feed extensively on the seeds of the thistle, but through most of its range depends almost entirely on the soft feathery down of the thistle-seed pod for lining its nest. Though the goldfinch has been known to use other material for nest lining, such as cattail fluff and milkweed down, many studies have shown that goldfinches will not nest where there is not an adequate thistle supply, even when the territory is otherwise suitable.

The goldfinch nests in fairly open bushy areas with a scattering of taller trees and an adequate supply of thistle, milkweed, and other food plants nearby. Apparently the goldfinch was originally confined to marshes, swampy margins of lakes, streams, and similar wet areas. Overgrown farms and pastures are much to its liking, and estates and well-landscaped housing developments are also used for nesting sites, provided there is a supply of thistle within a few hundred yards.

All through spring and early summer, caroling flocks of goldfinches frequent these favored areas. The song of the goldfinch is a loud canarylike outpouring of clear trilled notes interspersed in a jumbled musical carol. The beginning is similar to that of the indigo bunting, but the entire effort is much longer, richer, and less precisely patterned.

Because the goldfinch, unlike most other species, remains in flocks even when courting, it is not unusual at this season to find an entire treetop filled with singing male goldfinches.

With most songbirds, the male establishes a territory and then attracts a mate to it. But with the goldfinch, the pairs are already formed when in midsummer the birds begin nesting. Only now does the male establish a territory and show any signs of aggression toward other males. The territory includes nesting tree and immediate vicinity, but does not normally extend to feeding areas; these are still used communally by all nesting pairs in the neighborhood.

The nest itself is usually placed at the tip of a branch about 5 ft. from the ground in a dogwood, hawthorn, bittersweet, or similar small tree or woody shrub. In some areas where only taller trees are available, such as elms, the nest may be located from 20 to 30 ft. above ground.

The remarkable deep, cuplike nest is built almost entirely by the female in about a week's time; the basket is woven from milkweed or similar fiber, capped with a rim of fine bark, and lined with thistle, cattail, or milkweed down. Taking advantage of the fact that many species of birds have already completed nesting, the goldfinch often tears apart abandoned nests of other species, notably the yellow warbler and alder flycatcher, in order to obtain material.

The entire structure is tightly woven and bound with spider silk or caterpillar web, and when completed will actually hold rainwater for several hours.

The five bluish white eggs hatch in about 12 days, during which time the female remains almost constantly on the nest, fed by the male. Food for the nestlings is gathered by both parents, who swallow and partially digest it and then feed the young by regurgitation. When the nestlings hatch, food gathered by the male is usually passed to the female for presentation to the young. When the young reach the fledgling stage, the male will feed them directly, and in cases where there is to be a second brood, he takes over feeding the young entirely while the female begins constructing the second nest.

The goldfinch takes some animal food, mostly soft-bodied insects such as aphids and caterpillars, but it is primarily a seed eater, feeding on thistle, goldenrod, milkweed, sunflower, and a variety of other weeds. They occasionally do some crop damage, being fond of the seeds of lettuce and various garden flowers, but far offset this damage by consuming enormous quantities of noxious weed seeds such as ragweed and dandelion.

One of the most charming aspects of the goldfinch is its complete fearlessness while feeding. They generally forage among weed stalks a few feet off the ground, and when engrossed in this activity can be closely approached.

Later in the season when the weed-seed supply is depleted or covered by drifted snow, the goldfinch forages among tree branches, feeding on catkins of birch and alder, and cones of various evergreens. It may also be found on the ground at this season, hopping about in sheltered, sunny spots in search of fallen seeds.

By mid-September the goldfinch has raised its one or two broods, and the birds gather into flocks that will remain intact until the following summer. Some flocks drift southward into Mexico and southern

Florida, but the majority remain within the breeding range of the species. Commenting on the winter distribution of the species in Massachusetts, Nuttall wrote:

Although many of these birds which spend the summer here leave at the approach of winter, yet hungry flocks are seen to arrive in this part of New England throughout that season; and sometimes in company with the Snow Buntings, in the inclement months of January and February, they may be seen busily employed in gleaning a scanty pittance from the seeds of the taller weeds which rise above the deep and drifted snows.

During the winter goldfinches frequently associate with other small finches of similar feeding habits, notably the redpoll (p. 237) and pine siskin (p. 240). These three species are superficially similar in appearance, flight, and voice, but the goldfinch will always be known by its lack of streaking, pale horn-colored bill, and its clear *per-chick-o-ree* flight call, which is much more clear and tinkling than the rasping, burry, flight notes of the other two species. All three birds have an interrogatory lisping or rasping note at rest or feeding. The goldfinch's is a high-pitched, plaintive *"sheeeeee?"* (see pine siskin, p. 240).

During winter months goldfinches are somewhat more numerous in coastal areas; they also occur regularly inland and can be expected as regular visitors to feeding stations anywhere. They eat seeds almost exclusively. Sunflowers are their favorite, but they will take melon and squash seeds, millet, hemp, and a variety of other small seeds, as well as crumbs of bread, doughnuts, and cheese.

Description: Length, 5 in. Thick and conical bill; short, forked tail. Male: in spring, bright yellow with black cap, wings, and tail. Female: plain unstreaked yellow-buff above, paler yellow-white below. Male in winter as female, but black, spotted white wings. Flight strongly undulating. Occurs in flocks through most of the year. Male dark-backed goldfinch has a dark back, female is greener above and more yellow below; both show distinctive white wing-band in flight.

Incubation, 12 to 14 days; young stay 11 to 13 days in nest.

Size of eggs, 0.63–0.67 x 0.49–0.55 in.; one, sometimes two, broods per year.

RUFOUS-SIDED TOWHEE (*Pipilo erythrophthalmus*)

The difference in coloration between mates is enough to confuse even the experienced bird watcher, and beginning bird watchers are often thrown off by the extreme variations characteristic of some species. The towhee presents an example of sexual dimorphism, i.e., the female

SPOTTED

EASTERN

RUFOUS-SIDED TOWHEES

and the male have a differently colored plumage, a situation common among birds. Frequently the female is totally different from the male, as with the rose-breasted grosbeak, where the bright male with red on his breast appears in sharp contrast to the sparrowlike plumage of the female. In other species, such as the robin, the female is similar to the male but paler. In still others, as in the towhee, one color in the male, black, is replaced by a quite different color, brown, in the female.

Until 1957 the eastern and western towhees were considered separate species but are now considered a single plastic species that varies in plumage with the climate, changing gradually from region to region but is everywhere essentially the same in habits, voice, and actions.

The species ranges from coast to coast. It breeds in the Transition and Upper Austral life-zones from southern British Columbia, northern Minnesota, southern Ontario, and southern Maine to Guatemala, northern Oklahoma, southeastern Louisiana, and southern Florida. (It has bred in Louisiana only within the past 100 years, for it was unknown there to Audubon, who spent much time in the area.) It winters from southern British Columbia, Iowa, and New York south to the Gulf and Guatemala. North of its usual winter range, a few linger on each year in dense thickets or close to feeders, particularly near the coast.

In the West these towhees are often found some distance up the mountains. In New Mexico they breed at an altitude of 6,000 to 8,000 ft., principally at 6,500 to 7,500 ft. In late summer and fall they wander as high as 9,000 ft. Throughout the West those that have bred in the mountains descend to the valleys in winter.

In the New York City area this species arrives in bulk in mid-April, males preceding females. Summer residents in New England start south in August. Most migrants have left the Middle Atlantic area by late October. In South Carolina Low Country, winter visitors arrive from the north in October and leave in April. In the South and West some subspecies are largely resident and migrate little.

The rufous-sided towhee is the length of a catbird, but has a more robust body. The male in the East is distinguished by a black hood, reddish flanks, white underparts, and big white tail corners. Western males are similar, but have white spots on their backs and shoulders. In the northeast the birds have red eyes. In the southeast white eyes are the rule. Western subspecies, averaging a little smaller than the eastern races, are larger and darker in humid regions, and smaller and paler in drier areas. In some western races the females resemble the males much more than they do in the East.

Young towhees are brown above, buffy below, and have a streaked breast and back. They look like large sparrows, except for their big white tail corners. This juvenile plumage gives way in August and September to the first winter plumage, which is much like that of the adults. During this molt the birds often present a motley, piebald appearance. The first breeding plumage shows when dull feather tips wear off in winter. This reveals bright colors by spring. A complete postnuptial molt after the first breeding season results in the adult winter plumage.

The noisy, conspicuous towhee is the bird of dry woods. In spring and summer, even during the heat of the day, when almost every other species except the red-eyed vireo is silent, the song of the towhee comes clearly over rustling leaves: *Drink your TEA-E-E-E, drink your TEA-E-E-E*. From the pine and oak barrens of Cape Cod and New Jersey, over the oak and hickory slopes of the Middle Atlantic states, and up the lonely flanks of the Blue Ridge and Great Smoky Mountains this brisk, friendly song echoes.

In the East the rufous-sided towhee likes thickets, roadsides, ditch banks, vine-clad slopes, hedgerows, brushy fences, edges of fields and woods, abandoned fields, overgrown pastures, and forest clearings, as well as parks, yards, and gardens. In the West it also likes chaparral, canyons, slopes, and gulches. In Georgia the subspecies *rileyi* is partial to palmetto thickets in open pine woods. The towhee is a species that has benefited from wood cutting and lumbering. Fires and hurricanes create conditions favorable to it for several years. It is undoubtedly more common now than it was in Audubon's time. It occupies blow-downs and burnedover or cutover woodlands until the new forest canopy grows high and close enough to cover shrubby openings.

Frank M. Chapman has well described the habits and personality of the eastern subspecies:

There is a vigorousness about the Towhee's notes and actions which sug-gests both a bustling, energetic disposition and a good constitution. He entirely dominates the thicket or bushy undergrowth in which he makes his home. The dead leaves fly before his attack; his white-tipped tail-feathers flash in the gloom of his haunts. He greets all passers with a brisk, inquiring *chewink, towhee,* and if you pause to reply, with a *fluff-fluff* of his short, rounded wings he flies to a nearby limb better to inspect you.

Usually the towhee is a relatively solitary bird. Although in summer thousands may be scattered over miles of scrub barrens or dry uplands, they are well distributed. A small sample study in Yonkers, New York, found that the average foraging area for a pair was 1½ acres. In the

South, however, winter visitors from the north are seen in small flocks, sometimes in association with white-throated and fox sparrows (p. 287). Western birds are said to be shyer than eastern birds.

The normal flight of this species is short. The tail is fanned to show the wide white corners and flaps up and down as if it were hinged at the base, thus giving the bird a "broken-back" appearance. Migration is by night. An individual banded in northern New Jersey one September 28 was retrapped in South Carolina on October 17, suggesting that it moved in migration about 50 miles a day.

BROWN TOWHEE

When singing, the head is high, crown feathers slightly raised, and tail down. According to a small Wisconsin study, the lowest acceptable singing perch, with a ground cover 4 ft. high, is 11 ft. Males sometimes sing from housetops.

Edward Howe Forbush, the Massachusetts authority, is one of the few authors to refer to the courtship of this species. He simply says that in courtship the males chase the females, and both rapidly open and close their wings and tails.

The rufous-sided towhee breeds in scrub, sproutlands, open woods with shrubby undergrowth, and open swampy woodlands. In South Carolina, favorite nesting sites include clumps of yaupon and tangles of catbriers and roses. In Florida, the white-eyed subspecies frequently nests in yards and porch vines. The Oregon subspecies breeds in almost every rose thicket and blackberry patch in the humid parts of that state.

Nest sites are on the ground or near it. If on the ground, the nest is usually in open woods or the edge of woods, often concealed next to a tussock and protected by overhang. Sometimes the nest is sunk in the ground and partially roofed over. If above the ground it is seldom more than 5 to 8 ft. up. The bird often places its first nest of the season on the ground, and the second one off the ground, where it can be protected by growing vegetation of the advancing season. Such a nest may be in shrub, vine, or brush pile.

The well-cupped structure is made of twigs, weed stalks, grasses, rootlets, leaves, bark strips, and sometimes dead ferns or moss. It is lined with fine grasses, weed stalks, pine needles, and occasionally with hair.

A normal clutch of eggs varies in different parts of the country. In the East, four is usual, but sometimes it is five or six; in Florida, three is the rule, and there are three broods, in April, June, and August. The eggs are white or pinkish white, finely and usually evenly dotted with red-brown and lilac. Sometimes the markings are heavier. The four to five eggs of the western subspecies have a faint blue-green background with markings often massed around the large end. Incubation is principally by the female.

This mother bird is a close sitter. If an intruder approaches too closely, she will often slink away from a ground nest along a prepared runway in the surrounding grass. When some distance off, she will set up a disturbance to divert attention from the homesite. If, however, she is surprised on the nest, she will flop away with trailing wing and fanned tail, simulating a wounded bird.

After eggs hatch, the male helps feed the young. The young may leave the nest, as many ground-nesting birds do, before ready to fly. The family stays together until the young are fledged and can care for themselves, even a short time thereafter.

The rufous-sided towhee often sings from the top of a bush or small tree. The eastern subspecies has a brisk, dry song reminiscent of hot, dry summer days. It is variously written as *Drink your TEA-E-E-E-, See TowHEEEE, Sweet bird S-I-N-N-G*, or in the South, *cheap cheap CHEESE*. In Georgia, Norris recognized three songs: (1) *chuck-see-he-he-he-he-he*, (2) *chu-ke-e-e-e-e*, and (3) *we-e-e-e-e*.

The call, a crisp two-syllable affair, sounds like *towhee'* or *chewink'*, and in the South like *joree'*, *t'wee*, or a slurred *shrink*. Rarely a faint *scree* is heard. The voice of the subspecies *rileyi* is described as higher-pitched than the northern subspecies, with a distinctive questioning upslurring.

An Arkansas study of the length of song period found that this species sang from February 10 to August 15. It was the first species of the year to begin consistent singing and the fourth species in mid-summer to stop singing.

The food of the rufous-sided towhee is about one-third animal and two-thirds vegetable. The animal food consists of insects, spiders, and snails, including such varieties in different parts of its range as ants, bees, wasps, flies, grasshoppers, caterpillars, beetles, locusts, millipedes, sow bugs, tree hoppers, and alfalfa weevils.

The vegetable part includes weed seeds, wild fruit, mast, myrtle berries, holly, ragweed, and grasses. The bird is especially fond of bay-berries, blackberries, blueberries, huckleberries, pokeberries, raspber-ries, strawberries, and sumac. In South Carolina in spring it is said to feed on buds at the tops of deciduous trees.

Favorite feeder foods include scratch feed, shelled and broken pea-nuts, corn, and doughnuts. The species is fond of bathing in bird baths.

Description: Length, 7¼ to 8¾ in. Female smaller than male. Strong, short, conical bill; long, rounded tail; eyes red in North, straw color in Southeast and Florida, orange in West. Male: black upperparts and breast; chestnut flanks, sides, and undertail coverts; white wing mark-ings and belly; outer tail feathers with white tips conspicuous in flight. Female: brown replaces black of male, chestnut much paler. *Note*: western subspecies have much white spotting on back and wings; fe-males in some races have dusky hoods.

Incubation, 12 to 13 days; young stay 10 to 12 days in nest.

Size of eggs, 1.0 x 0.8 in.; one to three broods per year.

SLATE-COLORED JUNCO (*Junco hyemalis*)

The slate-colored junco breeds over most of Canada, northern New England, and in the mountains to Georgia. It also breeds in northern and central Alaska. Most of these Alaskan birds follow their ancestral route east and south in their autumnal migration. This junco winters throughout much of the United States, but it is rare along the Pacific coast and is absent from central and southern Florida. It is closely related to the Oregon junco (p. 258); hybrids between the two are frequently noted; so, too, but more rarely, are hybrids with the white-throated sparrow (p. 283).

The adult slate-colored junco, or "snow bird" as it is frequently called, has a white belly and outer tail feathers. The rest of its plumage is slate-gray. The young have streaked breasts that show their relationship to other members of the sparrow family.

This species has no spring molt, and the more sharply contrasting colors in summer are caused by the original brownish tips of the feathers wearing away. The first-year birds are browner than full adults, although they look much alike. An individual does not assume full-adult plumage for three years.

The first experiment to see what causes birds to migrate was carried out in the 1920s by William Rowan, an ornithologist of Edmonton, Alberta, who used the slate-colored junco for his experiment. He maintained two outside aviary cages full of these birds in the fall, long after the birds would normally have migrated south. The birds were well fed and kept in good condition. One cage was left alone. The other was subjected to artificial lighting for a longer period each day. This simulated the light conditions in springtime. Despite the fact that it was autumn and temperatures dropped to −50° F., the sex organs of the light-treated birds developed as they do in spring. When some birds were released in mid-winter, they disappeared and were thought possibly to have migrated.

The sex organs of the juncos in the untreated cage did not increase in size, and the birds stayed in the vicinity when released. Subsequent research has confirmed Rowan's findings that increased light causes an increase in the size of the sex organs. But conclusive evidence is still lacking to show that daylight is the cause of migration.

The slate-colored junco breeds in Canadian and Hudsonian life-zones, the zones of pine and spruce. In the mountains it breeds even above timber line. It is the only species of bird that nests on the summit of Mt. Washington in the White Mountains, the highest mountain in the northeast. In the breeding season it likes woodlands, ravines, and cut-over land. It is often seen about northern camps and summer resorts. It is found in both deciduous and coniferous woods, but is particularly identified with the great northern evergreen. During fall, winter, and spring we see the species far to the south in back yards, lawns, brush piles, thickets, hedgerows, roadsides, the edges of woods and fields, and overgrown fields and pastures.

This junco is tame, confiding, and social, and soon gathers near civilization. It is equally at home in a backyard in suburban Glenolden, Pennsylvania, or at the back door of the concession stand on top of Mt. Mitchell, North Carolina. Since it is a ground feeder it is dependent on open ground. Although it is active and flies about in snowstorms, heavy snows that cover the countryside will drive it farther south. Hence, its abundance in winter in parts of the South varies with the severity of the winter farther north. In some seasons flocks have even been seen combing the wrack line of coastal beaches, which was the only ground still left uncovered by a heavy snow.

When a flock lands on the ground to feed, its members scatter in all directions, then each intensively forages the area it has selected. It picks up seeds from the ground like the chipping sparrow and also scratches amid leaves and soil like a white-throated, though not so vigorously.

This junco sings from an elevated perch in bush, tree, or sapling. Except when nesting, it is gregarious and is regularly found in flocks, often with other sparrows. Its flight is somewhat undulating and seldom prolonged. For moderate distances the birds will usually fly from tree to tree or bush to bush, rather than flying directly to an objective. Such a tree-to-tree flight is usually accompanied by twittering and some flirting and tail spreading. When disturbed, the bird flies into a tree, often hiding in a conifer. Some individuals have been found roosting at night on the ground under yew trees.

The late afternoon flight of a flock of slate-colored juncos may differ from flights at other times of the day. Studies of one flock at Ithaca, New York, over a two month's period showed that, in the late afternoon, members of the flock followed a more ritualistic and stereotyped behavior pattern. The flock kept closer together, flew higher than usual, went in the same direction every day, and acted as if it had a common goal, possibly a common roost.

In their *Birds of Alaska*, Gabrielson and Lincoln say:

Once the birds are perched, they often escape detection by staying motionless on a branch usually close to the main trunk or in a tuft of foliage. The number that can fly into a tree and immediately disappear is astonishingly large. If, however, one watches quietly for some time, sooner or later one of the birds will become nervous and take off. This seems to be the signal, and gradually the balance of the flock will leave, first in ones and twos, and then in greater numbers until the tree is emptied. If such a flock is followed to its next stopping place, it will be apt to take alarm somewhat more quickly, but if not, the same process of relying on immobility will again operate on the nerves of some of the more timid individuals, causing the entire flock to start off again.

The species is subject to virus foot disease, which may result in the loss or clubbing of toes or feet. This disease apparently can be transmitted to white-throated, fox, and song sparrows, and to blue jays.

The rather bulky nest of the junco is usually placed on the ground, often under some cover. It is made of grass, moss, rootlets or bark shreds, and is lined with finer grasses, or cow or deer hair. A favored spot for the nest is under the lip of an overhanging bank, amid a tangle of roots from a blownover tree, in brushwood, dense vegetation, or moss.

The four to six eggs are bluish, greenish, or grayish white, heavily spotted with brown and lilac, and frequently wreathed at the larger end.

The birds build a new nest for a second brood. Each pair has a nesting territory. Both male and female incubate the eggs and both help in the care of the young.

After the breeding season, members of this species gradually assemble into flocks in which they spend the winter. The average number of birds in almost 400 flocks reported in Audubon Christmas censuses was 16. Slate-colored juncos in winter also often associate with towhees, myrtle warblers, fox and white-throated sparrows, and with other species of juncos. In the western part of their range, where they occur sparingly in winter, they are usually seen with Oregon juncos.

Slate-colored juncos are favorites with bird banders who have banded several hundred thousand of them. Information gathered by banders has revealed that many of the members of a flock may remain together in the same flock year after year.

The song of this junco is heard from late March to late July. It is a simple trill, or a series of rapid notes that are all on the same pitch. It is similar to the song of the chipping sparrow but is more musical and usually shorter and slower. When the notes are slow enough to be counted, they range from 8 to 20 in number. Sometimes there are slight variations in time and pitch. An individual bird, however, generally sings the same song without variation. Occasionally one bird may have a quite abnormal song; one such was described by Forbush as "a faint, whispering warble, usually much broken, but not without sweetness." Sometimes a number of birds will sing together.

The call note is a short, sharp *tsip*, sometimes described as a smacking or clicking note, or one that suggests the sound made by striking two coins together. The bird produces a pleasing twitter as it flies away. This is the same twitter uttered by individuals in a flock, supposed to help keep the flock together.

On a yearly basis, according to the researches of government biologists, 22 percent of this junco's diet is of animal origin and 78 percent vegetable. In summer the ratio is about 50:50. The animal food is made up of grasshoppers, caterpillars, leafhoppers, leaf beetles, click beetles, lacewing flies, weevils, ants, moths, and spiders. The vegetable food in winter consists of one-third grass seeds and one-third the seeds of ragweed and polygonum. Other plant material includes the seeds of crabgrass, pigeongrass, pigweed, broom sedge, Russian thistle, amaranth, wild sunflower, and such wild berries as blueberries and crowberries.

Favorite feeder food includes bread crumbs and small grains.

Description: Length to 6½ in. Female slightly smaller than male. Pinkish or horn-colored bill. White belly and outer tail feathers, rest of plumage slate-gray; female slightly lighter gray than male, sometimes brownish; immatures sometimes have pinkish brown on sides and brownish wash on back and breast; juveniles are streaked above and on breasts. (In the Oregon junco, the distinct brownish back and sides contrast much more sharply with the gray or black hood.)

Incubation, 12 days; young stay about 12 days in nest.

Size of eggs, 0.8 x 0.6 in.; one or two broods per year.

OREGON JUNCO

SLATE-COLORED JUNCO

OREGON JUNCO (*Junco oreganus*)

This junco has black or gray foreparts, a brown back, and pinkish sides. The outer tail feathers are white. The various subspecies are distinguished by whether the foreparts are gray or black and by the intensity of the colors on the back and sides. Females are somewhat paler than males of the same subspecies. The Oregon junco hybridizes regularly, both with the slate-colored junco (p. 253) and the gray-headed junco. Its habitat, habits, voice, nest, and eggs are very much like those of the slate-colored junco.

The Oregon junco breeds from southwestern Alaska and south-western Saskatchewan south to central California and northwestern Nevada. It winters from southern Alaska and southwestern Alberta to Lower California and central Texas.

The Point Pinos subspecies is a year-round resident in the coastal hills and mountains of central California, and does not migrate in the accepted sense of the word. However, many of these birds and other Oregon juncos in the western mountains may engage in altitudinal migration; i.e., birds breeding at high elevations will merely descend to neighboring lowlands for the winter, rather than migrate far to the South. Most members of the species, however, engage in widespread north-south migration. Bird-banding studies have shown that many migrant Oregon juncos return almost to the exact spot each winter.

Individuals that migrate put on a layer of fat prior to migration. This fat deposition is apparently induced by the increasing amount of daylight each day during late winter and early spring. Experiments have shown that this deposition can be artificially induced by increasing the amount of light on caged birds in late fall and early winter. Birds that do not migrate do not put on the layer of fat.

In *Birds of Oregon*, Gabrielson and Jewett say of the Oregon junco:

After the nesting season the birds roam the country in small family flocks that gradually merge into larger groups that sometimes number into the hundreds. The birds fly close to the ground, straggling along a few at a time unless flushed by some sudden disturbance. Once an observer has learned their characteristic flight note and sharp alarm note, he will hear them much more frequently than he will see them. If the flock is alarmed, the birds make a quick dash to a thick tree where they remain motionless, save for nervous twitchings of their tails, until the danger is past, and then the chattering note is again heard for some little time before the birds venture to return to their feeding place.

The nest, much like that of the slate-colored junco, is usually placed in a hollow, the edge flush with the surface of the ground. Favorite locations are under a low bush, among roots, or under an overhanging bank along a trail or stream; occasionally a pair builds in a woodpile. Occasionally also, and unlike the slate-colored junco, the nest is placed on a cliff or in some man-made structure that suggests a cliff, such as a niche in a shed.

The nest is of grass and rootlets and is often lined with cow hair. This species has an unusually long nesting period. In Oregon, for example, it breeds from the first of May to the middle of July.

The Oregon junco is one of the most common birds, in season, over large sections of the West, but in the East it is exceedingly rare and much prized at the winter feeder.

If one shows up—usually in a flock of other juncos—it may stay at the same feeder for weeks at a time. The diet of the species is similar to that of the slate-colored junco, and like the latter, its favorite feeder foods are bread crumbs and small grains.

Description: Length to 6 in. Female slightly smaller than male. Light bill; dark tail with conspicuous white outer tail feathers. Male: black or gray head; red-brown back; pink or rusty sides. Female: grayer head; duller back; pink sides contrast sharply with gray of hood. Juveniles have streaked breasts. (brownish wash on back or sides of immature slate-colored junco does not form a sharp contrast with gray of hood.)

Incubation, 12 days; young stay in nest about 12 days.

Size of eggs, 0.8 x 0.6 in.; one or two broods per year.

TREE SPARROW (*Spizella arborea*)

This sparrow breeds from Labrador to Alaska at and just north of the limit of trees. It winters over most of the United States and southern Canada, from eastern Washington to the Atlantic coast, and south to northern California, north Texas, and North Carolina. It is uncommon along the Pacific coast. In Colorado it winters up to 7,000 ft., occasionally to 9,000 ft. The chief winter concentration area is in the mid-South, but there is a heavy population also in Iowa and neighboring states, where a density of 1,000 birds to a square mile has sometimes been recorded. Studies have shown that, in some midwestern areas at least, the females winter farther south than the males.

The tree sparrow is our only sparrow with a reddish cap and a black spot on its breast. In summer it lives among the woody shrubs on the low-lying tundra and along its watercourses. In winter it frequents roadsides, weedy fields and pastures, brushy edges of fields, swampy thickets, orchards, open woods, chicken yards, barnyards, gardens, and feeding stations.

Gabrielson and Lincoln in their *Birds of Alaska* describe its activities in summer thus:

The tree sparrow is one of the abundant birds of the interior willow thickets. It is most numerous at or near timberline where the dwarfed willows form almost continuous patches that cover many acres. It also breeds at sea level, out on the tundra as far as the last patches of willows extend, and it follows the Colville and the Meade Rivers almost to the Arctic coast, again frequenting the willow patches. It is an exceedingly abundant bird throughout the interior country, and seems particularly numerous in the fall after the young are on the wing.

The tree sparrow sings from a perch, but forages and sometimes scratches for seeds on the ground. It progresses by hopping, not walking. It jumps up from the ground to snatch at seeds on unopened seed heads or climbs around the seed head and eats while hanging from it like a goldfinch. Its flight is somewhat undulating, graceful, and elevated.

Witmer Stone, the authority on birds in Cape May, New Jersey, says of its actions in winter:

We usually come upon flocks of tree sparrows feeding on the ground and they fly up into the bushes or trees as we approach, dropping back again when assured that danger has passed. This habit was the basis for the name of tree sparrow given to them by Alexander Wilson. As they perch they give a nervous flirt to the tail and the neck is craned up with the feathers of the crown slightly elevated. Other individuals settle themselves in a hunched attitude with all the plumage fluffed up.

Students of bird physiology and bird migration are interested in the amount of fat in the body of a bird in relation to the activities of the bird throughout the year. Investigations of banded tree sparrows have shown that body fat increases to a seasonal peak in late February (just before the spring migration) and decreases to a low in late July (when family cares are at a maximum). Under controlled temperature conditions, further investigations have shown that the average weight of a tree sparrow goes up as the temperature goes down. Thus at 62° F. the average weight is 0.64 oz., whereas at 18° F. the average weight is 0.79 oz.

This sparrow also has a daily change in weight. It is heaviest in the late afternoon (after a day of feeding) and weighs least in the early morning (after a night of fasting and energy consumed in keeping warm). Migration is a great consumer of fat. One study showed that the average tree sparrow in a single night of migration along the Atlantic coast lost about $\frac{1}{20}$ oz. of fat.

Courtship in this species seems to be a relatively simple rite. It is distinguished chiefly by the males pursuing the females over the tops and through the branches of the willows and alders.

The tree sparrow nests in thickets of shrubs on the level tundra and along the edges of streams. The bulky cupshaped nest is made of grass, rootlets, weed stalks, bark strips, and feathers (often ptarmigan feathers), and is lined with animal hair or fur. It is placed on the ground, often in a depression in a hummock, under a branch, or at the foot of a bush.

The four or five light green or ash-colored eggs are marked with light brown dots evenly distributed over the entire surface.

Family groups are moving about over their breeding range by late August. In September the birds begin to flock and most have left their summer homes by the end of the month. In the United States they arrive in October. Bird banders have noted that many individual birds come back to the same place each winter. One tree sparrow apparently returned to the Pleasant Valley Sanctuary in Lenox, Massachusetts, for eight successive years. Though not retrapped every year, it was recaptured on the fifth, sixth, seventh, and eighth years after it was first banded there. As the weather gets colder the birds become more common at suburban and even city feeders, where they are usually tame and seem unafraid of man.

Tree sparrows constitute the bulk of the winter sparrow flocks in many parts of the northern United States. Associated with them at various times may be chipping, field, fox, white-crowned, Lincoln's, savannah, song, swamp, and white-throated sparrows as well as juncos, redpolls, goldfinches, and myrtle warblers. An analysis of 451 presumably unmixed flocks of tree sparrows observed during Audubon Christmas censuses showed that the average flock was 18 birds.

According to the naturalist Ralph Hoffman, the song of the tree sparrow starts with four long notes, *whee-hee-ho-hee*, followed by a high, clear warble. Townsend and Allen give the song as *seet-seet, seet-iter-*

TREE SPARROW

CHIPPING SPARROW

sweet-sweet, with the first two notes higher than the last two. A. A. Saunders, the bird-song authority, says that "the first two or three notes are generally long, high-pitched, and extremely sweet in quality." In spring a number of birds often sing in concert. The tree sparrow is one of the few birds that actually sings when it is snowing.

The call note is a sharp *tseet* much like a similar *tsee* call of the field sparrow, but with a final consonant. When a flock is feeding together, the combined whistled, musical *teel-wet* or *teelo* notes make a most agreeable, jumbled, sweet twittering.

The winter food of the tree sparrow is weed seeds and grass seeds. Professor F. E. L. Beal, an authority on the food habits of birds, once estimated that each tree sparrow eats on an average of ¼ oz. of weed seeds a day. During its winter stay in Iowa, the species as a whole, he said, consumed 875 tons of weed seeds each year, the equivalent of the

FIELD SPARROW

tonnage carried by a long freight train. The favorite seeds of this sparrow include those of ragweed, lamb's quarters, chickweed, and sunflower. In summer it eats some insects, principally beetles, ants, caterpillars, and grasshoppers. On one occasion near New York City, tree sparrows were seen eating the seeds of the common giant reed, Phragmites, which are seldom touched by any other bird.

The favorite feeder foods include peanut hearts and scratch feed.

Description: Length to 6¼ in. Female slightly smaller than male. Bill, dark above and light below; tail somewhat notched. Cap, solid chestnut; cheeks and line over eye, gray; line through eye, brown; upperparts, streaked brown; two white wing bars; breast, plain whitish with black spot in center; a little white in tail. Autumn birds have yellowish wash on sides, and breast spot may be partially concealed; juveniles have a brown cap and a streaked breast. (Lark sparrow has much white in tail and a striped crown; chipping sparrow has white line over eye, black line through it, and no breast spot.)

Incubation, 11 to 14 days; young stay 12 to 14 days in nest.

Size of eggs, 0.75 x 0.55 in.; one brood per year.

CHIPPING SPARROW (*Spizella passerina*)

The chipping sparrow, or chippy, as it is familiarly called, is distinguished by its reddish crown, white line over the eye, black line through the eye, and notched tail. It is one of our trimmest and slimmest birds.

It breeds throughout North America from Mexico almost to the barren lands. It winters from Virginia and southern California south into Central America. In terms of ecology it nests in the Austral, Transition, and Canadian life-zones. In the western mountains it breeds commonly at 6,000 to 7,000 ft., frequently to 10,000 ft., and sometimes to timber line. After the young are fledged, some birds wander; in the mountains, often up to the timber line. For example, on Truchas Peak, New Mexico, chipping sparrows have been reported in mid-August at 12,300 ft. in the company of mountain bluebirds and red-shafted flickers.

This sparrow has a considerable range in time as well as in space. It goes back many thousand years. Its fossil remains have been found in the Pleistocene tar pits at Rancho La Brea near Los Angeles, California, where it was trapped in the tar along with such now-extinct forms as the dire wolf, monster vulture, and sabre-toothed tiger.

The chipping sparrow likes the vicinity of man. It is a bird of lawns, gardens, and parks, driveways, roadsides, and village streets, edges of fields and woods, brushy fields and clearings. It is also found in orchards, open woods, and pine groves. In the West it frequents the parklike groves and forests of yellow pine and Douglas fir as well as mountain meadows. In open places it is generally found near trees or hedgerows.

The maximum breeding population density of this species in Maryland in recent years has been 90 pairs per 100 acres in a "suburban type residential area (including small orchards and large expanses of lawn) in Prince George County in 1942." Similar population densities may well apply elsewhere in its range in similar habitats.

The chippy is the most domestic of our native sparrows. It is a tame, confiding bird that has increased its numbers since the settlement of the country. The substitution of the axe for tomahawk opened millions of new acres for chippy habitation, and the bird's fearlessness of man enabled it to occupy this habitat right up to the white man's doorstep. It is obviously tolerant of changing environmental conditions.

This native sparrow suffered considerably, however, from the great increase in the introduced house sparrow after 1880. With the decrease in this aggressive species in recent years, however, the number of chippies, in areas where the two species were in competition, has multiplied. In New England and elsewhere a considerable growth in the number of chipping sparrows is probably also due to the decline of agriculture and the development of residential areas.

The chipping sparrow usually sings from a perch at least 12 ft. high on a tree or wire. It forages on open ground, often almost at our feet, and does not scratch for its food amid leaves as do the fox and white-throated sparrows (pp. 282, 286). When flushed, the chippy flies to a perch on a bush, fence, or tree, rather than disappearing into a thicket, as do many other sparrows.

The chippy usually places its nest amid vines, in shrubbery, such as ornamental evergreens and windbreaks, or on the tip of the horizontal limb of a tree. The height from the ground is from 1 to 25 ft., rarely to 40 ft. Apple trees, red cedars, and pine trees are favorite locations. In the heyday of the horse, the nest was sometimes fashioned completely of horsehair. Today it is usually made of small twigs, weed stalks, grasses, and rootlets, and is lined with horsehair. When this is lacking, the bird uses deer or cow hair or fine grasses and rootlets. Chippies will readily accept hair that is put out for them. The pair builds the rather fragile nest in three or four days. Strong gusts of wind will sometimes blow it down. The female lays her eggs early in the morning, usually at the rate of one a day. Incubation starts the day before the last egg is laid. The female does most of the incubating, but the male does some.

The average number of eggs per clutch decreases as the season advances, as follows: May, 3.91; June, 3.69; July, 3.28; August, 3.00.

When first hatched, nestling chipping sparrows are cold-blooded. They do not acquire full control over their temperature and become warm-blooded until they are seven days old.

The chipping sparrow is one of the favorite host species for the brown-headed cowbird.

After breeding, the birds commence to gather in flocks, often with field sparrows and other sparrows. These mixed flocks wander over the countryside, where we flush them from open fields, pastures, and bushy fencerows throughout the winter. In the South, such flocks also often contain myrtle warblers (p. 159), song and savannah sparrows, and various other small birds of the thicket.

Individual chippies frequently winter in the same area year after year. W. P. Wharton who did extensive banding in South Carolina found that 20 percent of the birds he banded were recaptured in his traps in some subsequent winter. This was the highest percent of recaptures of any species he had banded.

The song of the chipping sparrow is one of the simplest. It is a plain, even series of notes, all on one pitch. It is somewhat like that of the worm-eating warbler (forest chippy), pine warbler (pinewoods chippy), palm warbler's, and various juncos; of all these songs, however, that of the chippy is the most mechanical. Sometimes the individual notes can be distinguished separately. Sometimes they run together so fast they are slurred. This song is frequently spoken of as a trill, though in the strict musical sense a trill is a series of two alternating notes, not just one.

Occasionally the bird will add or insert other notes or vary the pitch half a tone or more. Rarely, a song will vary from fast to slow or slow to fast. The dawn song is a series of short phrases, often of eight notes each, with a brief pause between each phrase. During its peak singing period, the bird sings five and a half songs per minute, or at the rate of 330 per hour. It has been estimated that in its 150-day singing season the bird sings a minimum of 200,000 songs, and probably twice that.

The call of this species is a short *tsip* or a slightly higher *tseet,* and as it flies away, a simple twitter. A thin *chip* much like the short *tsip* is used as a migration call note by night migrants.

The chippy sometimes sings at night and it is one of the earliest birds to pipe up at dawn. Its first song of the day is often heard half an hour before sunrise.

Young males begin to sing late in the season. Their songs are often a little different from those of their elders. Some are sweeter, some hoarser.

This species feeds primarily on insects and plant seeds. Through the year it averages 38 percent animal foods, 62 percent vegetable foods; but in summer, fully 90 percent is of animal origin, mostly insects. These include gypsy and brown-tail moths; beet, cabbage, army, and cankerworms; pea lice, various weevils, grasshoppers, locusts, and tent caterpillars. Half the plant seeds are grass seeds and about 10 percent are weed seeds, notably the seeds of plantain, purslane, and ragweed. Occasionally it eats wild berries and a few drone bees.

Like many species, the chipping sparrow comes to feeders most regularly in fall and winter. Its favorite feeder foods include bread crumbs and suet. The chippy can be trained to take food from the hand.

Description: Length, 5 in. Female slightly smaller than male. Black bill; notched tail. Streaked brown upperparts; unmarked grayish white underparts; red crown, white line over eye; black forehead and line through eye; gray rump; two thin white wing bars. Adults in winter and immatures: brownish bill, brown cap with pale central stripe and black streaks; no black forehead, brown ear patch (not bordered with black); gray rump; buffy (not white) underparts, cheeks, and line over eye. (Brewer's sparrow is paler; its crown is evenly streaked with black, no light central stripe, and ear patch is much paler than in chipping; tail seems longer, thinner. Rufous-crowned sparrow has black whiskers, no black line through eye.)

Incubation, 11 days in warm weather and 12.3 days in colder weather; young stay 9 to 10 days in nest.

Size of eggs, 0.7 x 0.5 in.; one to three broods per year.

IMMATURE SPARROWS

WHITE-CROWNED

CHIPPING

HARRIS'

WHITE-THROATED

GOLDEN-CROWNED

FIELD SPARROW (*Spizella pusilla*)

This sparrow summers in southeastern Canada and in much of the United States east of the Rockies. It winters from southern New England and Kansas south to the Gulf. In recent years it has been expanding its winter range slightly to the North.

The species is identified by its pink bill and reddish cap, a combination shared by no other North American sparrow. It is grayish white below, reddish brown above, and has two white wing bars.

In addition to fire scars and open overgrown fields, the field sparrow is also found in old pastures, dry bushy hillsides, weedy orchards, along roadsides, and by the edges of fields and woods.

The maximum breeding population density reported for Maryland in recent years was 80 pairs per 100 acres in "unsprayed apple orchards with unmowed ground cover" in Allegany County in 1948. Almost as high a population density was reported in "abandoned fields with an open growth of young scrub pines" in Prince George County in 1945. These figures may well be applicable to similar habitats in the bird's summer range in other states.

In the beech-maple forest-zone of northeast Ohio the field sparrow in summer is one of five dominant species in the early stage of vegetable development, "when sprouts and seedlings are from one to ten feet high, and there are large open spaces between the crowns." This is probably also true in the same zone elsewhere in the country. Since the habitat favored by the field sparrow is much more widespread now than it was in the days of the Pilgrims, the species probably is more common than it was then.

This sparrow sings from a perch on a shrub or small tree and forages on the ground beneath. Preliminary observations in Wisconsin have shown that 12 ft. is the minimum height acceptable to it for a singing perch when there is a ground cover of 2½ ft. The species is often seen on overhead wires and fences. It is sometimes heard singing at night, particularly by moonlight.

In fall and winter, field sparrows join in flocks with other species, particularly chipping sparrows. At these seasons they will frequently come to feeders.

The nest of this sparrow may be built on the ground, often beside a clod of earth or in a tuft of grass; or it may be placed in a low bush or tree up to 10 ft. above the ground, such as a huckleberry bush, berry patch, or the top tufts of a young pine. The nest is made of grasses, weed stalks, and rootlets, and is lined with fine grasses or a few hairs. An average of three days and a maximum of five is required to build the structure. The female lays three to five grayish white or bluish white eggs, generously dotted with light red-brown and lilac.

The average number of eggs in a clutch tends to decline with the progress of the season, as follows: May, 3.77; June, 3.69; July, 3.14; August, 3.00. The female can lay 18 eggs in one season. Incubation is largely if not entirely undertaken by the female, but the male helps care for the young.

For the first two days of their life the young are cold-blooded—as were their reptilian ancestors. They do not establish complete control of their temperature and become warm-blooded until seven days old.

The song of this sparrow starts off slowly with three, fairly long, clear notes. These are followed by a trill which becomes faster as it proceeds, at times rising or falling in pitch. We may write it *twee twee twee te-te-te-te-te-te*.

A. A. Saunders, in his *Guide to Bird Songs,* gives diagrams for 15 different varieties of the song. He says:

The song of the field sparrow is simple but of an exceedingly sweet, clear, whistled quality. It normally consists of a series of notes which are at first rather slow and long and gradually become shorter and more rapidly repeated till the song ends in a trill. The pitch usually rises or falls toward the end, but some songs are all on one pitch. In many songs the first notes slur downward; in some they slur upward; while in others they are not slurred at all. A few songs rise and fall in pitch, and some fall and then rise. But throughout these songs the extremely sweet, clear quality remains and distinguishes the species of the singer beyond question.

Each individual field sparrow usually sings but one song and varies it very little, so that individuals are easily marked and their singing habits followed. In late summer, birds often sing a longer song by simply repeating the song over two or three times. In such cases they often begin and end with rapid notes and put the slower notes in the middle of the song.

Rarely, at seasons other than late summer, the bird begins with a trill and sings its song in reverse, much to the puzzlement of even experienced ornithologists. The field sparrow's call note is a simple *tsip,* of slightly complaining quality and not so hard and sharp as that of the chipping sparrow.

The food of the field sparrow is largely weed and grass seeds and a little grain. Insects account for about 40 percent of its diet. These include beetles, grasshoppers, bugs, ants, flies, crickets, plant lice, tent caterpillars, and cankerworms.

The favorite food of this species at the feeder is a mixture of seeds.

Description: Length to 6 in. Female slightly smaller than male. Slim body, pink bill; tail fairly long and slightly notched; reddish cap and ear patch; white and narrow eye ring with dull gray border; two white wing bars; unspotted grayish white underparts, with brown wash on breast and sides. The young are finely streaked below but lack prominent head stripings. (Do not confuse with the tree sparrow, which has a dark spot on its breast and whiter wing bars, nor with the chipping sparrow, which has a white line over its eye.)

Incubation, 11 to 13 days; young stay 9 or 10 days in nest.

Size of eggs, 0.7 x 0.5 in.; one to three broods per year.

HARRIS' SPARROW (*Zonotrichia querula*)

This sparrow honors the memory of Edward Harris (1799–1863), a friend of John James Audubon. Harris collected specimens for Audubon, helped sell his books, and accompanied him on the Missouri River expedition in 1843.

Harris' sparrow is our largest sparrow and is the only one with a black cap, face, and throat. It is brownish above, white below; has streaks on its sides, two white wing bars and a longish tail. When flying away from the observer its back looks lighter than that of a song sparrow.

It breeds in the spruce forests and in the dwarf timber of the adjacent tundra in northern Manitoba, Saskatchewan, and the Northwest

Territories. John Bowman Semple and George Miksch Sutton, in an article in *Auk,* give an excellent account of this species on its breeding grounds as Churchill, Manitoba:

Frequently we found them feeding in tamarack trees; they appeared to be eating the buds. They were very graceful in their movements, climbing about on the slender, outermost twigs, and bowing this way and that like crossbills. Sometimes a single bird would fly suddenly from the ground under a bush, as if it had just come from a nest. Such a bird usually sought a rather high perch, often the top of a dead spruce near-by, where it would give itself over to a spasm of alarm notes, loud enough to summon all the yammering lesser yellowlegs from miles around; then it would dart away, to be seen no more. The habit of the birds, when frightened from the ground, of flying to rather high perches was characteristic.

Alexander Wetmore, onetime head of the Smithsonian Institution, in the *Migrations of Birds,* cites this as a species with limited distribution and migration:

In summer it nests in the Hudsonian zone, from Fort Churchill on Hudson's Bay westward. In September and early October it migrates south to a wintering ground from northern Kansas south to northern Texas (sometimes the Gulf coast). Migration is almost directly south and extends only through a comparatively narrow area along the eastern edge of the Great Plains. Stragglers come to eastern Colorado (sometimes California) on the west and central Wisconsin and Illinois (sometimes Ohio) on the east, but the full migration centers through a narrow region comprising eastern Kansas and western Missouri. Here this fine bird swarms in thickets and hedgerows during October, and again in April, filling the air with its rollicking whistled calls. At the height of the migration thousands may be seen in a single day, but outside this strip, which is barely 250 miles wide, the bird is casual or rare. The cause for this limited distribution is wholly obscure, for areas at either hand seem equally suited for the needs of the bird, which has the habits of its congeners. No other bird has this distribution, which lies along the lines where forms of the eastern half of the country begin to disappear and those of the west to appear.

In migration and in winter this is a bird of hedgerows, streamside thickets, brush piles, brushy undergrowth, vine tangles, edges of woods, and open woodlands. It scratches among leaves on the ground, where it often associates with its close relatives the white-throated and white-crowned sparrow and other winter sparrows. Its posture is upright and suggests that of the white-crowned.

Many of the birds are already mated by the time they reach their breeding grounds in late May. Nest building starts within a week after arrival. The nest is largely of grass with a lining of finer grass and is usually placed under a shrub on a mossy hummock with a southern exposure amid low spruce trees. The female lays three to five pale yellow-green eggs, spotted and scrawled with pecan-brown markings which sometimes form an irregular wreath about the larger end. The female incubates alone.

Semple and Sutton listened to the bird for almost six weeks on its breeding grounds; they say:

The song most frequently heard was single, whistled note, tenuous, fragile, a trifle quavering, and possessed of the plaintive character of the final *Peabody* phrases of the white-throated sparrow's lay. Sometimes this note was repeated once, twice, even four or five times, the notes trailing into each other uncertainly. Other songs were more elaborate, and consisted of two notes at one pitch followed by two or three notes two steps higher, or two or three steps lower. Often the notes struck were not quite in key, this frequently being responsible, no doubt, for the minor effect the songs produced.

Harris's sparrow has another, louder, and very striking song which we hear only occasionally. This song was so distinctively different from the usual whistle, and so suggestive of the songs of some of the other species of sparrows, that for some time we could not place it. It began with a fine, swiftly descending, rather tuneless whistle or squeal, and closed with a series of from three to six rough, buzzing, drawled notes which decidedly resembled the usual song of the clay-colored sparrow. We wrote the song down thus: *Eeeeeeeeee, zhee, zhee, zhee, zhee, zhee.* We noticed that the bird usually gave this song from a high perch and that, after it had sung, it dropped to the ground stealthily or flew off hurriedly.

On the breeding grounds, Harris' sparrows often sing in chorus, particularly from 8 to 10 A.M. and in the late afternoon. In fall and winter the birds also sometimes engage in chorus singing in the late afternoons. At times the female sings too, a somewhat softer song. The alarm note is a loud *wink,* louder than a similar note of the white-throated sparrow. There is also a chuckling, contented, musical note.

The food of Harris' sparrow, according to the studies of Department of Agriculture biologists, is 92 percent of vegetable origin and 8 percent of animal origin. Seeds of ragweed and polygonum make up about half the vegetable food; the balance is grass seeds, weed seeds, and some fruit. The nestlings are believed to be fed on insects.

In the East, records of this sparrow are casual to accidental. Most are at feeding stations where the bird—usually an individual—may stay for several weeks.

Description: Length, 6¾ to 7¾ in. Female slightly smaller than male. Pinkish bill; black cap, face, and throat. Spring adults: brownish upperparts, plain white underparts, gray cheeks, streaked sides, two white wing bars. Fall adult: black on cap and face; throat veiled with gray. First winter, crown is brown and spotted; face, flanks, and undertail coverts are buffy; white throat with necklace of brown streaks. Second winter similar to first winter, but with black blotch on chin.

Incubation, 12 to 14 days; young stay 13 to 15 days in nest.

Size of eggs, 0.95 x 0.65 in.; one brood per year.

WHITE-CROWNED SPARROW (*Zonotrichia leucophrys*)

The white-crowned sparrow is our most aristocratic of all sparrows. It is bold, handsome, upright in carriage, forthright in manner. Its relative rarity east of the Appalachians places it among those species especially esteemed by the eastern bird watcher. Its breeding grounds are chiefly in the remote north or high up in the mountains.

The sparrow is further distinguished by its large size, white crown, black-and-white head stripes and pearly breast. It breeds in Alaska, northern and western Canada, and in the western United States south to central California and northern New Mexico, principally in the mountains. It winters from southern British Columbia, Kansas, and western North Carolina south to central Mexico, the Gulf coast, and casually to Florida and Cuba. Its migration is largely west of the Appalachians.

Two of the western subspecies of this bird, Gambel's sparrow and Nuttall's sparrow, can be identified in the field and have long been known by these common names. In Gambel's sparrow, the white line over the eye reaches to the bill, whereas in the regular white-crowned sparrow, the space between the eye and the bill is black. In Nuttall's sparrow the white line also reaches the bill, but the white crown stripe is much narrower than in Gambel's.

Gambel's sparrow breeds from Alaska to northern Canada and winters from southern British Columbia and Kansas to northern Mexico. Nuttall's sparrow is resident along the Pacific coast, west of the Cascades, from Mendocino to Santa Barbara counties in California. The other subspecies, the Oregon white-crowned and the Puget Sound sparrow, breed in the Northwest, winter south into Mexico, and cannot readily be distinguished in the field from Gambel's sparrow. The modern practice, for general purposes, is to use the species name, white-crowned sparrow, for all forms and not be concerned with field identification of subspecies.

The white-crown breeds in the Hudsonian and Canadian life-zones, the zones of spruce and pine. Its favorite habitat in the North is the dwarf willows that line lakes and watercourses beyond the limit of trees and reach into the tundra. In Newfoundland it occurs in dwarf spruce and tamarack and in more open barrens. In the West it prefers shrubby mountain slopes, open uplands, and brushy subalpine meadows. In New Mexico it breeds as high as 11,000 ft. on Pecos Baldy. It also likes windy coastal areas with low shrubs.

In migration and in winter this sparrow frequents thickets, roadsides, hedgerows, edges of woods, weedy fields, and pastures, as well as dooryards and shrubby areas around farms and suburbs. Gabrielson and Jewett in *Birds of Oregon,* say: "during migration it forms a dominant element everywhere in the sparrow swarms that infest the fence rows and weed patches."

The white-crowned sparrow forages on the ground, scratches vigorously among the leaves, and when disturbed, takes refuge in a thicket. On the ground it can run rapidly. It usually sings from an elevated perch, but may sometimes give voice from inside a thicket. In the Arctic we hear its song from the top of the tallest shrub, in Newfoundland from a fence post, scrubby tree, or even a rock. Sometimes the bird sings at night, often continually.

When you see this bird it will often be at eye level or a little higher, in a shrub or brush pile. If you approach it slowly, you can study it at relative leisure. If it becomes aroused or alarmed, it will puff up its top-knot to display an ermine crown.

It is found in autumn and winter with other sparrows, such as the white-throated (p. 283), Harris' (p. 272), golden-crowned (p. 281), fox (p. 287), and song (p. 288) sparrows. In the colder months in the southern part of its range, a flock may settle down and spend the entire season in the weedy corner of a field or along a limited section of a railroad right-of-way.

In Yellowstone National Park, Gambel's sparrow is the most common of all birds. It arrives about May 1 at the 6,500-ft. level. By late June it has ascended to 9,000 ft., following the retreating snow. The Yellowstone is an excellent place to study altitudinal migration of this and other species.

In Maryland the peak of the white-crown's migration is May 5 to 15 and October 10 to 30. In recent years the bird has been extending its wintering range through central Maryland and sparingly down the Delmarva Peninsula. In New England it is more common, or rather less uncommon, in spring than in fall.

The nest of the white-crowned sparrow is placed on the ground at the foot of a shrub, often in a mossy area. Sometimes it is found low in a bush. The structure is made of small twigs, grass, leaves, rootlets, and moss, and is lined with fur, hair, fine grass, bark strips, or rootlets.

The female lays four or five (in the Arctic, sometimes six) greenish white or bluish white eggs. These are heavily marked with red-brown and purple-brown spots that often form somewhat of a wreath around the larger end. The female does all the incubating. The species is normally monogamous, but the male occasionally takes two mates.

As is the case with many species, the nesting season is shorter in the northern parts of the bird's range than in the south. Near the Canadian border, for example, the reproductive period is only two-thirds as long as it is in central California. The size of the average clutch of eggs varies with the subspecies. In the Puget Sound sparrow it is 4.00 eggs. In Nuttall's sparrow, only 3.65.

The song of the white-crowned sparrow is a short but attractive melody of five to seven notes sometimes immediately repeated. The beginning of the song is often said to suggest that of the white-throated sparrow. The first note is long and clear. To human ears it has some element of sadness or melancholy. C. W. Townsend renders the song as more *wet wetter wet chee zee*. Cruickshank writes it down as *pee bee bee bee chee zee zee*.

On its summer breeding grounds the white-crown sings into August. Sometimes 20 or more birds may sing at once, an extraordinarily pleasing performance. While the female is incubating, the male may sing from a nearby perch almost all day. Sometimes during a rainy morning and regularly in the autumn there is a whisper song that can be heard only a short distance away. Unlike most species of birds, the female occasionally also sings. The white-crown's call is a *chink* or *tsip* and a sharp *chip*.

A. A. Saunders, author of *Guide to Bird Songs*, describes the song of the white-crown as consisting of "long clear whistles at the beginning and husky whistles at the end."

In summer the food of the white-crown is largely spiders and insects such as caterpillars, ants, beetles, weevils, locusts, grasshoppers, and cutworms. Occasionally it catches insects in the air. During the rest of the year the bird subsists largely on a vegetable diet, which includes the seeds of ragweed and Johnson grass, other weed seeds, waste grain, a little wild fruit, some grapes, buds, blossoms, and berries such as crowberries.

Favorite feeder foods of the white-crown include crumbs and scratch grain. White-crowned sparrows will often stay at feeders through the winter, far north of their regular range.

Description: Length, 6½ to 7½ in. Female slightly smaller than male. Reddish bill. Adult: crown with black-and-white stripes, white center; streaked brownish upperparts; pearly neck and breast; two white wing bars. Immature: similar, but with pink bill, crown with red-brown and light gray-brown stripes, underparts with brown wash. (White-throated has a white throat and black bill; yellow before the eye, browner above. Golden-crowned has a golden crown and no white line over the eye; the immature golden-crown is browner and lacks the light gray-brown crown stripe of the immature white-crowned.)

Incubation, 12 to 14 days (15 to 16 in Alaska); young stay 15 to 16 days in nest.

Size of eggs, 0.85 x 0.65 in.; one brood per year.

GOLDEN-CROWNED SPARROW (*Zonotrichia atricapilla*)

Scientists group several species of similar birds into one genus. Members of a genus must all show signs of close relationship. The genus Zonotrichia, to which the golden-crowned sparrow belongs, includes the

HARRIS' SPARROW

white-throated, white-crowned, and Harris' sparrow, all of which are described in this book.

Two species, the white-throated and the white-crowned, have a coast-to-coast distribution, although the white-throated is more common in the East and the white-crowned more common in the West. The white-throated sparrow does not vary within its range. It has no subspecies.

The white-crowned, on the other hand, is more variable. It has given rise to four different subspecies, each of which in the future may develop into new species.

GOLDEN-CROWNED SPARROW

WHITE-CROWNED SPARROW

WHITE-THROATED SPARROW

The two other species of Zonotrichia, Harris' sparrow and the golden-crowned, have a limited range and no subspecies. Harris' sparrow is found along the centerline of the continent; the golden-crowned, along the Pacific coast. The golden-crowned looks as if it might have evolved from the white-crowned at some period in the past.

The large, handsome, golden-crowned sparrow is distinguished by the golden stripe over the middle of its crown and the heavy black stripe over its eye. On the back of its head the gold turns to a gray similar to its cheek and breast. Seen from the front the gold crown is conspicuous, but seen from the side it may be hidden; the big black stripe over the eye may tend to give the appearance of an all-black crown.

This sparrow breeds from western Alaska to southwestern Alberta and northern Washington and winters from southern British Columbia to northern Lower California, principally west of the Cascades and the Sierra Nevada. In Alaska, in summer it is most common south of the Alaska range, in the Alaska peninsula, and on Unimak, Kodiak, Kenai, and the Shumagin Islands.

On its breeding grounds in Alaska this species is partial to low willows and alders and dwarf firs. In migration and in winter it prefers brushy clearings, tangles, thickets, and canyons, chaparral-covered slopes, fencerows, and briar and weed patches.

The golden-crowned sparrow likes to forage on the ground, but it sings from an elevated perch, darting quickly into a thicket at the first sign of danger. It is more shy and retiring than the white-crowned. Over most of the range that the two species occupy in common, the golden-crowned is usually the less abundant. However, Florence Merriam Bailey, in her *Handbook of Birds of the Western United States*, writes:

In winter the golden-crowns are among the common birds of the San Francisco parks and cemeteries and are so tame they will hop over the grass and down the paths close to the bench on which you are sitting. The sparrow flock usually includes more white-crowns than goldens, but all are equally and delightfully familiar. In some of the parks the birds seem especially fond of sunning themselves on the budding *Laurestinus* bushes.

Gabrielson and Lincoln, in their *Birds of Alaska*, say:

No studies have been made of the nesting habits, so the length of the incubation period and the time the young remain in the nest are not known, although probably neither differs greatly from those of the Gambel's sparrow. Like that species, after the nesting season it gathers in loose flocks and migrates in company with others, sometimes forming a prominent element in the swarms of migrating sparrows that in late August and early September are such a conspicuous seasonal feature of the bird world in Alaska. In the spring, the golden moves up the coast, rather than through the interior as is done by so many other species, and it is a common migrant through southeastern Alaska. . . .

Like the Gambel's sparrow, this bird does not normally fly long distances but, when pressed closely, moves from one bush to another. It is adept at flying close to the ground from one patch of cover to gain access to another before becoming visible to an observer and is conspicuous only when it is in song during the breeding season and as an element of the feeding hordes of migrant sparrows in the fall.

In Washington, Oregon, and California the golden-crown is a common migrant in September and October and in April and May. It is also a regular winter visitor in those states, but only commonly from central Oregon south. In migration and in winter it often associates with white-crowned, white-throated, fox, and song sparrows.

The nest of the golden-crowned sparrow is placed near the ground in a low shrub or tree, on the ground in a depression or on a tussock. It is made of twigs and moss and lined with grass and fine roots. The female lays five buff, ashy, or pale greenish eggs with fine brown spots.

The children's round, "Three Blind Mice," suggests the three common whistled, flutelike notes in the plaintive song of this species. The phrases *"Oh, dear me"* or *"Oh, come here"* also catch well the timing and descending character of this unadorned song.

The food of the golden-crown is largely vegetable—almost entirely so according to one study, which set the figure at 99.1 percent. This may be too high, but as the study showed, weed seeds, waste grain, buds, and flowers do make up the bulk of the golden-crowned's diet. In the breeding season we may assume that insects for the young constitute some part of its food. In Alaska the bird takes many crowberries. A favorite feeder food is crumbs.

Description: Length, 6¾ in. Crown, stripe yellow in front, gray to rear; black broad stripe over eye; gray cheeks and underparts; olive brown upperparts with darker streaks; two white wing bars; sides with brown wash. Immature: dull brownish yellow crown stripe with fine dusky streaks front and back; brown broad stripe over eye, brownish above, whitish below. (The black stripe over the eye is not always complete. The immature rather resembles a big female house sparrow, but usually has a trace of yellow on crown, and is browner.)

Incubation, 12 to 14 days; young stay 13 to 15 days in nest.

Size of eggs, 0.66 x 0.47 in.; one brood per year.

WHITE-THROATED SPARROW (*Zonotrichia albicollis*)

Few bird songs are as typical of New England as the white-throated sparrow. New England, however, holds no monopoly on the species. From any northern thicket, coast to coast, the white-throat's melody greets the spring dawn from April onward. The species breeds from sea level to timber line in zones of spruce and pine in a broad belt across the continent, from the Yukon and British Columbia to Labrador and the mountains of Pennsylvania. It winters from Kansas and Massachusetts to the Gulf, primarily in the southeastern states.

The white-throated sparrow, jaunty and familiar, is our only sparrow with a bright white throat and a black-and-white striped crown. Many regard it as our most handsome sparrow, its song as our most beautiful sparrow song. It is a bird of thickets and tangles, brush piles, hedges, and second growth. It loves the edges of woods and ravines, overgrown pastures, swamps, streamsides, clearings, yards, and gardens. In spring migration these sparrows sometimes swarm in favored localities.

The white-throat hops rather than walks. It scratches among the ground litter with both feet, scattering leaves and humus, as does the fox sparrow, but not with equal noise or vigor. It can readily be "squeaked out" of the underbrush by kissing the back of one's hand. From the ground the bird flies up to a low branch where it remains relatively motionless and in full view until it has assessed the situation. If alarmed it seeks safety in the thicket. When it takes off on its short flights, we often hear an initial, faint whirring of its wings. At night it roosts on low or medium height branches.

The cupshaped nest of this sparrow is similar to that of the song sparrow, but larger. It is composed of grasses, twigs, leaves, and mosses, and lined with finer grasses, rootlets, or hair. The female alone builds it under a bush or log or, rarely, a foot or two up in a thick conifer. In primitive conditions the bird bred in glades of coniferous forests. Today favored nesting areas include cutover, brushy, and second-growth land and the edges of swamps, pastures, and woods.

The female white-throat lays four or five eggs marked with fine red-brown spots on a pale greenish, bluish, or whitish ground color. She does the incubating alone, but the male helps feed the young.

In the fall white-throats migrate in small flocks. They associate with juncos and other sparrows and, in winter in the South, mingle with Carolina wrens (p. 110) and cardinals (p. 200). The well-known ornithologist, Frank M. Chapman, writes of them in autumn in the New York City area as follows:

Few birds are more sociable than the White-throats. At this season they are always in little companies, and they frequently roost together in large numbers in the depths of dense thickets or clumps of evergreens. After they have retired one may hear the sharp *chink* of their "quarrier" chorus, and when darkness comes, with low, brooding notes of cozy companionship they are hushed for the night.

The white-throated sparrow is a favorite with bird banders because it enters traps readily. Birds trapped in the South are taken again, winter after winter, at the same banding station, often even in the same corner of the same yard. Over a number of years W. P. Wharton banded 3,112 individuals in Summerville, South Carolina. Of these, he retrapped 570 in the same area in succeeding seasons. Yet, each of these birds between trappings may have traveled a 3,000-mile round trip to its breeding grounds. Oddly enough, however, migrating sparrows are seldom recaptured in the same place en route. The birds apparently rarely take the same course, or do not stop over at the same places, from one year to the next.

Studies by Albert Wolfson of white-throats banded at Evanston, Illinois, showed that captive birds on the average used up 18 calories of energy per day and that the birds fatten up during the winter at two different times, once in midwinter and once again just before the spring migration. The midwinter increase in weight appears to be correlated in part with low temperatures and short days. In the premigratory increase, the bird is taking on fuel for its coming migration. Indeed, Wolfson found that birds before migrating in the wild add enough fat for a night flight of from 270 to 360 miles at 30 mph.

The highly distinctive song of the white-throat consists of one or two long introductory notes followed by three or four phrases of three notes each, which might be graphically portrayed thus, the length of the line suggesting the length of the note: — — —.— —.— —.—.

The bird sings from the ground or a low perch, and it frequently sings at night. In the South in midwinter, the song is often heard on mild or cloudy days. The autumnal chorus of the young learning to sing is unusually charming.

Often the first sign of a white-throat is not the song but a long *seeep* from a thicket. This high, incisive note enables us to distinguish the white-throat from all other sparrows. The bird also utters a distinctive, metallic *chip* or *chink*.

The chief foods of the white-throat are weed seeds, berries, and insects. The seeds include: ragweed and bindweed; the berries: alder, blackberry, dogweed, elder, poison ivy, smilax, spicebush, and yaupon; the insects: grasshoppers, beetles, ants, wasps, locusts, and boll weevils.

Favorite feeder foods of the white-throat are peanut hearts and scratch feed.

Description: Length, 7 in. Dark bill. Adult: crown with black and white stripes; white throat; yellow spot before eye; brownish back, streaked with black; two white wing bars; gray cheeks and underparts. Immature similar, but crown stripes are brown and white, and white on throat is duller. (White-crowned has grayish throat. Swamp sparrow is smaller; adult has reddish crown, immature lacks wing bars.)

Incubation, 12 to 14 days; young stay 12 to 14 days in nest.

Size of eggs, 0.8 x 0.6 in.; two broods per year.

FOX SPARROW (*Passerella iliaca*)

The song of the fox sparrow can be heard from many a suburban garden over most of the continental 49 states; *weeta weeta che che che*

che it goes, with some variations, particularly the last four notes. But few know the song well because it is heard only in migration in early spring.

The fox sparrow, so named for its foxlike color, is our largest and most distinctive sparrow, the one with the most heavily streaked underparts. The sexes look alike, although the female is slightly smaller. It is highly adaptable and readily given to developing distinctive local geographic variations. Indeed, next to the song sparrow, the fox sparrow has more recognized subspecies (18) than any other species of North American bird. Most of these are in the West; seven breed in Alaska. The subspecies range in appearance from large, dark brownish forms in southern Alaska and coastal British Columbia to grayer forms in

FOX SPARROW

California. The most widespread subspecies, the eastern fox sparrow, is the brightest. It is distinguished from other sparrows by its reddish-brown wings, rump, tail, and breast streaks, and by the gray on its head and cheeks.

The species as a whole breeds from Alaska to Newfoundland in the zone of evergreen forest and sometimes in adjacent tundra, particularly along shrubby borders of watercourses. It also breeds in the pine and spruce zones of western mountains. It winters southward to northern Lower California, the Gulf, and central Florida. In migration in any particular area, however, its numbers are likely to be irregular from year to year; sometimes scarce, sometimes abundant. It ranges in time back to the Pleistocene, its fossil remains of that epoch having been found in tar pits in California.

The fox sparrow is a bird of thickets, particularly woodland thickets. It is found in open, cutover, burnedover, or scrubby woods, wood edges, overgrown fields, hedgerows, and the bushy borders of gardens. In the West it is also found in chaparral thickets. When wintering in the South it favors thick, swampy woods. Eugene P. Bicknell, the ornithologist-banker who discovered Bicknell's thrush, writes of its habitat in the Middle Atlantic states:

In the early spring the fox sparrow is seen mostly about damp thickets and roadside shrubbery; later it takes more to woodsides, foraging on leaf-strewn slopes where there is little or no undergrowth, often associated with small parties of Juncos. On its return in the autumn it again becomes a common denizen of hedgerows and thickets, and also invades the weedy grainfields, rarely, however, straying far from some thickety cover. Sometimes large numbers congregate among withered growths of tall weeds, whence they emerge with a loud whirring of wings as their retreat is invaded, and hie away in tawny clouds, flock after flock.

The fox sparrow feeds in open grassy glades, surrounded by willows 10 to 12 ft. high, the branches of which it uses for singing perches.

On the ground the fox sparrow progresses by hopping, but the motions of its feet are so fast that it is hard to be sure that sometimes it may not also run a few steps. Everytime it hops it flicks its conspicuous red-brown tail. In its search for food this species scratches noisily among the leaves, using both feet at once. It sometimes jumps up in the air several inches, working both feet lustily as it comes down, sending a shower of leaves, dust, or sand backward a yard or more. If snow is on the ground, the bird will scratch through the snow to uncover leaves beneath. This ability to find food under snow permits the fox sparrow to migrate earlier and occupy its summer range sooner than a number of other birds not so generously endowed with long toes and claws.

If disturbed at its foraging on the ground, the bird flies up to a low branch that affords a wider view and an easier escape. It is a shy species, particularly in the breeding season, when it may be hard to flush from its chosen thicket, through which it scurries on the ground like a big red mouse. Although it flies long distances in migration, the flight we usually see is a short flitting from perch to cover or cover to perch. Such flight is jerky and nervous and is accompanied by pronounced tail flitting.

In the South, fox sparrows often arrive with a cold wave and are frequently seen in the company of towhees, white-throated sparrows, and juncos. In very severe weather they may invade towns in great numbers.

The fox sparrow usually builds its rather large nest on the ground in or near the northern evergreen forest. The structure is frequently placed under the shelter of a small tree or bush. Sometimes, however, the bird builds in a bush or tree up to a height of 12 ft., particularly early in the season when there may still be danger of late snow. The nest is cupshaped, made of grasses, mosses, leaves, bark shreds, weed stalks and rootlets, and is lined with hair, feathers, fine grass, or fine rootlets.

The three to five eggs of this sparrow have a pale green or blue background and are heavily spotted with rusty brown. The female does most of or all the incubation.

After the breeding season, fox sparrows collect in small flocks for post-breeding wandering and migration. A few go out on the tundra. The sparrows generally remain in smaller or larger flocks throughout the winter. In colder months an individual bird may live in one thicket for a protracted period.

The song of the fox sparrow that so delights us in migration is not its full song, which is heard only on breeding grounds. It is one of the strongest and loveliest of sparrow songs, and has been written down by various authors as *cher-ee, hear-her, hear-her, tellit;* or *to-whip, to-whee, oh-whee, buzz tellit;* or *tou-la, tou-la, tou-lit.* Allan Cruickshank, author of *A Pocket Guide to the Birds,* writes it as *Hear, hear, I sing sweet, sweeter, most sweetly,* which is an easy rendition to remember. Often a bird will sing with hardly a pause for almost 10 minutes. In Georgia and probably elsewhere in the South it sings its winter or migration song from late November until spring in cloudy and rainy weather.

The call note of this sparrow is a *smack* somewhat like that of a brown thrasher.

The food of the fox sparrow is primarily weed seeds. Ragweed and bindweed may constitute half of the total. It enjoys pokeberries and the berries of holly and cedar. The species consumes large numbers of worms and insects, notably millipedes, beetles, ants, and insect larvae found in the humus. Some birch, alder catkins, and wild fruit are also part of its diet. It is a regular visitor to feeders.

Description: Length to 7½ in. Female slightly smaller than male. Bill, dusky above, yellowish below; flesh-colored to clay-colored legs and feet; large and strong feet and claws; tail nearly square. Streaked red-brown above (on a gray background), brightest on wings, rump, and tail; white below, heavily streaked also with red-brown, often forming a dark spot in the middle of its breast; cheeks and head largely gray; two inconspicuous, narrow, white wing bars. (Hermit thrush has a thin bill, olive-brown, not reddish, head, no streaks on its back, and stands up straighter.)

Incubation, 12 to 14 days; young stay 11 to 13 days in nest.

Size of eggs, 0.9 x 0.7 in.; two broods per year.

SONG SPARROW (*Melospiza melodia*)

Originally a bird of bushy fields, briar tangles, and swampy thickets, the civilization of North America presented no problems for the song sparrow. Adapting quickly and easily to the changes brought about by man, it has become one of the most familiar of our North American birds, found everywhere from city backyards and vacant lots to brushy fencerows and roadsides in the farmlands.

Like most of our native sparrows it is a plain-looking bird with dull, brown, streaky upperparts. The underparts are dull whitish, heavily marked with dark streaks that run together to form the identifying mark of the song sparrow—a large dark blotch in the center of the breast. Sexes are alike.

The song sparrow occurs from the Aleutian Islands, southern Mackenzie, and the Gulf of St. Lawrence to northern Mexico in the West and southern Illinois, and to the mountains of northern Georgia and the coast of North Carolina in the East.

In winter it withdraws from the extreme northern portion of its range and is found southward to the Gulf coast and northern Florida. Song sparrows are present in at least small numbers throughout the year from southern New England southward. Originally it was thought that only a portion of the population migrated while a substantial number remained behind as permanent residents. But analysis of banding records indicates that only a few individuals actually winter in their nesting areas. Instead, they migrate southward a short distance and are replaced by birds from farther north.

Despite its nondescript appearance the song sparrow has a remarkable number of geographic variations; approximately 25 different races, or subspecies, have been described.

These variations do not occur haphazardly. They are the result of adaptation to temperature, humidity, and other local environmental factors, and can be shown to conform to certain general rules of evolutionary development.

For instance, individuals of northern populations tend to be larger than individuals of southern populations of the same species. The reason is that, other things being equal, a larger organism is better able to conserve body heat than is a small organism because of the more favorable ratio between total mass and total surface area. In between these size extremes may be any number of intermediate populations, each intergrading with populations of adjoining areas. The result is a gradation in which the extremes are obviously different, but the variation from link to link sometimes so slight as to be almost imperceptible.

Similarly, populations from humid areas tend to be darker in coloration than do populations from arid areas. Thus the large, dark song sparrows living in the damp cold of the Aleutians differ considerably in appearance from the small pale forms of the arid Southwest.

In late February, song sparrows that have drifted southward for the winter begin moving north, returning to the northern states by March and reaching the limit of their range in northern Canada by early April.

Together with the redwing and bluebird, the song sparrow is one of the first birds to be heard in the spring. Individuals that have remained in the north for the winter often begin singing as early as mid-February. By March, when the migrants have returned, the entire population is in full song, though winter is by no means over and much bad weather may lie ahead. As W. A. Stearns commented in *New England Bird Life*:

One of the most cheerful and persevering of songsters, as it is, this Sparrow often tunes its quivering pipe to the most dreary surroundings, the brief but hearty stave being one of the few snatches of bird-melody ever woven with "a winter's tale" in Puritanic stress of weather. The Song Sparrow flushes with music as soon as winter relaxes in the least, finding full voice in March when those who have worried through the cold greet the new arrivals from the south, and all together fill a chorus to which the shrubbery resounds unceasingly. . . .

SONG SPARROW

By early April the males have begun to establish territories, and solo performances replace the choral efforts of late winter. He may choose a roof top or utility pole as his singing perch, but usually it is some conspicuous perch nearer the ground; a fence post, bush, or tall weed stalk.

Like the bird itself, the voice of the song sparrow is rather plain and simple, but subject to remarkable variation. The basic pattern may be described as three, short, spaced notes, all on the same pitch, followed by a jumble of paired notes and trills with constant and rapid changes in pitch. But each individual sings at least three and sometimes as many as 20 different variations of his basic theme, all of which are at least slightly different from the songs of any other song sparrow. Certain regional differences are evident also; as a group, song sparrows of one area may have certain common vocal characteristics that distinguish them from birds of another area.

The call note, a very distinctive *chiff* or *chimp*, is difficult to describe but easily recognized by ear. Once known, it becomes a useful standard of comparison for recognizing the call notes of many other species.

As the breeding season advances the males become quite aggressive, chasing one another with a peculiar fluttering flight and occasionally buffeting and pecking with wings and bills. The female is courted in much the same manner, though less violently. The male pursues her with fluttering, sailing flight, occasionally hovering in mid-flight to give vent to his excitement in a rapid burst of song.

The nest is usually hidden in a clump of thick grass or tangle of briars on or near the ground, though occasionally song sparrows will build in a bush, low tree, or even a natural hollow or birdbox. They prefer a streamside or low swampy ground, but are perfectly willing to nest in dry brushy fields and similar locations, provided water is reasonably close by. The cupshaped nest, built by the female in about five or six days, is woven from grass, bark, and leaves, and lined with rootlets, hair, or similar soft material. The number of eggs vary from three to seven; the usual clutch is four or five. They are greenish white, variably speckled and blotched shades of brown and reddish.

Some males incubate; others leave this chore entirely to the female.

The eggs hatch in about 10 or 12 days. There are two, three, or even four broods per year.

The young are fed almost entirely on insects, mostly beetles, grasshoppers, crickets, and various caterpillars and other larvae found on or near the ground.

Like most ground-nesting birds, young song sparrows develop very rapidly. They usually leave the nest before they are able to fly and are fed by the male while the female begins laying the second clutch of eggs. Though snakes and other predators capture many of them, these flightless chicks can scamper about in the tall grass with great agility and are surprisingly able to avoid danger. By the time the male leaves them to begin caring for the second brood, they are able to fly and fend for themselves.

In early August the long nesting season is finally over, and for a few weeks the song sparrow is silent as it begins a complete molt into the dusky-tipped plumage of winter.

During the warm days of early autumn, song sparrows again begin to sing, though more softly and sporadically than during the exuberant outbursts of spring. This fall singing apparently is not of a functional nature, but seems simply an outlet for nervous energy or a recrudescence of a stimulus (song) no longer overridden by others (brood-raising).

In late September song sparrows that migrate begin to drift southward. The peak of the movement comes in October, and by mid-November the winter populations are essentially stabilized.

About two-thirds of the annual diet of the song sparrow consists of weed and grass seed, including crab grass, dandelion, knotweed, ragweed, sorrel, and many other plants that infest croplands and the lawns of suburbanites. The total of grain and other crops taken is negligible. Animal food taken by the adults consists mostly of the ground-dwelling insects mentioned previously as nestling food. Through most of the year song sparrows forage on the ground under thickets, brushpiles, and similar cover, seldom venturing far from a safe retreat. But in late fall and winter they become bolder and will venture out onto lawns and open fields to search for grass seeds.

Song sparrows are regular visitors to feeding stations throughout the northern states. Although once they become accustomed to their surroundings they will fly up to a tray or hanging feeder, they are more inclined to remain on the ground, feeding on fallen seeds. It is a good practice to scatter some seed on the ground for them and for other species with similar habits. If possible, do this close to shrubbery and brush piles so that the birds are close to a safe retreat if startled.

Song sparrows will eat any of the smaller seeds in a typical wildbird food mix, but seem to prefer hemp and millet. They will also take doughnut or similar greasy crumbs, peanut butter, and occasionally cracked corn or suet.

Description: Length, 6¼ in. Thick, conical bill; rather long tail, somewhat rounded. Above: brown, russet brown, or gray-brown streaked darker and lighter. Crown with dull gray stripes. Below: whitish, heavily marked with dark streakings that merge into a conspicuous blotch in midbreast. Sexes alike. Vesper sparrow is similar but grayer, with white eye ring and outer tail feathers. Savannah sparrow has more conspicuous head stripes and a yellow eye line. The flight of the song sparrow is somewhat labored; it pumps its tail. Flight of similar birds is more free and direct; tail is held still.

Incubation, 10 to 12 days; young stay 8 to 10 days in nest.

Size of eggs, 0.80 x 0.60 in.; two to four broods per year.

Suggested Readings

BOOKS

AMERICAN ORNITHOLOGISTS' UNION, *The A.O.U. Check-list of North American Birds,* 5th ed., 1957.

BAILEY, FLORENCE MERRIAM. *Handbook of Birds of the Western United States.* Boston: Houghton Mifflin Co., 1902.

BAKER, JOHN H. *The Audubon Guide to Attracting Birds.* New York: Doubleday & Co., Inc., 1941.

BENT, ARTHUR C. *Bent's Life Histories of North American Birds,* 20 vols. Washington, D.C.: U. S. National Museum, 1919–1958.

BULL, JOHN. *Birds of the New York Area.* New York: Harper & Row, 1964.

COLLINS, HENRY HILL, JR. *Complete Field Guide to American Wildlife: East, Central & North.* New York: Harper & Row, 1959.

CRUICKSHANK, ALLAN D. *Birds Around New York City.* New York: American Museum of Natural History, 1942.

———. *Cruickshank's Pocket Guide to the Birds.* New York: Dodd, Mead & Co., 1953.

DAWSON, WILLIAM LEON. *The Birds of California.* San Diego: South Moulton Co., 1923.

FORBUSH, EDWARD HOWE. *Birds of Massachusetts and Other New England States,* 3 vols. Boston: Massachusetts Department of Agriculture, 1925, 1927, 1929.

GABRIELSON, I. N., and JEWETT, S. G. *Birds of Oregon.* Corvallis: Oregon State College, 1940.

GABRIELSON, I. N., and LINCOLN, FREDERIC C. *Birds of Alaska.* Washington: Wildlife Management Institute, 1959.

GRINNELL, JOSEPH, and MILLER, A. *Distribution of the Birds of California.* Berkeley: Cooper Ornithological Club, 1944.

HOFFMAN, RALPH. *Birds of the Pacific States.* Boston: Houghton Mifflin Co., 1927.

HOWARD, HENRY ELIOT. *An Introduction to the Study of Bird Behavior.* New York: The Macmillan Co., 1929.

JEWETT, S. G., TAYLOR, W. P., SHAW, W. T., and ALDRICH, J. W. *Birds of Washington State.* Seattle: University of Washington Press, 1953.

LINCOLN, FREDERIC C. *The Migration of North American Birds.* New York: Doubleday & Co., Inc., 1939.

MATHEWS, F. SCHUYLER. *Field Guide of Wild Birds and Their Music.* New York: G. P. Putnam & Sons, 1921.

NUTTALL, THOMAS. *Popular Handbook of the Birds of the United States and Canada.* Boston: Little Brown & Co., 1903.

PEARSON, T. GILBERT. *Birds of America.* New York: Garden City Publishing Company, 1936.

PETERSON, ROGER TORY. *A Field Guide to the Birds,* 2nd rev. ed. Boston: Houghton Mifflin Co., 1947.

————. *A Field Guide to Western Birds,* 2nd ed. Boston: Houghton Mifflin Co., 1961.

POUGH, RICHARD H. *Audubon Bird Guide—Eastern Land Birds.* New York: Doubleday & Co., Inc., 1946.

————. *Audubon Western Bird Giude.* New York: Doubleday & Co., Inc., 1957.

RANSOM, JAY ELLIS. *Western Field Guide to American Wildlife.* New York: Harper & Row, 1966 (in process).

ROWAN, WILLIAM. *The Riddle of Migration.* Baltimore: The Williams & Wilkins Co., 1931.

SAUNDERS, ARETAS A. *Guide to Bird Songs.* New York: Doubleday & Co., Inc., 1951.

SIMMONS, GEORGE FINLAY. *Birds of the Austin Region.* Austin: The University of Texas, 1925.

STONE, WITMER. *Bird Studies at Old Cape May,* 2 vols. Philadelphia: Delaware Valley Ornithology Club, 1937.

TERRES, J. K. *Songbirds in Your Garden.* New York: Thomas Y. Crowell Co., 1953.

WETMORE, ALEXANDER. *Migrations of Birds.* Cambridge: Harvard University Press, 1926.

PERIODICALS

Audubon Magazine (bimonthly), National Audubon Society, 1130 Fifth Avenue, New York, New York.

The Auk (quarterly), American Ornithologists' Union, Intelligencer Printing Co., Lancaster, Pennsylvania.

The Condor (quarterly), Cooper Ornithological Club, Berkeley, California.

The Wilson Bulletin (quarterly), Wilson Ornithological Society, Lawrence, Kansas.

Index

This index includes all common English names of species, as well as scientific names of families and species covered in the book. A **boldface** roman numeral indicates the number of the color plate on which the species is illustrated; arabic numbers in **boldface** indicate black and white illustrations.